Francis

May this bring back
memories
of
past years and
may it bring pleasure
for
many, many years
to
come.

Norman Small
1995.

SPIT, POLISH AND TEARS

Spit, Polish and Tears

A. N. Small

The Pentland Press
Edinburgh – Cambridge – Durham – USA

© A. N. Small, 1995
First published in 1995 by
The Pentland Press Ltd
1 Hutton Close
South Church
Bishop Auckland
Durham

ISBN 1-85821-307-X

Typeset by Carnegie Publishing, 18 Maynard St, Preston
Printed and bound in Great Britain by Bookcraft (Bath) Ltd

This book, *Spit, Polish and Tears*, is dedicated to Elizabeth and to every woman who served in the WAAF during World War II. To them I say thank you and may this book show in a small way the admiration I have for you.

. . . And in the Morning

Shall we remember through long aching years
The heartbreak in laughter, rare, comforting tears,
The silence of sorrow, deep uplifting pride,
Soft whispered consolings of those who have died?

Mollie Wilson Whiteside
(The Little Corporal)

CONTENTS

LIST OF ILLUSTRATIONS

FOREWORD

The last few years before the outbreak of the Second World War – Hitler's War – were times of ever-increasing foreboding for anyone who was living in Britain at that time. Was Hitler really trying to drive the world into another conflict on an unimaginable scale? To be on the safe side, and for the first time in its history, Britain introduced universal conscription.

This universal conscription covered women as well as men, with service able to be given in the armed forces, in auxiliary services such as ambulance, fire or auxiliary rescue services, or else in industry. While the Royal Navy already had its women's branch in the WRN, and the Army in its ATS, the RAF had never had a women's service until May 1939, when the Women's Auxiliary Air Force was set up. With uniforms made from the same blue-grey material as were the men's RAF uniforms, the concept of service in the WAAF soon appealed to many women and volunteers immediately offered themselves from all walks of life.

Service in the WAAF brought some women closer to the actual fighting than perhaps many of them had expected, for service on an operational station, be it for fighters, coastal, transport or night-bomber squadrons, often meant that the aircrew on the station almost daily went off to war, from which some might never return . . . Members of the WAAF assisted in almost every activity needed to keep the planes flying, from spark-plug testing to meteorological services, from cooking to clerk/typist, from truck driver to parachute packer – the WAAF carried out all such jobs routinely, and with great efficiency and devotion.

Service in the WAAF therefore placed these women in situations that were quite different from those experienced by their sisters in the other women's services because of that close involvement in the frontline activities of their station. The inevitable result of this was that they often experienced a sudden and traumatic transition from a happy off-duty hour spent in some typical English country pub one night, to finding that their boy-friend from last night was 'missing in action' the next night. This was a constant and unnerving burden for any woman to have to endure.

Norman Small met his future wife, Elizabeth, under wartime circumstances of this nature, but following her recent decease after a long and happy marriage, he decided to give thanks and honour to her memory by producing this remarkable book. His persistence in this quest of honour has gathered together several hundred contributions that detail the recollections of other women who served in the WAAF during the war. He has since done me the honour of asking me to write this foreword, which I am very glad to do because I am also able to add my own tribute to another WAAF, one who has been my lovely wife for fifty years.

To any future historian seeking to write about the spirit of those far-off days, my advice is to overlook any bits of service jargon that they may encounter in these pages, and read all of this very carefully and then to take in a deep, deep breath – what they will find here is the true spirit and atmosphere of those days. For myself, I say all honour and thanks to the wonderful women of the Women's Auxiliary Air Force.

S/Ldr R.B. Osborn, DSO, DFC (Ret.)
460 (RAAF) Squadron, Breighton 1942/3

ACKNOWLEDGEMENTS

My thanks go to all who helped with the stories found in *Spit, Polish &
Tears*. The following wrote, some two or three times; others phoned and
told of their experiences. Not all of these were former WAAFs. Some were
men: brothers, husbands and, in a few cases, men who could tell me of
losses from 460 Squadron.

M. P. and M. E. Aldrich, R. Allard, V. Allen, M. Allwright, W. L.
Andrew, A. Archibald, G. and J. Armitage, M. J. Atkins, F. M. Back-
hurst, J. Bale, J. Ball, M. Barber, B. A. Barnes, E. Barton, A. Bask-
erville, A. Bates, D. Beasty, I. Beattie, P. Becker, J. Bolton, K. Boreham,
– Bradbury, P. Bradshaw, K. M. Brassington, P. Brimson, C. Brothers,
K. Browne (Curator of Private Records, Canberra), J. Britenshaw, P.
M. Caley- Cullum, D. Catten, M. Clowes, S. Coburn, N. Cook, M.
Coombs, I. Cronie, J. Coutts, C. De la Torre, F. Denby, W. Denyer,
M. Dice, E. C. Dodsworth, J. Dudeney, J. Dwyer, M. Edwards, D.
Ellis, L. Elms, D. A. Evans, G. Finch, R. B. Fisher, S. Fisher, N.
Foster, M. Foster, E. M. Francis, B. Gardener, J. and E. Gascoigne,
A. A. Gauley, P. Gibby, J. Glossop, G. Grace, B. Grant, E. Gray, M.
D. Griffiths, L. Groom, E. R. Halfyard, N. Hargreaves, J. Harriott, B.
Harrison, J. Harrison, – Harvey, V. Harvey, C. Haugh, P. L. Hayes,
M. Hendry, J. Herring, L. Hill, D. Hobson, M. Holdcroft, D. V.
Holmes, M. Howden, J. Hughes, K. Humphrey, M. Hubbard, M.
Irving, V. and E. Jacobs, D. James, C. Jenner-Akehurst, P. Jones, S.
G. M. Jones, J. Kaye, M. Kelly, G. Kilvington, G. W. King, P. Kirby,
M. J. Knight, E. Kup, I. Lallemant, D. Laverne-Smith, M. G.
Lawrence, P. M. Leary, I. Lewis, M. Lewis, R. G. Lewis, D. Lindo,
J. Lindsay, R. Lister, P. Lloyd, M. Lovell, S. MacPhail, F. Mahoney,
V. Mallert, A. S. Manning, F. Martin, F. Martin-Smith, J. May, J.
McCague, D. McCandless, L. McConnell, J. McDonald, L. McDonald,
W. and B. McKay, M. McPherson, L. Mill, J. Milne, M. Moore, E.
Morrison, M. Morarecky, J. Morton, D. Moss, P. Mulligan, M. Mur-

phy, L. G. Nind, K. J. Olszewski, R. Osborn, S. Orrell, R. Orton, S. Overend, B. Partridge, P. and J. Paylor, A. Pennock, A. Pickering, O. Piercy, B. Powell, J. Quantrill, E. Redfern, M. Rhodes, J. Richards, F. Robinson, M. Rushton, B. Sara, K. Scoffin, R. Seltzer, B. Seton-Hodges, C. A. Simpson, D. L. Sims, G. Smith, J. D. Smith, M. A. Smith, M. L. Snashall, K. R. Southworth, E. Spark, V. Spence, P. Spencer, B. Stuart, J. Studdard, M. Summer, S. Sims, A. Taylor, G. W. Taylor, M. Tempest, I. J. Theobald, N. Thomson, D. Toamy, A. Toole, J. Tucker, I. Turrill, V. Tunner, M. Underwood, W. Vickerstaff, L. Vittles, F. Walker, F. D. Walker, P. Walker, M. Woolnough, E. Waye, G. P. Webb, J. Weeks, P. M. Whetton, M. Whiteside, K. Wilkinson, D. A. Williams, J. B. Williams, D. B. Wilson, E. Withers, M. Whitlam, B. Woods, N. Watling.

In relation to the foregoing names, I would have liked to be able to give maiden names, but most did not give these. A few did, and they also gave their numbers, for they remembered them proudly.

I am indebted to the following for publishing my appeal for stories from former WAAFs: The *Australian Weekly Times*; British Provincial Newspapers – I have not listed these as in some cases I am not sure whether publication was made; BBC Scotland for broadcasting an appeal; 3AW Radio Station Melbourne.

To my old school friend, John Hodson, Secretary, Victorian Branch of 460 Squadron Association, I must say a sincere thank you for bearing with me and assisting in the tracing of airmen who served. This was something that came as a result of the appeals being published.

To the Melbourne Branch of the Royal Air Force Association I send my thanks as they gave coverage in the newsletters.

The Commonwealth War Graves Commission in Canberra, Australia provided information on the grave of an Australian airman and this brought to a conclusion the long, heart-rending search by an Irish former WAAF who had hoped to marry that airman.

The Ouyen Primary School came to my aid on many occasions with photocopies.

Christine Ianson who wrote the poem 'For All Second World War Heroes' was not a WAAF but her father Ivor Hayes was a member of Richard Osborn's crew. S/Ldr R. B. Osborn, DSO, DFC (ret) 460, (RAAF) Squadron, Breighton 1942/3, wrote the Foreword and I am most grateful to him for this and for his interest, advice and encouragement.

Finally I am most grateful to Rhonda Young, Secretary, Ouyen Primary School, for her persistence, care and good humour as she typed the whole of *Spit, Polish & Tears*. This was no mean task as she had to cope with my efforts in editing so many letters from WAAFs.

Norman Small
Editor

APOLOGIES

This is an apology to the former WAAFs whose stories I typed out and incorrectly spelled the name or names of your stations. I have a pocket Bartholomew's Atlas of the British Isles which I used fifty years ago on cross country flights. When I was not sure of the spelling of a particular station, I looked it up, but must admit that I was not always successful. Perhaps we can share the blame for incorrect spelling as sometimes your writing, like mine, was a little hard to read.

Even the spelling of names I may have confused. This was entirely my fault as I was the typist, the secretary and the general dogsbody with *Spit, Polish & Tears*, so my apologies.

EDITORIAL

When I visited Britain during April – May of 1944, I found that among the WAAFs of the Second World War there was still, even fifty years on, that grand spirit of comradeship, of sharing and of optimism, which I knew and understood as a young Australian airman serving in the RAF. Those WAAFs whom I met opened their hearts and their homes and I am most grateful. Indeed, that welcome came from all who wrote and from all to whom I spoke on the telephone.

When the first thoughts of writing about the WAAF came to me, I wrote to nearly sixty newspapers in Britain asking for publication of an appeal to former WAAFs who wished to share their wartime experiences and have them recorded in *Spit, Polish & Tears*. Almost three hundred replies came from all over England, Scotland, Northern Ireland, Canada, New Zealand and Australia. Letters from WAAfs in Britain crossed oceans to WAAF friends in the Commonwealth to tell of the appeal and then, as the message was passed on, the stories flooded in. A former Yorkshire lass, on receiving a copy of an appeal from a friend in Britain, sat down during all of her spare time in the big freeze of the Canadian winter and wrote her story.

In Derby and Yarmouth, I had the pleasure of addressing former WAAFs at their Association meetings. It was like old times. The friendship, the good humour and the charm of the girls were still there. We all looked older, perhaps some of us looked a little wiser; some were a little bent with years but the old spirit of the Royal Air Force was present. A number gave me hospitality and many more offered it, but it was impossible to visit everyone in a limited time. To those with whom I stayed or shared a day or a few hours, I must say a sincere thank you. Your welcome to one from down under made me proud to know you and proud to have served with you in Britain.

To all of those British newspapers who published my appeal, to BBC Scotland and particularly to Nancy Nicholson and Anne Bates who arranged an interview for broadcasting, to the *Australian Weekly Times* and June Alexander, to Tony Charlton of 3AW, I say a sincere thank you.

So overwhelming was the response to the appeal for stories that many who wrote will be disappointed to find that their stories have not been published, but let me hasten to add, not this time, for there is enough material for another collection of stories, perhaps a second 'Spit'. Also, eventually your stories will be sent to the Australian War Memorial Museum who have requested memorabilia.

In most cases, the words and the style of the contributors' writings have been kept. I have tried to preserve the facts, the drama and the humour as recorded by the thoughts of the loves and sometimes losses of those memorable times. They flowed so freely, were written down and given to be shared. Occasionally, I trimmed. In the case of a WAAF who told me that she climbed down into the bomb hatchet of a Lancaster, I gave it the chop. Another lass told me that she fell over a cow but he didn't mind. I had to do a little gender mending to cut out the bull!

During the whole of the operation of drawing together these stories, I have tried to keep in the forefront the original motivation: the honouring of Elizabeth, my late wife, and then in turn every WAAF who served, whether on the most menial or the most sophisticated or even secret assignments. The book is a thank you to every woman who served in the WAAF.

A number of books have been written about the WAAF, some recording in great detail the history, others telling individual stories, and some, like this one, a collection of stories. However, all of those that I have seen have been written by women. Now, here is one from a different viewpoint. You will find an Australian bias. Indeed, a few stories are about Australians and there is a leaning towards 460 Squadron, an Australian Squadron of Bomber Command stationed in Binbrook in Lincolnshire. It was on that station that Elizabeth and I met and where we later married in June 1945.

As you read, you will see that Australians were always made so welcome in the Royal Air Force in spite of the fact that they were hard to handle and had their own way of letting off steam. They did things which their parents would not believe. At 460 there was tremendous pride in being part of that Squadron. For a time Hughie Edwards, a great Australian who was awarded the Victorian Cross, the Distinguished Service Cross and the Distinguished Flying Cross, was Commanding Officer of the Squadron. He showed that he could handle Aussies with a relaxed and easy style and they responded with nothing but the best when he called for it.

Of late much has been written about serving King and country, honouring our flag and so on. I make no apologies for here giving the views of this great Australian who served. Peter Firkins in his book *Heroes Have Wings* records some of the remarks of the late Hughie Edwards, who said of his fellow Australians:

> They had a fierce national pride and there is no doubt that Australians were conscious of the Anzac spirit and reputation, and for these reasons were consistently brave and afraid of being thought otherwise. I think their main concern was to do their stuff with a minimum of interference from the powers-that-be, complete a tour and get back to Australia. I'm sure they didn't feel they were fighting for King, Country or Commonwealth or held any high sounding principles on the policy of the war or their opponents. They were part of a struggle and they wanted . . . to survive.

Now let us think again of the WAAF. A great deal of what was said there can be applied to them. They served alongside these men; they were consistently brave; they wanted to do their stuff; they had a great pride. They will have to say whether they were fighting for King and country, I cannot answer there, but I do know they wanted to do their duty and felt it an honour to wear the uniform; they were part of the struggle and they too wanted to survive. Quite a number didn't survive because they served in areas where there was constant danger from the enemy and even from their own aircraft.

Some girls were deliberately discouraged from joining the WAAF by parents who had all sorts of doubts and fears, but even these difficulties were overcome by very young girls who wanted to play their part, who wanted to join their mates and wanted to prove that they too could have the impossible dream, the dream of being true to themselves no matter what the odds.

Some have said, 'Thank God for the RAF.' Let me say in conclusion, I salute you, Elizabeth, and every WAAF – THANK GOD FOR THE WAAF! If *Spit, Polish & Tears* has brought a better appreciation of the WAAF, then the operation has been successful and the target has been hit.

Norman Small
Editor

SAY IT AGAIN

At the risk of repeating my appeal to ex WAAFs to tell me their stories, I would like to say again what came to me soon after Elizabeth left us. These were the thoughts and words which set me on the road to Damascus. This longing to say thank you to Elizabeth had to be written down. I really needed no conversion but what I did need was to express in words what this WAAF, a shy Scot, had meant to me over forty-eight years.

Like most men, I seldom said the words, but for all that dumbness I was now game to have a try: to honour her and to say thank you to the thousands of her mates who gave us so much when we most needed an arm around us and a word of good cheer, so that we could press on regardless.

Waafs at War

In front of my late wife's photograph lies a Royal Air Force cap badge which she wore for almost five years during World War II. As I touch it, into my mind flood scenes of the many hundreds of times it was polished. The details of the crown are worn flat and some of the leaves surrounding the letters RAF have lost their shape.

When Elizabeth was first issued with this brass badge at Bridgnorth, Shropshire, in 1941, she had to work hard with Brasso, rag and button stick to make it gleam. Time and time again it would be cleaned till it gleamed.

It went with Elizabeth to Dyce in Scotland for a year and a half and then to Binbrook, Lincolnshire.

There at Binbrook, in early 1945, Elizabeth and I met. Going down a hill from the camp to Binbrook village was a steep road edged by a deep, grassy ditch. In that ditch we met – Elizabeth, dazed and stunned by the blast from an exploding aircraft, scrabbled around with two other WAAFs. A Beaufighter in trying to land at Binbrook had hit a hill at the side of the village. The explosion of a torpedo on the aircraft caused the huge blast and shock wave which carried the three girls into the ditch.

Our engineer and I raced towards the aircraft but were stopped short by exploding ammunition. As we backed off, we found the girls shocked and in floods of tears. That was the beginning of a great interest which I took in the girls of the 'Tailors' Shop'.

Elizabeth was the most beautiful and from that tearful beginning, we had forty-eight years of happy married life. When Elizabeth left us in August, it was my turn for tears.

As my fingers glide over the cap badge, I feel again the love, warmth and devotion that Elizabeth gave to all that she did. The brass glows; it gleams; and as with Elizabeth it gives me back what is given, the light of good works. She has gone but left me with memories, so many of them beautiful, some sad, but always I see her smiling face, the gleam in her eye, and I hear again the quick whip-like wit of a Scottish lass, who could devastate this Aussie in seconds if she so wished.

Now, as I read again our Squadron history, *Strike and Return* by Peter Firkins, the scenes of the war-time bomber station flood back. I feel again the contrast of living: one moment flying through hellish flak and then a few hours later sitting in the station cinema cuddling Lizzie. Perhaps later there would be a pub crawl on bikes or a trip to Tealby Castle, when we sat in a pub that was the front room of a house and the locals eyed us off with great suspicion.

When I wrote Elizabeth's obituary for our local newspaper, I pointed out that only those who were on an operational squadron in Britain during World War II would know of the dangers faced by WAAF personnel. Much has been written about fighter pilots and other Air Force heroes, but not nearly enough tribute has been given to those thousands of women who gave so much support to Australian ground staff and air crews while they served in Britain. These girls supported not only Australians but also British, Canadians, Free French, Poles, Dutch and many other Allied airman. Their lives were always in danger; they could not take to the air; they stuck it out and prayed.

As a tribute to Elizabeth, I am writing some of the stories in the WAAF. However, there are so many other women who served in the WAAF and their stories are worth telling and need to be told. There are those who worked in the R/T and perhaps heard the very last words of so many airman; there are those who worked as MT drivers who drove airmen to the aircraft and with tears farewelled them for the last time; there are those who wept tears of joy when boyfriends who were given up as lost suddenly and unexpectedly returned; there are those who perhaps sewed another 'ring' on the sleeve of an airman only to find that he never returned to claim the garment. Yes, so many gave so much and those stories ought to be told.

Norm Small
460 Squadron RAAF Binbrook
Lincolnshire, 1945

WELL OILED

Dorothy wanted to be in the WAAF at least eighteen months before she was signed on. She was nineteen when she left her job as a telephonist/typist and by that time most of her friends were in the Forces. Although there were buckets of tears when she first joined, she had a wonderful time and really hated to leave when the war came to an end. Here is Dorothy's story:

When at last I left the office to join the WAAF, I cried my eyes out. They were all so kind; in fact, the cashier made up a poem about me:

Ode to Dot
by Lucy Lastic (Hugh Macallum)

A WAAF our Dot has got to be,
Dressed in Air Force blue.
But judging from the tears she shed,
The Navy ought to do!
For when she left the office staff,
She gave us all the jumps;
The staff put on their Wellingtons
And shouted, 'Man the Pumps!'

Dot no more would say, 'Engaged',
Or that the lines are crossed;
Nor Mrs R. will get enraged,
When her call is lost.

For Dot will not know
Of these things,
When once she is a WAAF,
She'll only know
Of bombs and wings,
And mostly pilots' chaff.

Anyhow the office staff
Wish her the best of luck,

And send a pin to keep her tie,
From dangling in the muck.
For when ground staff and aircrew,
On the aerodome are standing,
It would not do for any WAAF
Her 'spirits' to abandon.

Unfortunately, this pin and also a Swan fountain pen were stolen while I was in hospital. I had a tooth filled while on camp at Hednesford. Later it was extracted and then I had septicaemia and was transferred to the RAF Hospital at Cosford. I had two operations in one week. My parents were notified and they stayed with me in the hospital until I was taken off the danger list.

If I may go back to the beginning: war was declared two days before my sixteenth birthday. I had left school at fourteen years of age and was employed as a clerk and relief telephonist at the Education Offices in Sheffield. When I was 17½, I left my job to go as a telephonist/typist for a building contractor. The office staff were all very nice but I hated the boss, a woman.

I wanted to leave but my mother said that I must stay. I wanted to volunteer for the WAAF but my father insisted that I stay at home. My work was not far away and my wages were good, even so I was miserable as most young people were in the forces.

When I was eighteen, I had to register and be interviewed at the Employment Exchange. I had to wait until I was nineteen years old before I was called up and I was happy to join the WAAF. My next problem was deciding just what I should do. I didn't want office work and it seemed that with everything else that I wanted, there were no vacancies. At last the Office suggested Flight Mechanic and I jumped at the chance. I enjoyed the training at Hednesford Technical School and everything went fine until I had the tooth extracted.

I was posted to Spitalgate near Grantham, where I went to work in the Minor Repairs Hangar. At first, I was sent to help an LAC fit a new stern-frame into a Blenheim and as time went on more WAAFs came along, and the airmen were posted. The Technical Officer decided that the new girls, and there were three of us, would have to have a practical test before we could work on our own. So my friend Violet and I had to rivet new legs on the inside of the centre section of the mainplane.

We started work and I had to stand on a tool box because I couldn't reach. The Flight Sergeant and Technical Officer were breathing down our necks. They were so close and didn't speak a single word either to us or to each other. At last we finished and turned to them. The Officer congratulated us on a job well done. He said that it was the best riveting he had seen on the station. We heaved a sigh of relief for we had passed the test, and now we were on our own.

Now, we had to sign for the work we did, whereas previously the airman with whom we worked had to sign. I enjoyed my work as an airframe mechanic, but I longed for hot water. We were billeted in peace-time married quarters which were old houses where it was necessary to light an old boiler to get any hot water for washing. There were no showers and we were out at work all day, starting at 7.00 a.m., and then after tea scrounging for coal, wood etc. to light the fire.

We grumbled to the WAAF Officer and we flight mechanics were eventually moved into modern billets with central heating. It was like being in heaven. The airmen had to move out to let us girls in. We were a jolly lot. I came back one night rather late. The lights were off and I felt my way to the bed to find that the sheet was half-way up, tin hats down the middle and old brushes and other things piled on. I turned to my neighbour's bed with the intention of tipping it and her over, but she wasn't in it. She must have had an idea what I would do, so she spent the night with a friend, squashed up together while I slept in her bed. The next morning I stacked my own bed and left hers so I think I came off OK.

When we first started working in the hangars, the men didn't want us doing their jobs. One day we had to work overtime and I was the only WAAF working with seven men. When we had finished, we walked down to the cook-house for a very belated tea. After being served, I went to sit in the WAAF section. It felt so strange being alone in that huge place. I had just started eating when one of the men called me, saying, 'If you are good enough to work with, you are good enough to eat with. Come and join us.' So I did. I felt that they had now accepted me as a fellow Flight Mechanic.

The Officer who eighteen months previously had congratulated me on the riveting, now accused me of nearly chopping his head off. We went to work as usual but there was only one aircraft in the hangar – very unusual. The WAAFs had just moved into a lean-to smoke room and there was a big notice on the door: 'No Men Allowed'. It was a place where we could hang our overalls instead of keeping them in our tool boxes. On this occasion it was about 11.00 a.m. before anyone bothered us, when a Corporal popped his head round the corner to say, 'All out on this kite.' We all went outside and the Corporal told me to go on the brakes. So I did. The rest of the girls pushed and we all were going along well, when I saw the Technical Officer coming along on his bike. He slowed down and was very annoyed at the lack of overalls – not one of us was wearing them. I thought to myself that I must be sharp on the brakes or I should be the next to be lectured, so when the Corporal shouted, 'Brakes', I was on the ball. The plane stopped dead. Unfortunately, the Officer didn't. His bike went under the main plane but he didn't. It caught him on the throat and down he went. I didn't dare get out of the cockpit so I waited a while. The WAAFs who had been pushing just looked at him sprawling on the ground and turned around and walked back to the hangar. However, he shouted, 'Come back here. I haven't finished with you yet!' They came back and stood in a semi-circle. He was going on about the overalls and I thought that I could get out and creep behind him. I did, but he turned, pointed his finger at me and yelled, 'You! You nearly chopped my head off!' I was scared and I said, 'I'm sorry, Sir.' Then I laughed and laughed. I couldn't stop. Perhaps I should stop the story for a little and tell you about our overalls. They were men's boiler suits. I usually managed to get a pair to fit a man 6 feet 2 inches – I was 5 feet 2 inches. We had to roll up the sleeves and the legs and finally the body. The crutch usually came around my knees. I'm sure we all looked very glamorous.

I thought the Officer would put me on a charge when I laughed, but he didn't and when I thought about it later, it was his own fault. I heard the Corporal shout, 'Brakes!' so he should have heard. After all, I was in the cockpit and he was outside the aircraft.

One day, I was doing my job and I came across a WAAF who was standing in the fuselage doing nothing. I said, 'Is there anything wrong?'

'I have to check the cables in the fuselage but I don't know how to get down there.'

'You'll have to crawl through as I do.' She tried but got stuck. I didn't think she was so fat. Well, she laughed and I did too. The more she laughed, the more the gun turret turned around and squeezed her. We did get her out, but her job now was to splice the cables. She was very good at it and I was very glad that I didn't have to do that part.

One day, I was tightening the nuts on the wheels when the spanner slipped and I fell backwards into a tray of oil that had come out of the engine. I was soaked right though, my overalls, slacks, pants, the lot! Was my bottom black! I had to scrub it.

I sometimes went with the men to the belly-flop landings where perhaps the pilot had forgotten to lower the undercarriage or perhaps it was faulty. The men had to sling ropes about the aircraft and the mobile crane would lift it up. My job was to sit in the cockpit and lower the undercarriage by manual pumping, then it was inspected for faults. I enjoyed going on these little trips away from the airfield.

As mechanics we were sent to go with the pilot for a trip when he tested the aircraft. I thoroughly enjoyed flying. In fact, I had my first flight when I was thirteen years old – a five-shilling trip from the beach at Southport. The first time I had a chance to fly in the WAAF, I was so excited and rushed off to the parachute section to draw a parachute. It was pushed towards me by a WAAF. I put my arms around and found that it was heavier and bulkier than I had expected. I thought, I'll never carry this back to the hangar, so had an idea – I'll sling it on my back as the pilots do. I felt around for something to grip and slung it. What a surprise! Should I say SHOCK! There, lying on the ground, were yards and yards of material. I had pulled the rip cord. I felt such a fool. I had to take it back and get another one. There seemed to be miles and miles of silk in that parachute and I had to gather it all up. When I went back, I said to the WAAF, 'Well, it did work!' She simply handed me another one.

I did enjoy my flight. We visited another airfield and we flew for about fifty minutes there and back.

One day I was camouflaging new elevators which had been fitted, when suddenly, I realized that it was quiet in the hangar. I looked around but couldn't see or hear anyone. Must be NAAFI up! Off I went to get a cup of coffee and a wad. The hut was packed with RAF and WAAF. I managed a coffee and wad and sat on the concrete floor. I had just taken a bite out of the wad when the Corporal shouted, 'Back to work!' Everyone moved except me. He came over and repeated, 'Back to work.' I said, 'I've only just come. I'll come when I've eaten my wad and drunk my coffee.' He put me on a charge. I was marched in to see the Officer and I explained why I was late and luckily I was let off. The Officer said that I should have gone back when he ordered me. I said that if I had done so at the time I would not have been able to eat my wad or drink my coffee for which I had paid.

I hated winter and trying to push Blenheims into a hangar from where they had been parked. Our feet slipped on the icy ground and our hands and feet were frozen. I remember the beginning of 1944. It was very cold and we had to sweep the snow off the main planes and the hoods on the top of the cockpit were frozen shut. Our Sergeant had a stove in his office and we, the workers, were invited in to get warm. We all crowded in and I was near the stove. I burned a hole in my trousers as big as the palm of my hand. I didn't feel the heat until I smelled my clothes burning.

As we were not as strong as the men, we did things differently, for instance when putting the wheels back on an aircraft. The men lifted the wheels up to slot the axles into the olo legs. The girls lowered the aircraft into the axles. We could fit the perspex and triplex windows in the cockpit. The men in doing the same job often used too much force and smashed the perspex.

One day, a plane came into the hangar and everyone gathered around to lift the fuselage onto the trestle. This we did by bending down and getting our backs under it. The only men in the hangar were NCOs and all the mechanics were WAAFs. I was to work on the plane. I sat around and waited for someone to come to help me trestle up the front of the plane and get it into rigging position. I waited and waited and got fed up so I decided that I would do it myself. I got the crab jack, pulled the trestles under the centre section and bit by bit I got the plane into the rigging position. Some time later the Corporal came around and he was surprised to see the plane already trestled up. He asked who had helped me. When I said that I had done it myself, I don't think he believed me as he went around the other mechnics asking who had helped. They all said, 'No.' When the Flight Sergeant got his breath back he told me that I shouldn't have done it. There could have been an accident. I didn't think anything could go wrong.

Looking back now, I realize what a big job it was for a WAAF. I knew exactly what I was doing and I was full of confidence and it was OK.

I was posted to Hixon in Staffordshire along with a lot of friends. Spitalgale was closing down. It was early in 1944. Hixon was a dispersed camp and everyone was issued with a bicycle. If you couldn't ride a bike you had to learn or walk. We worked on Blenheims and Beauforts. I was used to Blenheims but the Beauforts were bigger. I could just manage the wheels which we had to take to the tyre bay, where they would be examined and new brake shoes fitted if needed.

Just after the war ended, one day at lunch time, the Sergeant told us to go to lunch and come back in our best blues – tunics and skirts. We wondered why but did as we were told. When we arrived back at the hangar, we were amazed: not a plane in sight and the hangar floor was spotless. Tables and chairs were scattered around. We soon found out. Lancasters carrying thirty-five men were landing and bringing men who had been POWs in Germany back to England. Before we came in contact with them, they had to be sprayed with DDT powder. They all looked bedraggled and not very talkative. Our job was to help them and try to get them to talk to us. They all seemed very quiet. How could I understand how they felt? Some of them had endured years of captivity, torment and degradation, some since Dunkirk. One man gave me a German coin and a box of German matches. I still have those.

After we had talked to the men, lorries came and they were taken to the cook-house. We WAAFs had to follow on bicycles. We served bacon and eggs and tomatoes to these soldiers. Then they all piled into lorries and left as we waved goodbye and good luck. We didn't know where they went. Some of them were in very poor health and one died as he was trying to get out of the plane. Some of them were in a daze and couldn't believe what was happening. For me this was a sad day but a happy one also.

I was married in June 1944 to George. He was in the RAF as a Wireless Operator. We had to live with my parents until we got a home of our own. I was then nearly twenty-two years old.

Dorothy Hobson
Gulgong, NSW, Australia

PUSH BIKES

This year, 1994, it is fifty years since I arrived in Britain as an Empire Air Trainee destined for service in the Royal Air Force.

I began service life as a foot slogger in the Australian Army and marched and staggered over many miles, but never had the chance to try pedalling along.

1943 and some of 1944 were years spent in training in the Royal Australian Air Force at Somers in Australia, Mossbank on the prairies in Canada and then Winnipeg. At Somers no push bikes, but plenty of push – we doubled everywhere. Everybody seemed in a great hurry to push us off to make room for yet another course of young men bound for glory.

Looking back, it disappoints me that those in Australia took the war so

Murray Nottle's crew at Seighford, 1944.

seriously: posting pickets or guards, as they were in the middle of nowhere; having constant kit inspections; playing at war. Yet, when we got to where the real action was, and men were dying not just in ones and twos but in hundreds every night, then the bull dust ceased.

Of course there were some who thought we were dodging war – Jap dodgers, they called us. Men who were facing hellish flak night after night received from Australia white feathers. O those of little faith! Twice as many men were lost on one Australian squadron in Britain in World War II as were lost by Australia in Vietnam.

Yes, we were pushing it uphill against the wind right from when we Aussies were sent overseas to Europe. Blame Bob Menzies; blame whom you like, but the fact remains that Europe was one hell of a training ground for Aussies to bring their skills back to the Pacific War.

In England, I met five other Aussies who became mates in a crew but also the greatest mate I ever had – Elizabeth. She and I were crewed up for forty-eight years until she left last August.

Buck, Bluey, Johnno, Brownie and Murray, all Aussies, met for the first time in August 1944. Not so long after we were crewed up at Hixon, Staffordshire, our crew moved to Seighford. From Seighford six of us in Murray Nottle's crew rode bikes through Newport to Wellington.

Little did I know at the time that we were so close to Bridgnorth where Elizabeth had received her initial training.

We had made it a pub crawl, so by the time we turned back, it was not only late in the day but we were a little tired. Somehow we became separated and I found myself with Buck, the rear gunner. Neither of us knew the way home so as it became darker and darker, we realized that we were completely lost. I suppose when one is lost, then being completely lost is no different.

A haystack swam into view in the fading light and we made for the side sheltered from the wind. It was a glorious feeling to sink down into that sweet smelling, dry hay. Not for long! My uprising was both rapid and colourful. I am not sure what I said, but it was couched in Aussie language. A great rat plunged out from under my left shoulder and scampered away. After that I always advised Aussies to keep away from haystacks, be they in Shropshire or any other part of Britain.

Later, when we reached Binbrook in early 1945, as a crew we did a couple of bike trips to Caistor about eight miles away. There at Caistor, we discovered a tobacconist who sold many types of pipe tobacco. It was all loose so you could ask for a bit of this and a bit of that to make a ripe and interesting mixture.

When I met Elizabeth and we started courting, we went touring, pedalling around the Lincolnshire Wolds. On one occasion, we went to Tealby Castle, where Lord Tennyson lived at one stage. Unfortunately we were unable to go right up to the building, but it aroused great memories for me as I had studied the poetry of Tennyson and Wordsworth at High School and could spout great slabs of Morte d'Arthur. Poor Elizabeth had to put up with a crazy airman who wanted to reel off lines learned just a few years before. Well, she was long suffering as I was still spouting forty-eight years later.

With all of the bike riding Elizabeth and I did, even later in Australia, it did not occur to me to ask how she learned to ride a bike so well. Many years later she told me of her first attempts while at Dyce in Scotland.

When she was posted straight from initial training to Dyce, near Aberdeen, she was billeted at a private home some distance from the camp site. She was issued with a bike and told to ride in each day. This was no mean task to ride miles before breakfast to the mess in sometimes freezing conditions.

Elizabeth had never ridden a bike before. There she was, miles from camp and not a clue how to ride a bike. Elizabeth's description of her first efforts had me in fits. She got on; fell off; got on again; wobbled a few yards; went head over turkey into a field; tried again and again and out of sheer desperation mastered it. She would be twenty-two at the time. It always amused me that she said 'into a field'. It was not 'paddock' as an Aussie would describe it, but 'field', with a Scottish accent. That word rings in my ears now.

Early in my meanderings around Britain, I learned that a push bike was the thing to have on RAF stations as ablutions, messes, lecture rooms and tarmacs were usually scattered over vast areas. At Hixon, in Staffordshire, there was a whole village smack in the middle of everything else. We marched past the village church, past cottages, past ponds, past sheep and cattle, past villagers and finally arrived to have a wash. Do all of that again in another direction and you came to the mess, to eat.

Almost at the very end of the runway, there was a railway line. Prang after prang took place on the line from Stafford. I was always glad that our crew was posted to the satellite – Seighford.

It was at Hixon that I bought my first bike in England. Each time we were posted, I sold up and bought another at the next station. Since Seighford was just the other side of Stafford from Hixon, several of us decided to ride across, while our gear went in the truck provided.

We all have magical and memorable moments and it was during that ride to Seighford that one came to me. It was almost dusk and the road from Stafford out was very hilly, dipping in waves. As I went down one dip I sud- denly found myself in thick fog. It wrapped around you like a warm, fluffy, security blanket – like love – and then, suddenly, you rose out of it to catch your breath.

It was such a different feeling to flying in and out of cloud. Always in cloud I was asking myself, 'Who else is in this cloud? Will they keep out of our way?' The fighter pilot sometimes looked for cloud. It was a place to hide but it always scared the pants off me.

When I try to summon up visions of Elizabeth as I knew her then, I am looking at a smiling, happy lass whose grey skirt rides up; her tunic flaps and her beautiful hair streams out as she pedals beside me.

I wonder, does God have push bikes in heaven? Is there snow and are there country lanes with winding grass verges, where Elizabeth and I can once again hold hands across the track as we pedal on to the next hamlet?

At seventy-three I still ride a bike. I am practising just in case.

DAM BUSTERS

Kathleen Olszewski (née Fitchett) is a natural story teller and she has sent a number of stories – some sad, some joyous. Here are some tales of 617 squadron at Scampton:

I was a WAAF stationed at Scampton, 1941–45, with the Dam Busters and the then not so famous Guy Gibson whom I saw every day.

As an MT driver I used to be on Dispersal which entailed driving the air crews out to their kites and picking them up on their return. They were days of great sadness and joy. The sad times were when I used to wait on the tarmac and many didn't return.

I lost many friends during those dark days, and we had just got used to one squadron of young boys when they went for a 'burton' and a new lot came in.

The WAAF sleeping quarters were next to the bomb dump. When you think about it, that wasn't too bad, for if Jerry had dropped a bomb on it the whole of Lincoln would have gone up so we didn't think about it.

All was not gloom and doom. We had our camp dances. Lincoln was only a few miles down the road and life was sweet.

We got used to crews not returning but one sad day for me was when driving past our makeshift morgue. I stopped as I saw an airman standing there and looking glum.

'Are you OK?' I asked. He took my arm and without much ado, led me inside. There were the bodies of the whole crew of a Lancaster. They had pranged somewhere and been brought back to base.

They had a military burial of course. Two were Canadians and I know that somewhere out in that lonely cemetery lie two of my friends who will never be forgotten.

I also remember the day that Guy Gibson's dog, Nigger, was killed by a civilian driver. Guy took the dog everywhere and it roamed the camp freely. I'm glad that I didn't have to break the news to him.

I could go on and on but the memory grows dim as the years go by. One incident that springs to mind is the day that two squadrons were breaking up to be posted elsewhere.

We had taken the crews out to their planes and were watching them take off. Each aircraft circled the drome in a farewell gesture. I noted that each plane came lower for a while but I began to feel uneasy about the last one. It seemed to be making straight for us. It was. 'Run for your life,' the Sergeant who was standing beside me yelled. I did.

I felt the hair on the back of my neck stand on end as the Lancaster zoomed over us. The back wheel scraped the roof of a Nissen hut beside which we stood and the plane landed on top of a troop of RAF Regiment, who had been drilling a few moments earlier. All were killed as well as the crew and some ground staff who were taking a lift. All of our luggage which had been in the Nissen hut was destroyed. The smell of burning stayed in my nostrils for days.

Once, I hitched a lift in a Lancaster – only twenty minutes in the air, but it put me off flying forever.

Kathleen Olszewski (née Fitchett)
Nottingham

COMRADESHIP

When I read Elsie's letter, certain parts leapt out. She had expressed, in a far better way that I could, her thoughts about the spirit that still prevails among those who served in the WAAF and the RAF. She has been to many national reunions of WAAFs and is able to write with real knowledge of comradeship that has lasted so many years. Here is her story:

I write to you as an ex-WAAF to extend and continue the common bond which brought, and has kept, so many thousands of us together. That bond was forged during World War II.

Over the past six years, I have attended three national reunions, when hundreds of us get together, for a three-day spell, to relive, rekindle and enjoy the comradeship and lasting friendships we made over fifty years ago. During the last reunion when four hundred of us gathered, after having seven hundred in 1989, we found that our numbers were reduced but the spirit still prevailed.

I was a Flight Mechanic working on the airframe sections of the aircraft. These were mostly Wellingtons and Mosquitoes. We did a four and a half months' course, identical to airman, including hydraulics, pneumatics, metal and wood repairs, riveting and welding, theory of flight, airfield procedures and splicing.

Very often, we lived in exposed Nissen huts on WAAF sites and worked in draughty hangars or in the open on flights in the elements of winter's lowest temperatures. However, in retrospect, none of us would have missed it.

Elsie M. Gascoigne (née Williamson)
LACW 2148932

DAKOTAS TO CAEN

Ted Dodsworth of Stourbridge, Worcestershire had a sister Dorothy who was a Nursing Orderly in the WAAF. Sadly, Dorothy died some years ago and Ted has written to tell of her work with 48 and 271 Squadrons:

My sister served as a WAAF during World War II. Sadly, she died of leukaemia some years ago. Dorothy served as a LAC Nursing Orderly and was based at RAF Down Ampney, Gloucestershire, where she flew in

Debriefing after a trip to Caen for wounded.
Dorothy Dodsworth with the crew of a Dakota.

Dakotas with 48 and 271 Squadrons. Often, she would fly twice daily to Caen and other airfields to recover wounded troops of all nationalities, even occasionally German POWs.

Her pilot on many trips was the comedian, the late Jimmy Edwards of handlebar moustache fame. Before accommodation was completed for WAAFs at Down Ampney, Dorothy was billeted in the New Inn of Gloucester.

I have a portrait photograph of her plus another of her in flying kit, Mae West, flying boots etc. Also there are photographs of her as she sat with the flight crew around a stove, either briefing and debriefing.

Ted Dodsworth
Stourbridge

I am most grateful to Ted for his letter and the photographs he enclosed.

DIRECTION FINDERS

When Olive first wrote to me, she told me two things which stuck in my mind. The First was that she had worked on Direction Finders and the second was that when she went on duty she had to carry a bucket of water. She tells about the Direction Finder but I am still left puzzling about that bucket of water. I am leaving that for you to puzzle out. Here is Olive's story:

The Direction Finders were just a big compass. We were not allowed to draw them or write anything. The sounds gave you the readings. There were two sounds which we had to learn and I found the job nerve-racking.

I trained at Cranwell which was the ace place. I met an airman who was on the advanced course. While we danced, I would question him about some of the things which were not clear to me. This helped me and I passed.

When I went to Scotland, the CO at Charter Hall thought it was a good idea for the Radio Telephonists to do a couple of days in the canteen. Who should come in but the airman whose brains I had picked. He thought I had failed and had been put on the cook-house staff. He was happy to discover that my canteen work was just a fill-in.

In Scotland, I was issued with a cycle and there were some beautiful spots to visit. Transport out of the camp was not good and had to be paid for. When we went on leave one of the boys would catch a rabbit and this became a help with rations at home.

When we came back from a dance at Kelso, we would cycle along the runway. Fortunately we were never caught. Probably, this was more good luck than management.

Olive Piercy
Reepham

A BRIEF ACCOUNT OF MY LIFE
IN THE WAAF, 1939–46

On 11 May I met Grace at her home, had a chat and saw the book in which she wrote up each raid in shorthand. One of these accounts is given in Vera Lynn's book, The Women who Won the War.

Of all the descriptions of life on a bomber squadron, this one given by Grace is the most detailed. As I read it, I live again the build-up to an operation – the tension, the hopes and the fears. Of the many things I learned from Grace one of the outstanding was her love of the Lancaster aircraft.

I joined the WAAF in August 1939. I was living in Coventry at the time, and it was obvious that war was imminent. I'd been wondering what sort of war service I could do, when I saw a life-size model of a WAAF in full uniform in the window of the RAF Recruiting Office in the centre of the town. That did it. The uniform! Absolutely smashing! I couldn't resist it, so in I went, and signed on the dotted line there and then.

Once war was declared I waited impatiently for my calling-up papers. They came on 12 September, and I had to report in ten days time to RAF Castle Bromwich, near Birmingham.

I duly reported there, with about twenty other rookie WAAFs from all over the Midlands. I'd expected to be kitted out with full uniform immediately on arrival, but to the intense disappointment of us all, there wasn't any uniform – it hadn't yet been mass produced for women. So all we were issued with was an airman's greatcoat and a beret. Well, at least it was something.

We stayed there for a few days, learning elementary drill, RAF Regulations, and being interviewed to find out for which branch of service we were fitted. Having been a fully qualified secretary in civilian life, I was labelled 'Clerk'. We were also told to which RAF Stations we were being posted. I was sent, with half a dozen others, to Wittering, a Fighter Station between Peterborough and Stamford, and I spent two very happy years there, meeting my future husband within a few months of arriving. (He was on 25 Squadron, flying Beaufighters at that time.)

In the early days at Wittering there was obviously no proper WAAF accommodation, and we had to live in airmen's married quarters – rows of little two-up and two-down houses. We lived four to a house. There was no bathroom – just a long zinc bath, which we had to fill with hot water, having first filled the copper and lit a fire under it. There was also no WAAF mess, and our meals arrived in a field kitchen, which we had to dash out (in all weathers) to collect, and dash back in to eat before it got stone cold.

Over the next few months the uniform arrived bit by bit, and we had to go to the Equipment Section to collect each item after we'd been notified in daily routine orders that a particular article of clothing had arrived. One week it would be a skirt, the next maybe a couple of shirts; then grey lisle stockings; a tie; a hat; three pairs of passion-killers (knickers); and finally, best of all – the jacket, and at last we were real-live-fully-kitted-WAAFs. Wonderful!

As a qualified shorthand-typist I was put first of all into the office of the Station Engineer Officer, and worked for him alone; then later on for the Station Commander. It was very interesting work, and as you can imagine our Fighter Pilots were kept very busy indeed. When I first went there the planes were Hurricanes, Defiants and Beaufighters; then came the incomparable Spitfires.

There's lots I could write about my stay at Wittering, but I'd better hurry on to my next posting. When I'd been there two years, the CO called me in and told me he was recommending me for a Commission. (I was a Corporal by that time and had just received notice that I was to be posted to HQ Fighter Command at Stanmore as a Sergeant). I went before a Commissioning Board at Air Ministry, and to my great joy was informed that after an Officers' Training Course (at RAF Benson) and an Intelligence Course at Medmenham (near Maidenhead), I would be commissioned as an Intelligence Officer. So I duly attended these courses, which were extremely interesting, and I shall never forget the thrill of wearing Officer's uniform for the first time, and being saluted, after two years of my saluting Officers. It's quite embarrassing at first, and you feel it's all wrong.

At the end of the Intelligence Course we were all informed where we would be posted. When I learned that I was going to the Air Ministry, my first reaction was – WOW! – I really thought it would be absolutely marvellous. There I'd be, in Whitehall, right at the heart of things, a <u>real</u> part of the war effort, and I might just be lucky enough to catch sight of the great man himself – Winston Churchill. But how wrong can you be? I've never been so bored in all my life. I was in Whitehall all right, but in a depressing office seemingly miles underground; I was the only RAF person in that office, the others, male and female, being Civil Servants. They hadn't got a clue about Service life, or what it was like to be on an RAF Station. And the work I was given was excruciatingly boring. I had to wade through acres of files and draw up lists of where all the Intelligence Officers were located; whether male or female; whether married, single or otherwise; what their particular jobs were; how long they'd been there; were they due for posting, and so on, and so on, and so on, until I could have gone screaming down Whitehall, shouting, 'Who the blazes cares?'

Anyway, after about nine months I couldn't stick it any longer, so I put in an application for a posting back to a Station. I realized I could be jeopardising my future in the WAAF, but I felt that <u>anything</u> would be better than the Air Ministry.

I waited fearfully for news of my posting, and when it came it wasn't as bad as it might have been, but wasn't quite what I'd hoped for. It was to HQ 92 Group at Winslow, a pretty little village between Aylesbury and Buckingham. I was to be one of three Duty Intelligence Officers in the Operations Room. 92 Group (a Bomber Group) consisted of seven Stations, at that time flying Wellingtons. It was a Training Group, and most of the pilots and crews had done their training in Canada; their spell in 92 Group was their final training before being posted to a fully operational Station. My work was now totally different from what I'd done at Wittering and the Air Ministry, and also far more interesting. I worked three shifts in the Operations Room – the first shift was from 13.00 hours to 20.00; then the next morning from 08.00 to 13.00; and then an all-night shift from 20.00 to 08.00 the following morning. We had our own switchboard in the Ops room, and were in immediate touch with all our Stations; we had to take down all the details of the training flights the crews were carrying out, and pass them on to HQ 12 Group at Nottingham, who then passed them on to Bomber Command. It was interesting to visit each Station on days off, and get to know the other Intelligence Officers that you'd only known by voice over the phone. As a point of interest, when the first 1,000 bomber raid on Cologne took place on the night of 30 May 1942, forty aircraft from our Training Stations were included, and three of them failed to return. (Altogether Bomber Command lost forty-four aircraft that night.)

I stayed at Winslow for a year and a half, and then came what was to be my last posting – to RAF Kirmingham in Lincolnshire. There were three Stations working more or less as one – Elsham Wolds, Kirminton, and Killingholme. By then they were all flying Lancasters, and how the crews loved them! Once again I was working in the Ops Room, and the shift-times were the same, except that when the crews were operating there was no fixed 'signing-on' and 'signing-off' time. Once the gen came through from Bomber Command, giving us the night's target (in code, of course), the number of aircraft required, the route to be taken, the bomb load, the amount of fuel needed, the time over target, the take-off time, etc. etc., then the Intelligence Officers had to notify the Station Commander, the Squadron Commander, the Armament Officer, the Bombing Leader, the Navigation Officer, the Engineer Officer, the Signals Officer, the Met. Office, Photographic Section, Flying Control, and so on. Then we'd have to work out briefing time, and notify the Officers' and Sergeants' messes what time to have a pre-briefing meal ready.

Once everybody had been notified, we then had to prepare the Briefing Room. On a huge map of Europe covering one wall, the target would be marked, and the outward and homeward routes pinned up with red tape. It was always fascinating to watch the faces of the aircrews as they entered the Briefing Room and saw for the first time where they were going. Sometimes it was a look of relief, if they'd been before and hadn't encountered much opposition; but it could also be a look of horror if it was Berlin or Nuremburg or the Ruhr. At Briefing, the Station Commander would have his little say first; then the Squadron Commander; then the Duty Intelligence Officer, followed by each of the Specialist Officers. Any questions the crews asked would be answered, then they would be dismissed to collect their target maps and escape and survival kits, and hand in any personal belongings that could identify them in case of capture. The crew buses would then ferry them out to their respective aircraft at dispersal points around the airfield.

Very often, if I wasn't the particular officer on duty, I would accompany the Squadron Commander (if he wasn't on the operations himself that night) as he drove around to each crew in turn to chat with them and wish them well. I got to know most of them very well indeed, and some of them seemed so young, and looked so small standing beside their massive Lancasters. We had a lot of Canadians and New Zealanders, and several Norwegians – all of them absolutely great.

Having visited each crew at Dispersal, we would then go up into the Flying Control Tower to watch take-off, and <u>what</u> a joy that was. If they were taking off in daylight on a summer evening, it was a wonderful sight to see those beautiful Lancasters taxiing round the perimeter tracks, turning on to the runway, waiting for the green flare signal to take off, and then roaring down the runway, and rising so gracefully into the evening sky.

After they were all airborne, the next job was to get the Briefing Room ready for Interrogation when they returned. Tables, chairs, pro-formas, etc. all had to be at the ready. If it was a long trip lasting for five, six or seven hours, only one Intelligence Officer remained in the Ops Room (and there were always umpteen jobs to do); the others could go to bed and get some well-earned sleep. The Duty WAAF Watchkeeper (we had three, all Sergeants) would ring the sleeping Ops Officers in good time to get to the Briefing Room before the first kite landed. Sometimes a crew would have to return early, perhaps with engine trouble, and the duty Intelligence Officer would brief that crew and send them off to the mess for a meal and to bed.

After interrogating the first few crews it would become clear whether the raid had been successful or not. Either they were elated because everything had gone according to plan, and they'd got back safely; or there was too much cloud to identify the target, and the markers hadn't helped very much, and the flak and the fighters had been a nightmare. One by one the landing times would be chalked up on the large blackboard in the Ops Room, and not until every space was filled in did we give a sigh of relief and thank the good Lord that all 'our boys' were safely home. But when that <u>didn't</u> happen, I used to weep inwardly at the thought of the wives, sweethearts and parents, who would have to be told that the one they loved was 'missing'. This illustrated the big difference between being on a Fighter Station and a Bomber Station. At Wittering I rarely came into contact with the pilots, and therefore with any losses that we sustained, although I felt sad, I didn't feel <u>personally</u> involved. But with the Bomber crews I knew every one; I'd joked with them in the mess, I'd chatted to them before briefing, I'd learnt about their families, their hopes, their fears

– I felt they were all my brothers, so that whenever any of them failed to return, it was like a knife in my heart.

I had many a flight in a Lancaster bomber. Quite often when a crew wasn't needed for an operational flight they would have to do a 'cross-country' flight and the pilot would usually ask me if I'd like to fly with them. If I wasn't on duty, I accepted the invitation without hesitation.

When the war with Germany was over (5 May 1945) we were able to brief the crews for far happier missions than bombing enemy territory. Some of our aircraft were on 'Operation Manna' (known as 'Spam-trips' by the crews) which involved low-level flights over Holland, dropping food to the starving Dutch. Other aircraft were on 'Operation Exodus' – which was ferrying POWs from camps in Belgium, Italy and the Middle East.

When these trips were all completed Bomber Command gave permission for all Intelligence Personnel (if they wished) to be flown over Germany to see for themselves what damage had been done by our 'boys', and to know that in some small way we had contributed to the many scenes of desolation and wholesale destruction. It was an amazing experience. The pilot told me to go into the nose of the aircraft (where the bomb-aimer would be during a raid), and to lie on my tummy and look down through the perspex. As he flew at very low-level over city after city, I didn't know whether to rejoice or cry. In some places it seemed that nothing was left standing – just ugly, jagged ruins, and empty, lifeless streets. I had to keep reminding myself of Coventry and Plymouth, Portsmouth and London; and all the other areas of my own country that had been at the receiving end of the German bombers.

I was asked by the Chief Commandant of the WAAF if I would stay on indefinitely, but now that the really interesting work of an Intelligence Officer was over, I saw no future in it. In any case I had already put in an application to the Allied Control Commission for Germany, asking if there was any possibility of a post over there. I'd done this because my husband (we'd married in 1944) was in the Far East and wasn't expected back to UK for another twelve to eighteen months. I was accepted by the Control Commission, and worked in Germany until October 1947, when my husband and I were at last reunited. He was a Regular in the RAF, having joined as an Apprentice when he left school, so I was delighted that my association with the Air Force life would continue indefinitely. He finally retired as a Wing Commander after forty years in the RAF.

Sadly, he died three years ago, otherwise this year we would have celebrated our Golden Wedding.

I think this is a suitable place to end my little account of 'Life in the WAAF in Wartime'.

Grace Finch

PERILS OF HITCH HIKING

Nowadays, hitch hiking for girls is a very dangerous practice but during the war thousands of WAAFs got home or got to the local railway station or the local hop this way. Joyce, stationed at Grantham at the time, decided to hitch to Nottingham. She admitted to going through life in a dream but she little dreamed as to who would be driving the car she flagged down.

This story is the only one in the book where I sat down and took notes. I was able to do that since Joyce and her husband Dennis kindly gave me hospitality during my visit to Britain in April–May 1994. I was able to spend several days at their home, and I was most grateful for the visit to Binbrook which they made possible. We visited Binbrook airfield, Binbrook village and Swinhope, the WAAF site on which Elizabeth was billeted. Now, here is a brief account of Joyce's experiences:

I went through life in a dream and the very first day at Bridgnorth I was asked by a Sergeant to black-lead a stove. What a beginning! Somehow I found that I was always put in the middle of a group when we went marching. Perhaps this was so that I didn't get lost as often on such occasions my mind would wander and so would I. On one occasion, and it was an important one, we were marching past and I made a proper mess of things as suddenly my gas cape unfurled and I dragged it along with me.

On one leave I missed the bus back to camp and was picked up by the MPs. One MP took pity on me and took me home to sleep and then his wife gave me breakfast – an egg. What a luxury!

When I set out to hitch hike to Nottingham I got some distance from camp, saw a car coming and hailed it. A head came out of the window and to my horror it belonged to the CO of the camp. I was given a right royal lecture on the dangers of hitching. I remember the motto of a Rhodesian Squadron with whom I later worked, 'Always Bloody Something'. Yes.

For six months I worked in the Met. Office at Waddington in Yorkshire. There we prepared maps after gathering information and passed this on. While I was there, Guy Gibson of Dam Buster fame visited the station and he was treated like a film star.

While at 5 Group HQ the ops room was in an old house with the Met. Office next door. When I first joined all Met. Officers were civilians. Of course I went to Bridgnorth and Morecambe and I went to London for Met. training. I still remember the balloons which were on top of Barclay's Bank in London.

I remember the Dam Buster raid and how one of the aircraft had to turn back because the wind-screen was broken by a seagull crashing into it.

Joyce Dudeney (née Sayner)
Grimsby

THE WEATHER GIRLS

Joan Weeks, who served at Topcliff, Yorkshire, wrote to me twice – firstly telling of her postings and then later of the work of the meteorologist in the WAAF. She later became an RAF wife and spent five years overseas with her husband. Here are her stories:

I joined in 1942 and became a meteorological assistant in the WAAF. I had previously worked as a laboratory assistant so possessed a somewhat scientific mind.

After six months or so of training I was posted to Topcliffe, Yorkshire, which was part of the Royal Canadian Air Force Group. This I enjoyed immensely. They were a great lot. After a year or so I became a Corporal and was posted to RCAF Group HQ, where there were Canadian WAAFs or WDs as they were called.

Here I stayed until the end of the war in Europe when all the RCAF went home. I then moved to HQ 1 Group Bawtry for six months and then to Abingdon, near Oxford.

After being demobbed, I was offered the same job as a civilian and accepted. This was lucky as I would not otherwise have met my husband. I enjoyed life as an RAF wife very much, particularly the travelling with 2½ years in Ceylon and later, another 2½ years in Singapore.

When I wrote to Joan asking her to tell more about her work as a met. assistant, she sent along these details.

In response to your question, the WAAF met. assistants were not sufficiently qualified to do briefings. Only the forecasters did that. Our job was to trot up to the roof of the building containing our office – normally the Flying Control, on the edge of the airfield – every hour to observe the weather. This meant noting the types of cloud and how much, the visibility, wind speed and direction and any other phenomena that were present. The temperature was also noted.

Back in the office again, we coded this information into five figure groups, adding a few more items in the process, and sent it off by teleprinter to Dunstable, the Head Office.

About ten minutes later, all the observations were sent back from all the British Isles stations. Every three hours, we plotted a chart with the information. This is what the forecasters used for their forecast.

Of course, we also kept them going with cups of tea and coffee. Occasionally a kind Canadian would bring us some cake which had been sent in a food parcel. We gave them cups of tea too.

We worked shifts, 0800–1700, 1700–2300 and 2300–0800, two days of each. After that we had two days off. We needed it too.

My maiden name was Irving and I believe I may have some relations in the Melbourne area in Australia. I hope you enjoy your visit to Yorkshire.

Joan Weeks
Kings Lynn

I certainly did, Joan, and I fell in love with the beautiful Yorkshire dales.

NITS TO YOU!

What a wonderful expression: 'Nits to you!' I must admit I haven't heard it for years. Before I go on with this nitty story, I must thank Diana Lindo (LACW Tait) for bringing nits to mind when she discussed FFIs in her book, *A WAAF at War*.

Early in the preparation of this book Diana sent me a copy of her book and I spent one of the most enjoyable evenings for a long time lapping up her wartime jottings of a WAAF driver. She had me roaring with laughter as she rollicked through the fifty-two thousand miles of driving, seven RAF stations, a couple of boyfriends, a few snotty-nosed WAAF Officers and five years of fun spent in the RAF. Even Diana had tears to tell about when she worked with an Aussie Officer investigating aircraft crashes in Britain. She often mentioned 'polish' and button sticks, but I didn't read about 'spit'. Perhaps she had a better way of polishing shoes. Thank you, Diana. You have inspired me – double-declutched me and now I hope to stay in top gear.

Back to the nits. When masses of WAAFs gathered at Bridgnorth to have what to some would be their first medical, it would be a normal thing for some to have nits. Elizabeth mentioned this to me when she had me in fits describing that embarrassing first medical. The types with nits in their hair need not have come from poor working class homes. Many did and conditions prewar and early war in parts of what some think of as a green and lovely land were anything but lovely. After working with children for over forty years, I know that nits do not make distinctions. You can be young, pretty or a bit older and ugly. Nits go for your nut just the same.

If you've had a nitty nut, the nits have chosen you as someone special. They may be thankful for a good home, no matter how temporary.

SALOME—SALOME!

Jeanne Denise Smith (née Ditchburn) now of Torpoint, Cornwall, writes:

My life in blue started in 1942. After the initial kitting out and square bashing at Innsworth, Gloucester, I was posted to RAF Pucklechurch, a balloon centre, a few miles from Bristol, where I was to spend eleven weeks training for my future role and learning how to splice rope and wire, how to deflate a balloon and inspect, repair and drive a winch. All this took place in a large hangar. The day arrived when the 'monster' was taken outside to be flown.

After training, we were sent to an operational training site to get the 'feel' of things to come. Those of us who passed all exams were sent to operational sites proper. I had been posted to one just outside Bristol and then to No 72 site by Clifton Suspension Bridge, Bristol, and this is where my story begins:

A crew was made up of twelve operators and two NCOs, all of whom were to show their courage in the face of the enemy.

Our billet was a Nissen hut with the proverbial iron stove in the centre for warmth. A wooden recreation room and a kitchen/diner were situated a few feet away and the ablutions much further. This was the accommodation scene.

The balloon was either 'bedded' on a concrete base, or flying 'at point of attachment', ready for the inevitable phone call: 'Fly balloon at – feet. Enemy aircraft approaching.' Having been given our instructions by the NCOs, we would set off, usually in the dark, to get 'Salome' into the sky, at the same time tripping over wires, concrete blocks and sand bags, causing bruises and scraped knees to most of the crew . . . Jerry had arrived. Spewing down on the City of Bristol came the deadly loads of bombs and incendiaries. Anti-aircraft guns roared, searchlights blazed, skimming the skies and often shining upon a lone plane heading towards a balloon's deadly cable. Our duties completed, all we could do was wait and watch.

Then the All Clear would sound. Another night was over and we retired to our beds, leaving two girls on guard duty. It wasn't only Jerry who kept us on our toes at night. Gale warnings would bring out all the crew to our Salome. Often the girls only had time to put on boots and steel helmets and, clad in pyjamas, went forth in the pouring rain and high winds to ensure that Salome was made safe. We got soaking wet!

This is only a brief account of life as a balloon operator. However, despite the dangers we endured, it brought us the most precious things in life . . . comradeship, heartache, compassion and, above all, friendship. All of these were to follow me for the rest of my Air Force career.

Now, fifty years on, I have memories that will never die and although I am a war disabled veteran I still wonder where my friends are now.

Jeanne Denise Smith (née Ditchburn)

A LIGHT-HEARTED ACCOUNT OF A WARTIME FRIEND I WILL NEVER FORGET

Emily came into my life when, as a WAAF, I was posted to Fradley Aerodrome, Lichfield, and found myself billeted with a strange girl who sat up in bed with her hat on!

I was the product of a sheltered upbringing, vulnerable, prone to blushing and uneasy in the company of men. I stayed in camp, a willing hairdresser for those with dates, and was consequently always on hand when trouble brewed. Emily was my opposite. She liked a good time. She was a Plain Jane, small and rotund with mousy hair rolled tightly round the then fashionable bootlace. But she had a 'way with her' – she liked the boys and they liked her. In my innocence I did not then appreciate the reason why! She crept back into camp many a time in the wee small hours of the morning (her 'blackouts' shredded on the barbed wire) confident that I would be covering up for her.

One incident concerning Emily is seared into my memory. I was preparing for bed one night when a loud banging came upon the door of the billet. I opened it to find the duty SP propping up a limp, rag-doll figure which he informed me, with disgust, had been deposited at the Guard Room by a Yank. It was Emily, blotto! His last words as he handed her over were that she was to be on duty the next morning or she would be put on a charge.

I flopped this figure onto her bed and divested her of her outer clothing, heaving a sigh of relief at the success of my wrangling as she finally lay at peace; but with a loud snore her mouth dropped open and I gazed in fascinated horror at her toothless gums. Where, oh where, were those pearls she flashed at the boys?

She was oblivious and at peace but my night was spent worrying about her teeth. Come the crack of dawn, I rushed across to the Guard Room to report their loss, dreading the ribald laughter that I felt sure would greet me. I knocked timidly at the door and turned the knob, my nose coming up against the chest of the departing Duty Officer. Quickly my hand went up to the salute but there it froze as I gaped at the sight that confronted me. Grinning back from the polished table in front of the Sergeant was a set of false teeth. The blood suffused my face, bright red above my starched collar, as I asked timidly if they were Emily's. The Sergeant laughed as he handed me the gruesome objects . . . naked! I took them queasily, wishing that he had put them in a bag. He informed me that they had been retrieved by a public-spirited citizen after Emily had sicked them up in Lichfield's public loo.

Turning, I fled back to the billet and hurriedly proceeded to dress the still jelly-like figure. Why I had undressed her in the first place I will never know. My task was made difficult because, as each garment was pulled into place, Emily sank back onto the bed with a groan. Finally I rammed the offending teeth into her receptive mouth and her sunken features once more assumed the contours of a young girl.

I staggered outside with Emily and tried to mount her on her RAF issue cycle. There was no other transport. She wobbled and fell off. Finally, after a few pushes, her legs started to pedal and off she went. I pedalled after her only to find her falling off in front of me. This set the pattern for the four-mile journey to the aerodrome. I never knew how we made it, but we did, and I had her propped in front of her teleprinter at the correct time – saved from Jankers!

I spent the morning in the control tower running backwards and forwards doing my own job on the switchboard and hers on the teleprinter. By the time she had sobered up I was ready to pass out through sheer exhaustion.

Thus, in the haze of half-forgotten faces from Service life, the memory and the face of Emily linger on.

Lucille Elms

GET FELL IN THERE!

Mollie Whiteside of Co. Tyrone, Northern Ireland needs no introduction to her work. She is a natural story teller so here is yet another from her.

When I was young, you couldn't stop me writing poetry, scribbling all the time, after I went into the Forces even. Girls serving with me in the WAAF agreed I was an oddity. 'You think too much,' they said. I wrote a poem then. Eighteen I was and sad, feeling the weight of others' grief, of my own grief to come.

And in the Morning

Shall we remember through long aching years
The heartbreak in laughter, rare, comforting tears,
The silence of sorrow, deep uplifting pride,
Soft whispered consolings of those who have died?

Shall we remember how planes throb at night,
How swift bursting shells pattern darkness with light?
Shall we remember the flame ridden skies,
Or picture the sadness in some mother's eyes?

Shall we remember the horrors of hate,
The unflaunted courage of those who must wait,
Remember the ramping of rough hungry seas,
See shadows on graves under sheltering trees?

Shall we remember staunch weary-eyed youth,
Remember the bleakness of ungilded truth,
Remember eternal grim soul-burning sand,
The full-hearted grasp of an unfettered hand?

Shall we remember in purpled content
The mud and the blood and the bugle's lament,
Remember who secretly unsolaced weep,
While death swathes their sons in cold unwaking sleep?

Shall we remember as long as we live
Remember though loving we still must forgive?
Shall we remember for ever? – And yet
If this is our destiny, can we forget?

In school, while I was still too young to do my bit, I worried all the time, knitting socks and balaclava helmets under the desk among my books, writing sad bewildered verse. Hitler had taken over most of Europe right across France. The day Paris fell I tried vainly to concentrate on lessons while in the park outside our window soldiers drilled and wheeled, marching up and down, singing brave rude patriotic songs. From Dunkirk, other troops in full retreat waded out into the sea right up to their chins, waiting for a fleet of bold foolish incredible little boats to take them off. Mates not so lucky fell on the beaches or filled the prison camps. I wrote to some of them, keeping them in touch, and they said I got more on an airgraph than anybody you ever met. Young boys in their teens and early twenties took to the air, fighting off German bombers that swept in wave on wave, pounding our cities into rubble. German invasion armies poised on the shores of Europe. Casualty lists grew longer and longer and whole families mourned. The Japanese took Singapore, advancing then into Burma, menacing India. Things were so awful you'd wonder how even hope managed to survive.

Across the water here in Ulster, too, Dad's Armies trained with broomsticks, guarding the home front. St John's held First Aid classes in every town and every village. Because I was skinny and no weight, I was a regular 'patient', bandaged and splinted from head to foot, carted about on a stretcher to give them practice. Voluntary bodies worked and gathered up, sending off huge parcels of woollies and things to military depots everywhere. Everybody cared. Everybody tried to do his or her share. One by one, young people, some not so young, slipped quietly away.

My sister and my two brothers went charging off to join the Air Force and I went too. I was a wee little thing then, scared stiff they wouldn't take me. 'Sure, look at the size of you,' they said, 'we're not that desperate yet!' and they laughed, teasing, not meaning any harm. But I wanted so much to help, I couldn't rest, rushing off as soon as school exams were finished, knowing that we had to stop this trouble soon. They sent me for medicals to Omagh, to Glasgow, then to London where bombs fell like rain, 'You're thin,' they told me, 'but fit enough. What can you do?' I breathed again. 'Anything,' I said, 'I'll do anything,' so they put me in Signals and I made Corporal before it was all over. 'The little corporal', they called me, or sometimes, 'Napoleon', making fun. I was too shy and diffident for promotion but being a corporal was just fine.

My elder brother trained as a pilot in America, called at my camp, bright new wings on his tunic front. The girls flocked around him, 'a smasher,' they said, 'an absolute doll.' You know what girls are like. Always a hit with them he was, full of wit and charm. Wild about small children too. 'Wee scaldies', he called them. You could picture him as a husband and father, nice young wife, little ones on his knee. Not for him though. He was twenty-two when he died in his blazing plane, shot down over Holland. They sent us the dreaded telegram, 'We regret to inform you . . . ', the bleak ungilded truth I'd sensed in my poem. Afterwards, I gave up writing altogether. My parents, hiding their distress, kept a happy cheerful home for the rest of us, who had to press on regardless.

When it ended at last, you could see it was a war we'd had to fight and had to win, worse, far worse than anyone had ever dreamed. You don't mention Belsen any more or Dachau or Auschwitz or Buchenwald, gas ovens and incinerators, six million Jews alone transported in padlocked cattle trucks to mass extermination centres, death railways in the Far East built on British bones. Gathered round the Cenotaph each Armistice, laying our poppy wreaths, we remember our dead of two world wars in sorrow and gratitude, trying to put the horrors behind us. For our tomorrow they gave their today. We owe them everything we have.

Mollie Wilson Whiteside
Northern Ireland

FOR ALL SECOND WORLD WAR HEROES

I wasn't born, I wasn't there.
Thank God that it was so –
That does not mean I cannot thank
The ones that had to go.

To war that is, that dreadful war
That shaped our world today;
You made it safe for me to live –
A debt I can't repay.

It's thanks to you that I am here,
My lovely children too;
You made it safe for us to live
At tragic loss to you.

You lost your friends and family,
You fought that war so true;
But, please, it was not all in vain –
Our lives, our thanks, to you.

To all unseen heroes,
I'll make sure my children know
You gave us back this lovely world
For us to live and grow.

Christine Ianson
(Ivor Hayes's second daughter)

TEARS

Not all the tears I saw shed while in Britain were those of children, girls or women. Let me tell you just what happened three days after our last bombing raid on Berchesgarten on 25 April 1945.

Although the war was not officially over, many Allied POWs had either been released or had escaped from prison camps and were being brought to Brussels in Belgium. The RAF was given the task of picking up these men and bringing them home to Britain.

Lancasters were not built as passenger or troop transport craft. You could not pack men into bomb bays, but it was surprising how many could be packed in from the bomb aimer's position in the nose, around the skipper and the engineer, around the navigator and wireless operator and then back behind the main spar right to the rear gunner's turret.

On two occasions, one before VE day and one a few days after, our crew went to Brussels to pick up POWs. The official name given to this exercise was 'Operation Exodus'.

Of course we all wanted to get leave in Brussels and have a look around. We had seen a great deal of Europe from the air, but had never been on the ground. We tried hard and actually got a 'flattie', a flat tyre on the undercarriage when we landed. No luck! We were sent home in another Lancaster along with POWs. This was the first time we as a crew had even entrusted ourselves to another skipper. However, he was a 460 bod and that speaks volumes.

When we did have POWs on board, two of them came down with me into the bomb hatch. There, the three of us lay flat and probably had the best view through the perspex of the Lancaster's nose.

It was difficult to speak to these men. As a crew, we could communicate all the time through our RT. I tried to yell at them and they tried to yell back but the roar of the four Merlins made it an impossible task. It was like trying to communicate while at a modern rock concert.

I gazed at these boys. They were wan, shaky, apprehensive but in better shape than we had expected after hearing the horrific stories which were coming out of Europe at that time.

It was a great feeling to be doing something really humane and to be helping those who had suffered so much. The couple of men I had in the front hatch were men from the British Army and they had spent years in POW camp following Dunkirk. Their story was in their eyes.

They had been through God knows what and they tired easily, so just lay back either dozing or looking at the inside of the aircraft. I think they had never flown before and the front of a Lancaster was not the best place to start.

The war was still on, so my eyes were sweeping left and right, up and down and away in front for aircraft, friendly or foe. There were a few around. A Spitfire gave us a hell of a fright at Brussels. When we came in to land, this Spit swept underneath us and landed. We had to overshoot

– that is give the four Merlins full throttle and gain height to go around again. Of course, you always did something else when you had to over-shoot – prayed, hard!

As we were over the English Channel, the white cliffs of Dover in all their magnificence shone out. I shook the shoulder of one man and pointed. He turned. He stared out. I saw his eyes moisten, then fill up. He turned away. There was no need for him to do that. 'Where breathes the man with soul so dead . . . this is my own, my native land.' With more than moistened eyes I turned to him and in a firm grip grasped his hand. Yes, men can and do have tears.

Down through the years since that time, when I listen over and over again to Vera Lynn, those words of the 'White Cliffs of Dover' bring to mind that scene in the bomb hatch of the Lancaster and my eyes again tell the story.

> There'll be blue birds over the white cliffs of Dover,
> Tomorrow just you wait and see.
> There'll be love and laughter and peace ever after,
> Tomorrow when the world is free.

I sit here now and wonder. Were we the 'blue birds' over those white cliffs? We were bringing home fathers, sweethearts, brothers, uncles and cousins to love and laughter. What a hell of a pity there has not been peace ever after. Surely we don't want to change those wonderful words and say, 'There'll be tears ever after'.

THEY ALSO SERVED

Some WAAFs were well away from any operational action and locked into such duties as administration or even typing pools where the hours were long and the heating and lighting poor. Marjory, a Yorkshire girl, was one who for years laboured on without, as she said, having any exciting times. I must differ with this opinion for many of these girls made their own fun and when it came down to it, enjoyed their life in the WAAF. They were part of the great team which helped to keep the aircraft flying and they were every bit as important as mechanics, fitters, electricians, radar bods or aircrew. In several letters Marjory had this to tell us:

I was a WAAF and was stationed at No 16 Maintenance Unit at Stafford.

I was well away from any action and locked in a typing pool. I don't have any exciting tales to tell, nevertheless we worked very hard, long hours night and day to keep the aircraft in the air both at home and abroad.

I found life very exciting during the war although there was always the feeling of uncertainty around. In the 4½ years of my service, I learned a lot about life and met so many interesting people from various walks of life and I feel sure that the experience gained was beneficial to me.

On the day that Victory in Europe was declared, work stopped and we were allowed out of camp without passes so we could stay out without any fear of being put on a charge for being AWOL. Dorothy and I went into Stafford where all the celebrations were in the market square. We finally arrived back in camp at some unearthly hour to find that we were the last in that hut. Also, we found our beds missing – gone completely, nothing there! We collapsed into fits of laughter and woke everybody up. I think they were all awake and waiting for us. Then all the lights went on and after great hilarity and help our beds were produced and restored to their proper places.

A few hours later, there was another commotion when Officers arrived with a cup of tea for each of us. I wonder if they were disillusioned when they saw us with our hair in pins and our unglamorous striped pyjamas.

I shall always remember VJ night when I sat on a stool entertaining those around me with the things I was saying. On the way home from that celebration, I had to walk through woods and across a stream by a single plank of wood. How I did it, I shall never know. I had left Stafford by this time and was only a few miles away, demobbing men from overseas.

Marjory Rhodes (née Camwell)
Yorkshire

RATTLES IN THE NIGHT

Margaret Coombs of Saltdean tells of the hectic life on the south coast and of bogus messages that came through on WT. She had some near misses with rockets. Here then is her story:

I joined up in 1942, going to Bridgnorth for square bashing and being sorted out for a trade. I wanted to be a map reader but was sent to Wireless

Op training at Compton Bassett in Wiltshire for six months. Then I had a short spell in Scotland which was a rest station for squadrons so there were Poles, Australians and New Zealanders. My mother became ill and I was allowed to be in Brighton, my home town, for three months. Brighton was where aircrews came when they had been 'naughty boys' and they had some retraining and lots of lectures. I was on the reception desk as there was no need for a wireless op. That was the end of my easy time.

Next, I went to HQ Coastal Command at Northwood. We were well underground and security was No. 1. It was also doodle bug time and we were hardly free even for a day. I was in hospital in a ward so crowded with civilian victims that beds were on the floor between other beds. In many beds were Londoners with such wonderful humour and yet some were very badly injured.

I went back to WT and it was just prior to D-Day. We were picking up all sorts of messages from ditched pilots – some bogus. I got one and when it was deciphered it read, 'A submarine is coming up Watford Road!' That one took some living down. Then one night after we kept getting 'snowballs' it was the Allied invasion of Normandy. We were not aware of that until we came out of our rabbit warren and had to parade. We were told that we had worked through the night and that it was D-Day at last.

I was then posted to North Weald, Essex, Fighter Command and went to the Ops Block at Blake Hall. By then rockets were coming mainly in Essex and one landed in the grounds near us. The blast went over us and just blew our door in. We were all deaf for some time and it was horrifying to see the hole where a cottage had been with the gardener and his four children – just a hole!

I have one lovely memory from there. Douglas Bader was released from POW camp and flown into North Weald. He came to Blake Hall which was a lovely old house with wide wooden stairs. We wondered how he would manage. He gave a grin and literally bounded up those stairs – no problem.

My last posting was to a radar van on the cliffs at Fairlight Glen, Hastings . . . just two WAAFs and a High Frequency Direction Finding post. We did twenty-four hours on and twenty-four hours off. Billeted in the village, we had German POWs all around us and they were allowed to wander. One was useful as I had a problem with my generator – no generator, no lights, no little cook-ups – nothing. He got it going but I was worried as I had a feeling of being taken over.

Then I thought I had been, as about 2.00 a.m., my petrol cans under the van started rattling so I rang up North Weald. I was told to investigate. I did eventually and found it was a horse. I hadn't seen one around before, but by morning it was gone.

Eight Americans had run that post before two WAAFs took over. I did send in one reciprocal bearing before correcting myself – the poor pilot would have gone back to France.

Looking at your wife's photo brought back so many memories. I think I looked a similar type. You can always tell a serviceman or woman – there is something about them.

Margaret Coombs
Saltdean, Sussex

CHASED BY A BUZZ BOMB

Jo Bale, who now lives in Castlemaine, Victoria, Australia, describes her five years spent in the WAAF as times of happy fellowship and great interest, which she was glad to have for they made her stand on her own two feet and taught her about the real world. Five years in the WAAF was not enough, for she then went to Germany to help with rehabilitation. She wrote me a very long story and here is some of it:

I joined in 1941 and was sent to Harrogate for enlistment and then to Innsworth Lane, Gloucester for square bashing. There I landed in hospital with vaccine fever so I missed a posting. Later came a posting to HQ Coastal Command Northwood Hills which is near London. I did not like that outfit for I felt that it was only a showpiece with a lot of social people trying to be useful. After asking for a posting, I was sent to RAF Debden, Essex, 11 Group which was a busy active sector. We worked in four watches, A, B, C and D, doing a week of each duty – early morning, afternoon, evening and night. Half-way through each week we had thirty-six hours off and after night duties, seventy-two hours.

Life at times was hectic and busy but then it could become slow and dull mainly due to the weather conditions. In this area we had many near misses. Our fighters had to keep the raiders away from London if possible.

During my time we had the unfortunate raid on Arnhem which went very wrong and we had great losses.

The fall of Singapore and Pearl Harbour brought great gloom to our sector. Enter the Americans, who were sent to take over our Station at Debden. We had to stay to train them and this was not an easy task as discipline was very lax.

By this time I was a DF teller and had a crew of new boys. When the air raid sirens went they put on helmets and dived under the table. The RAF bods showed shock and surprise and I remember leaning under the table and the red faces of our brave allies came up. The Americans were at first very unpopular with our men but gradually they improved.

We went to RAF Sandwich which was then a satellite of Manston. By this time radar was getting going and we were situated outside the town overlooking Dover – a lovely spot.

It was outside here that the Mulberry Docks were made. Of course we used to see these strange objects but no one knew what they were. Then came Hitler's secret weapon – buzz bombs. They were scary and we saw fighters chasing them day and night. For defence, back came the barrage balloons. Up went the searchlights and the fighters were chasing them out to sea. Tension ran high when we heard the buzz and it was a great relief when they were shot down before they did harm.

I recall one evening when four of us WAAFs were returning from an outing on our bikes. We were on the coast road when a buzz bomb appeared almost over us and seemed to be chasing us. We did not fall off our bikes but I remember sending up a little prayer. Then, thankfully, an aircraft appeared.

On another occasion two of us were on the beach at Sandwich Bay and had a nice swim. Suddenly, the guns from the French side of the Channel opened up. We soon got going. Shots never did hit us but they kept us awake at night.

There were red faces once when the RAF Regiment shot up our aerials thinking there was going to be an invasion. When at long last came our turn to invade, all our leave was cancelled and no one was allowed to leave Sandwich. The town filled up with troops who were confined to quarters. We at least could go to our usual haunts – but not out of Sandwich. Lots of 'Brass' arrived and tension built up. At first the weather was against us but then came the break. I was on night duty when it became clear that it was on its way. We all felt tense; no one spoke; we were all trying to keep calm and do our job. We were all very busy with all the activities and by early morning it became clear that all was going well. We were on our way. We came off duty feeling relieved and fairly happy, but we were not allowed to talk about the D-Day invasion until it was announced by the BBC. Later, we had heavy bombers taking off for Berlin and plotted them across our sector.

Things gradually ran down and two of my close friends were posted overseas and I went to Biggin Hill and finally on to Birmingham for demob. This for me ended five years of happy fellowship.

A lot of WAAFs went on to Germany after demob, joining the CCG – Control Commission Germany. I was one and I saw the awful aftermath of war. We thought that we in Britain had had it bad, but the civilian population in Germany were in terrible conditions. There was, in some places, nothing – no shops, no transport – nothing! I was in Education, researching and trying to get things started. It was here in Westphalia that I met my future husband who was an Army chaplain. We returned to the UK in the late forties and married.

Looking back on my long life of eighty-three years, I realize that it has been an interesting life and I have so much to say thank you for. Yes, I have again polished my cap badge and intend to wear it on a chain.

Jo Bale
Castlemaine, Australia

A WAAF OFFICER AT BINBROOK

I am most grateful to John Hodson, the Secretary 460 Squadron Association in Victoria, Australia, for his request to Anne Baskerville to write of her experiences at Binbrook, Lincolnshire, where Elizabeth and I were stationed. Anne was a WAAF Officer, Signals, who came back to Binbrook in November 1944. Her story gives an excellent account of life for an officer on a bomber squadron. Anne met her husband F/O Alan Henry Baskerville DFC while he was on 460 Squadron during 1944. Before marriage her name was Brooke-Wright. She now lives in Hillcrest, Queensland, Australia.

I arrived at Binbrook in November 1944, after four years working as a WAAF 'Plonk', in small radar units detecting aircraft/shipping etc., mainly around Kent and Sussex in CH (Chain Home) and CHL (Chain Home Low Flying), and with the radar installation at Trimmingham on the Norfolk coast. I did a year's technical training in General Signals and then came to a posting to Binbrook, Headquarters of No. 1 Group Bomber Command in Lincolnshire.

There were seven other WAAF Officers besides myself at Binbrook. The WAAF Officers' mess, where we lived, was a Nissen hut constructed like a half circle on a concrete base. There were eight small individual bedrooms, each containing a bed, a wardrobe and a small cast-iron, pot-belly stove. It used to be very cold and damp and I always placed my clothes to wear for the next day under the blankets or they would be damp, almost wet. We had a bathroom and a fairly large kitchen with a big Aga stove. It was always a lovely warm room and helped to heat the place. The fire never went out and large circular lids, five inches thick, covered each cooking hot plate. These could be lifted on a hinge if you wanted to cook. This type of Aga was standard RAF equipment. To have an Aga in Britain was then, and I believe still is, the state of the art for kitchen cooking. There was a small dining-room off the kitchen for us, ending with the mess living room with its comfortable chairs, pot-belly fire and windows on three sides.

Every Sunday afternoon the WAAF Officers used to have 'open house' for the 'Oz' Officers. Two days after I arrived, one such Sunday afternoon came and I told the other girls I was not too keen on the idea and to count me out. 'Impossible,' they said, 'we're always all in this together.' So . . .

On Sunday 26 November 1944, I met my husband to be, Henry Baskerville, at a Sunday afternoon tea party. Incidently, he told me later that most of the guys weren't too keen either but they were urged on by the CO.

Occasionally, the various operational 'flights' would hold a party. There were A, B and C Flights. Henry was in B Flight. In early December, B Flight held a party. My sister, a civilian in the Land Army, was visiting me and came along. 'What's all this water running across the floor?' she asked. I replied, 'That's not water, it's beer from the keg. Someone has left the tap on.' Mind you, English beer was about 2% at that time and almost water. That night I remember three absolutely huge kegs of beer with a help yourself tap in each of them.

All WAAFs who wanted could come to these affairs and I remember Henry's bat-women, Ruby and Jean, being among the girls present.

Henry was about three-quarters of the way through his tour of ops at this time and 460 was sending out aircraft nearly every night, and now, as the Second Front proceeded, during the day also.

On 16 December 1944, the Group Captain, Hughie Edwards VC, was farewelled at a party to end all parties. 'Foggo' the Intelligence Officer did his stuff on a table with a mug of beer on his head. As we gathered around and sang the ditty, 'The Muffin Man', Foggo took all his clothes off except his red and white striped underpants. As he undressed, always with the mug still on his head, he went round and round the table. It was always the centrepiece of any party.

Groupie Edwards, who had won his VC on a daring low level attack, had lost a very good friend on ops. When he died, Groupie Edwards married his widow.

But Christmas was getting close and I had been on the station a month – a lifetime in those days – and the WAAFs were decorating the place with holly gathered from the nearby woods. It was a great Christmas with feasting and dancing. I remember going to a Christmas church service at that time.

One of my duties as a WAAF Officer was being present from time to time in the WAAFs' mess and with the duty Sergeant to walk up and down the tables asking, 'Any complaints?' Another duty was to walk down 'Lovers Lane' at midnight and to see that everyone was getting to the huts etc. Lovers Lane was the lane from the RAF quarters to the WAAF quarters. I was only twenty-one at the time and the youngest of all the WAAF Officers. I would walk one way, lightly tap the guy on the shoulder and say, 'Don't be here when I walk back.' Often it would be someone I knew. Then I would walk up to the end of the lane, turn around and slowly walk back. If anyone was still there, which was hardly ever, I'd have to say something a bit stronger.

Elizabeth and I were often in Lovers Lane at Binbrook but we must have watched the time as I cannot remember ever being tapped on the shoulder. Among my many souvenirs is a photograph of that lane. Ed.

Boxing Day came along and I did Duty Signals Officer on my own for the first time. Gilly, the RAF Signals Officer, had taken me to several ops briefings and we sat and listened as the aircrew were briefed on the op that night. All the wireless operators were issued with the call signs of the day and all the necessary signals information for the flight. Later, as they landed and came to interrogation, they were questioned as a crew together and then the wireless operators would come to the Signals Officer. So I used frequently to go to briefing and then later to de-briefing. Most of the wireless operators were young, some even younger than me. One guy I spoke to on that Boxing Night was in trembling shock. They had been attacked by fighters on the way back and the engineer was killed. The lad kept saying to me, 'The plane's got holes all over it just like a colander.'

If I wasn't involved in this side of things, I used to hand out hot coffee, cigarettes and a tot of rum to returning crews. Very few had the rum but they loved the coffee and cigarettes. Dee Delius would wake me up in the night and together we would go up to the de-briefing hut and look after the hot drinks until all of the crews had landed. They came in like Brown's Cows – F/O Olley and crew always wanted to get back first and often did. As the crews landed, the surname of the pilot was written up on a blackboard.

One night, all names were up except Baskerville. When Harry Ellis, Henry's wireless operator, walked in, I just about blew his head off! Who did he think he was! . . . But they were down. They were safe. They had had a mix-up with wind velocity and their ground speed was much slower than they realized. A hazardous situation but all was well.

Henry finished his tour at the end of December 1944. The relief on Harry's face could be seen. But Harry was twenty-eight and the others nineteen, twenty and twenty-one and they thought of Harry as a genera-tion removed from them. Harry understood the risks and he knew he would be going home.

Henry walked me back to the WAAF mess that night and his reaction wasn't like Harry's at all. In fact, he seemed disappointed that it was all over for him. He was then posted from 460 Squadron Binbrook to HQ Bomber Command, High Wycombe. He seemed to have access to small Oxford planes and flew up to Binbrook a number of times. We were still operational and still losing crews. We would be dancing in the mess one night and the guy was gone the next.

One morning, the WAAF Intelligence Officer, Val, woke me up and asked if I'd like to go on a sight-seeing trip in a Lancaster over the bomb-devastated cities of Germany. I was in my clothes, pants and battle-dress like a shot and without breakfast out to the plane. Squadron Leader Frank Lawrence was the pilot, from Maryborough, Queensland. As I can remember not many WAAFs had this privilege; Val and I were the only ones I knew from Binbrook.

As soon as we were aboard the Lancaster, Frank told me to stand up behind him (no parachute) so I did have a wonderful view as we took off and made for Holland, flying in over the Zuider Zee marshes. We went first of all to the Ruhr Valley in Germany and flew over Essen and other cities in the Ruhr. Then we followed the Rhine down south as far as

Wiesbaden. As I looked down out of the pilot's windows, I could see little 'ants' of people slowly moving about. In the cities it seemed as if every building had no roof – just three or four walls standing and rubble, rubble everywhere. How Germany recovered I cannot imagine; yet she did recover and recovered to be one of the major powers in Europe. There are no real victors in war. The individuals who are devastated, tortured, maimed, orphaned or killed are soon forgotten on both sides.

When we got back to Wiesbaden, Frank changed course and we flew back over France, over the south-east and central areas of country which presented a very different sight. We looked out over calm rivers, green forests and rolling country fields. Then we went on north over the North Sea and back to Binbrook.

About lunch time when we were still flying, I said to Frank, 'Any lunch?' and he gave me a Mars Bar. I was horrified – a Mars Bar for lunch! By this time, my legs were very tired of standing and there seemed to be a protruding ledge through the black curtain behind me. It was warm and I realized much later it was the H2S box.

When we eventually landed, I felt as though I had done a hard day's work and needed to go to bed fast. We as WAAF Officers had been taken up in small planes for various training aspects of our course, but nothing previous had prepared me for that long haul to 'Happy Valley' and back. The war was heading to a close and the authorities worked overtime to keep their service personnel occupied. At Binbrook we had a large sports meeting to commemorate 6,000 sorties by 460. I was partnered in the three-legged race by Group Captain Keith Parsons – the CO and well over 6 feet. When the whistle blew, he tucked his 5 feet 1 inch WAAF Officer under his arm and ran for the tape. We won! We had discussions and seminars and the like . . . everything was winding down.

VE Day in May, and I celebrated late into the night in Piccadilly Circus with Henry. Crowds everywhere. Back at Binbrook, they had a merry old time, setting fire to furniture in the Officers' mess, burning the lot outside the ante-room. Soon it was all over. Henry sailed for Oz and I followed a year later in 1946.

We have six children, four boys and two girls – all married and twenty-three grandchildren. What a tribe!

Anne Baskerville

So many to be proud of their grandparents.

A YORKSHIRE LASS

One of the most prolific of writers of all WAAFs who sent stories to me has been Mona Clowes, a Yorkshire lass who now lives in Canada. She has spared no details and pulled no punches in her graphic account of life in the WAAF.

All the winter of 1994, she sat and wrote, doing a little at a time. The days of the Canadian winter may have been dark and dreary but her story sparkles with life and fun. So to Mona, a warm thank you from the Editor.

Here is Mona's story:

Too dismal to cry, I sat on the steps of a shed, one of hundreds in the camp of new recruits. Come Christmas 1942, there had been many griefs and I wanted change, but in that dark stony hour, I had wondered about that. But it was the right move. I saw many places; met many youngsters and learned to drive and behave myself.

We stood in interminable queues for medicals and then for our gear. Thousands of girls everywhere and when a lone man came by embarrassed or haughty, we'd acknowledge him loudly. Girls marching in squads looked a bit 'off' to me, but it was therapeutic and fun to 'get' it at last. There was spit and polish but always company to chat with while you did it.

'What do you want to do?' asked an Officer.

'Drive,' I said.

'Why drive when you are in nursing?' he asked, 'go into medical.'

I didn't tell him about the big change I wanted, but I said that my father was a chauffeur for a steel firm. It was good for us to have a choice. Training, I was told, would be at Blackpool but not yet!

The school was full so a few of us were sent to Elsham Wolds in Lincolnshire, where I washed long tables in the Airmen's mess for weeks. It was in the depth of winter in the English countryside. Nobody bothered me in the mess for this was a man's world.

A sweet spring came. A friend and I biked through the tiny roads finding lovely old churches, and once the sun was so warm we lay in a meadow hearing and then spying out skylarks. They flew very high. My friend was twenty-two and I was nineteen and I was a bit in awe of her.

She had recently been widowed at Driffield and didn't laugh much. I

Mona Clowes, the Yorkshire lass who now lives in Canada.

thought she was perpetually weeping until she told me that she had a tear duct problem. She was tall and slim.

My second friend was the opposite, a year younger than me, short and full of fun. She was going to be an MT too and we couldn't wait. She saw a van standing by the bike rack and said, 'Get in!' She took her shoes off to get the feel of it and drove singing, 'Moonlight Becomes You' – her favourite song. She didn't do badly either. I was amazed. She would have made a good pilot.

We never got to the airfield where the young gods dwelt, so we'd take the bus to Brigg, a small, pretty market town, where there were Canadian and American fliers. One day we went to meet some mess hall lads there, but we missed them and were picked up by two American boys. They bought us a lot of whisky but the mess boys turned up and there was nearly a fight. They bundled us on a bus back to camp.

On one occasion when we went with Americans, we missed the bus and spent the night on armchairs in the lounge of a women's hostel as it was full. We took the early bus back to camp and went over the fence. We'd been missed in the billet and were called onto the carpet. 'Say we were in the ablutions,' whispered pretty mischief. So we did and got away with it. I went back to my first friend and the bikes and the fields. She made Leading Aircraft Woman after driving school. I didn't.

I couldn't get out of my next scrape which came after I had been driving a year or two. A young ground crew lad had for his pride and joy and penury a magnificent bought bike, with everything on it. Out on flights, I was waiting, parked under the nose of a plane where the radar lads were working and this lad laid his bike out of my vision. Of course, I was reading a novel. My boys finished up, jumped in the back of the van and off I went. What a horrible sound! We all stood around as if at a grave-side. There's nothing that looks more demolished to me than a run-over bike. The lad ranted and raved and I knew he was within his rights, but had to suppress a smile when he snatched his cap off, flung it down and jumped on it.

I wasn't smiling for many pay days after that as I sheepishly scooped up the few coins from the pay-master's desk. He looked a bit sheepish too. They gave me two weeks jankers also, shifting dirt evenings and weekends.

But I'm ahead of events. From the mess hall our Blackpool posting came through, for driving lessons, but not yet. The school was still full. The private billets were poor, not enough food and we were put to picking potatoes at a nearby farm. We took our shirts off in the hot sun and ended up in sick bay. What young numbskulls the service had to put up with! But we were in a different world! The holiday season was at its height and the constant stream of merrymakers below the windows kept us awake. The swimming baths were out of bounds as airmen swam naked there, or so we were told.

We mastered double declutching on the hills and went on a dismal convoy to Wales where we were billeted in a wretched hotel in the small hours. It was lovely to see blue sky, puffy Welsh clouds and little waves through the window next day. It was a stressful drive and I don't recall just how we went back.

Our final posting was to Topcliffe in the countryside, near Thirsk, Ripon, Harrogate, Leeds and Sutton Bank. Some Bank – one in four grading in places.

There's a pub in Topcliffe village called the Black Bull, where we'd go and sit with a beer pretending we weren't looking at the lads. There was a stone pub up a little road called the Leg of Mutton. It had rambling roses out front, but inside wooden seats were empty as the very old couple who kept it had to labour down a cellar for beer by the jug – very slow.

Topcliffe camp was a conversion unit for RCAF, 6 Group. Bomber lads learned to handle four-engined bombers and how to work as a crew. There were three flights of three planes spread out around the perimeter from Flight Control. We had billets in peacetime married quarters. They were neat but got very cold as winter was coming and we'd sleep fully dressed and find frost on the blanket near our noses. Yet I remember that February we were once out on flights in shirt sleeves and the tarmac was hazy with heat. We got half a sack of coal per week for the tiny fireplace. For one evening we were warm and there was water for a bath. Our LAC got the bath. I didn't mind as she polished the billet floor each week till it glowed red in the firelight.

Nearby Thirsk is a cobbled market town with a fine hotel called the Golden Fleece. This is sheep country and very beautiful as Herriot's TV vet series has told the world. So we saved for some fine dining in the Fleece. It was all right, another mate drove us out in style. The main course was jugged hare, exotic and strange. Strange indeed when I learned it really was jugged, then buried for – I don't know how long, weeks come to mind – to make it tender. The weather was becoming nice again and on the wall of the lounge where we had coffee and port, half a tree of laburnum blossom was spread.

Sutton Bank was surely a bank, looking deceptively low rising from the Vale of York. There was only one way to get down it on bikes – recklessly. We saw a gaggle of geese run down a slope and take off with a tremendous noise, then cackle excitedly as they flopped below. Half-way up was a still small lake enfolded in dark banks as if it never felt the sun – weird feeling!

And we found Rievaulx Abbey, a tracery of pale ruin in its sylvan setting, and debated what it would look like in the moonlight. We traced the water intake from its little river and its outflow. The monks were people again and not wraiths.

Ripon is another market town with a fine old cathedral, more impressive than York's. We counted twenty-one pubs on one street, but quit sampling as we would have liked to do, when the pavement became wavy.

Sitting on a railway trolley at the train station, I taught a young gunner to play snobs. He taught me crap. We laughed and were young. Within the week he went missing over Germany. I sneaked a drive over to his mess at Skipton camp. No news and the boys in the lounge looked askance.

They were quiet, realizing now death as not alien to the young. From being 'proudly friended', they saw the empty beds appearing in the billet with sickening regularity.

I never saw a crash but ugly plumes of smoke in the area told the tale. I saw a belly landing once. The pilot did a good job, touching the great thing down and shrieking to a stop in a shower of sparks. The crew got into the truck with rubber knees and one of them was sick.

Harrogate is also a lovely town, where I worked for a while early in the war, in a nursing home, so I would go over to visit patient friends. The valley gardens were still lovely but the dance pavilion was closed up and I walked through the pine woods into the wild country beyond.

I don't know if Topcliffe was ever bombed; it was strafed a couple of times late in the war. Under the furniture we'd go. There was no mistaking the racket of the guns. We lost a good friend while she was on night duty, bullets down the side of her body. It was ironic as she had taken night duty to get off on leave next day with an MT Corporal to get married. He volunteered to go out East. I forget her name, but oh the fun we had – three of us doing silly marching steps to the mess on frosty clear mornings. Our LAC fussed about some of us going to the funeral but to no effect.

We had a small hut near the MT section called Waffery. It had double bunks, a toilet and small stove where we would goof off to get warm until a Corporal turned us out to sweep vehicle bays. It was a frosty winter, not much snow.

There was a Valentine's dance and a lorry of costumes came for us. I fancied myself as Joan of Arc. We had prunes stuffed with peanut butter. We discovered that only blacks and Englishmen can dance. Does anyone remember NAAFI beer in greasy glasses?

Canadians could all drive though and had motor savvy. Their Officers would forestall a stall up Sutton Bank by happily pushing. Some types on long trips would stop for tea and once I was fed and given a bed in a nice country hotel. There were soft sheets, of course. They tried the door but I had locked it. Another locked door was on an American drome. They gave me fruit salad and a nurse's room. She was away. Lovely sheets again and a sniff of lovely perfume in the air. They were a decent lot.

Our LAC never made Sergeant but she should have. Her influence caused us to listen to the BBC news in the NAAFI at 1.00 p.m. What was going on out East? Some of the girls went there after VE Day.

Sent on a long trip with a lorry, I looked at the route form and found that it passed my home. Why not swank and call on the family. Mum said, 'You're not going all that way on your own.' So I put my great-coat on her and off we went. A married sister was *en route* too. As we went tootling down the Great North Road which at the time was empty, a fussy little RAF Officer, moustache and all, pulled us over and looked at our papers. Eyeing Mum suspiciously, he said, 'Where's your hats?' Mum grabbed mine on the seat between us and plonked it on her head, covering her thin grey hair. I said that mine was in the back and he let us go in disgust, shadowing us for a while. If he stopped us again I knew that it would be jankers for me. I think Mum had her teeth in.

Blissfully stupid, I noticed a fenced yard near my sister's house in Nottingham and put the lorry in charge of a mystified man there. It was supper time, so I stayed the night at my sister's. Off bright and early, dead on 8 a.m., I continued to Leamington to find two Officers impatiently waiting. 'Where have you been?' I told them and one that came back with me, RAF type, spoke not a word, made no stop, and clutched a parcel between his knees all the way back to Topcliffe, the last three hours crawling through a dense fog in the wee small hours. I was just thankful nothing came of it, save they got rid of me on what turned out to be a wonderful job. It was driving for a Conversion Unit. There were three fitters who would fix our planes on American stations down south, forced down from damage ops over Germany. Our base was at Thorney Island on the south coast where there were beautiful poplar trees scenting the air. There were several units so the boys and we girls would go into Chichester for beer and onion sandwiches and chocolates and fags which they shared. One became a particular friend and we'd go long walks in the hazy moonlight and compose poetry. He didn't like kissing but that was fine with me.

We got around a lot – St Neots, Grandson Lodge, Middle Wallop, Stanstead and Manston Friston. Our Dispatcher Officer took me up for a flight once. Our work was patchy – too busy and too slow in turns, depending on what turned up or turned down rather.

Then we were sent back to Topcliffe, where circuits and bumps, landings and take offs were being practised, I was put on twenty-four hour duty, working on flights out on the air field. There wasn't much to do between the flying sessions, and the lads raised rabbits out there, the wild ones coming in for supper too. There was a flight hut where we lay on unbelievably dirty blankets to sleep a little when the aircrews went on cross country training. We'd hear them coming back and go out to see if they were all back safely. Once I crossed the runway just as a plane roared

over me. I didn't see him coming in. I don't think he was aware of me –
I heard nothing of it. I could've caused a nasty accident.

On one twenty-four-hour leave we went to Leeds to a dance and I stood
by the wall amazed at the black boys jitter-bugging with the local girls.
We couldn't do that – old time medleys, quicksteps, slow foxtrots and
waltzes were our forte.

Then back in the Waafery I went on a drive taking boys to get firewood
for the CO. We went to a little picture postcard village called Coxwold,
near where the woodcarver, 'The Mouse Man', lived at Kilburn. He
always put a mouse on his carvings. Standing by the wood in Coxwold a
gentle snow began to fall and the church bell to ring. One of the lads
stood transfixed. The snow was Canadian snow and the bell a Canadian
train for a moment. He told us and I understood. He would soon be going
home. They were a great lot.

One murky night, when to get off the tarmac was a disaster because of
the winter mud, Tom, my future husband, rocked the vehicle and got us
back on land. I fell in love. We biked and walked; went for leaves to my
home and to his parent's families who were in Devon.

Things were winding down and we married around VE Day. The flags
were out and our mates came and stayed at my uncle's pub in Stockport.
So did Tom's Aunt and Uncle from Devon. Tom's Mum sent jellies and
tinned fruit; a friend of Mum's made a cake. Tess's husband, a butcher,
bought pork pies. My four-year-old nephew got ill drinking gin under the
table and of course, it rained.

A WAAF mate loaned me a white satin dress; an aunt made a veil and
my LAC friend gave me a satin slip, pants and nightgown – peace. We
lived blissfully off camp in cramped but adequate bed-sitters, biking to
work each morning. Soon VJ Day came – victory in that far away Japan.
Of course it was good but there was rather a violent sadness at the end
of carefree fun and there came a feeling of being part of a great goal
which had brought also a great waste of young life.

It was exciting to think of going to Canada, but hard to leave beautiful
Yorkshire, where I was born. The last words to those who never left in
body, be it from bombs, crashes or accidents and those who left their few
belongings there to be sent to sorrowing families, wives and sweethearts.
WE WHO WERE THERE WILL ALWAYS REMEMBER.

Mona Clowes
Orangeville, Ontario, Canada

UP IN THE 'GODS' FOR HALF A CROWN

Rosemary who now lives in Orange, NSW, Australia was at one time stationed in Dyce in Scotland. At nearby Aberdeen, previews of London plays were staged and it was then that Rosemary sat in the 'Gods'.

My name was Rosemary Flint when I joined the WAAF from King's Lynn in Norfolk and my number was 481277. I was married in July 1945 and became R.M. Lister. Luckily I still have my Service and Release Book as my memory is rather hazy.

My first few weeks were spent somewhere near Gloucester and I later completed a course for wireless mechanics at Shrewsbury and Bolton. When I was posted to Dyce I was struck by the cold weather but enjoyed life in the Highlands. Dyce was a training station at that time. My work was repairing wireless sets from Mosquito aircraft. I was thrilled to be taken for a flight one day.

The late supper provided by volunteer ladies in a canteen made a welcome change after RAF food. Occasionally we went to Aberdeen to visit the 'Gods' in a theatre to see previews of London plays for just half a crown. They were really good and we afterwards enjoyed coffee in a small café.

We took our bicycles north by train because we had a lovely weekend along the River Dee, cycling through Braemar to within sight of Balmoral, where we saw deer in the wild.

After a year and a half my unit moved to Haverfordwest in Wales, near the pretty town of Tenby. The European war was coming to an end and I was given a compassionate posting to Feresfield in Norfolk as I was planning to marry a glider pilot who was expecting embarkation leave for the Far East. When the atomic bomb fell on Japan he was sent to Port Said, Egypt and Palestine.

As you will see I was never in dangerous situations as was your Elizabeth but I hope my memories of Dyce will be of interest.

Rosemary Lister
Orange, Australia

AUSTRALIAN BORN

It would be most interesting to know just how many Australian born girls joined the WAAF. Gladys was Australian born, her mother was English and her father Australian. She returned to England when she was quite young.

I am of Australian birth for my father was Australian and my mother English. We returned to England when I was very young after the death of my father.

We lived in London and after the war broke out I joined the WAAF in 1940. I served in Uxbridge for eleven months and was then posted to Beckham in Norfolk. This was just a few miles from where I live now. West Beckham was a radar station and I served as a telephonist in the receiving block.

While I was there, I met my husband who was a Commando. I also had to face up to the trauma of losing my mother and both grandparents in one of London's first bombings with rockets. Fortunately I was given support by the CO and by a family in the area.

Our CO was a most caring man and on one occasion went to great trouble to find oranges for a WAAF who was dying with TB.

Gladys Smith (née Knee)
Norfolk

AN AUSSIE GIRL IN THE WAAF

Edith was born in Wentworth in New South Wales; she went to England in 1934 and during the war became a WAAF. As she was older than most of the girls, they called her 'Mum', and I have no doubt that she looked after them like a mother.

I went to England in 1934 and lived in Leeds in Yorkshire until the war. I joined in 1941 and had a short stay at two stations before being posted to Edzell in Scotland. As our station was a Maintenance Unit we were never bombed.

I was born in Wentworth, NSW in 3 March 1911. I have no family to pass these souvenirs to and I thought you may find them interesting. I was a Corporal cook in charge of the Sergeants' mess. I came back to Australia in 1949.

Edith Morrison
Swan Hill, Australia

I am most grateful to Edith for her Service and Release Book, a Christmas Menu, photographs and postcards. Swan Hill is very close to Ouyen in Victoria and I was able to speak to Edith on the phone. It was then that she told me she was affectionately known as 'Mum'.

BALLOON OPERATOR OR CARPENTER?

Of all the girls who sent in stories only one tells of becoming a carpenter and that was Leah from County Antrim, Northern Ireland. Leah had very long service both in the WAAF and the WRAF and she now is doing sterling work in the Northern Ireland ex WAAF Association. Here is her story:

I was born in the Lakes District of County Fermanagh and enlisted in the WAAF as a Balloon Operator in June 1942. After the usual square bashing and balloon operating courses, I was posted to 936 Squadron, Newcastle-on-Tyne, and then to Glasgow and Clydebank.

When balloons became obsolete, I was forced to take another trade and chose a Carpentry course. I returned to Gloucester for training and then had a posting to Bishopcourt. From there I went to five other stations. When the war ended I was at Aldergrove and three of us decided to transfer to the WRAF for a further two years. It was March 1949 before I left the Service. The latter years were spent as a Clerk in the Chief Technical Officer's office. I must say that I enjoyed my Service and the wonderful comradeship which I greatly missed on return to civvy street.

Early in 1980 some of the Northern Ireland WAAFs got together for a meeting at which we started to plan our first week-end reunion. It was held in October of that year at the King's Arms Hotel in Larne. It was a wonderful success and now every two years, we have a similar reunion. I am a member of the Committee of the Northern Ireland ex WAAF Association, and a member of the RAFA so I keep myself busy with these activities.

Leah McConnell (née Graham)
County Antrim, N. Ireland

FLOWERS IN THE BILLET

Not many WAAF billets had flowers brought by boyfriends. When S. Coburn was at Ballyhalbert in Northern Ireland, she met a boy who brought her flowers from his mother's home. Here is her story:

I joined the WAAF in 1942 and went first to Bridgnorth and then to Blackpool in England. Pocklington in Yorkshire was my next posting. I returned to Northern Ireland and Ballyhalbert. After Annan in Scotland I finally went to Boscombe Down from where I was demobbed.

I was an Assistant Armourer and remustered to Fabric Worker. It was then that I became an LACW. Before joining up I had worked in a munition factory here in Belfast for 1½ years.

Although a very shy person, I enjoyed my time in the WAAF and I came out in 1946. My husband was a Corporal Armourer in the RAF. I must say that it took me at least three months to get used to life in the WAAF as it was surely different.

As you probably know, we were issued with bicycles if our billets were a long way from our work place. I always had punctures on the country roads. There was a young man who seemed to be around to help by taking my bicycle to the repair shop. This was the young man whom I married in 1946.

Our billet was the only one which had flowers as this young man brought flowers from his mother's garden every time he went home. I still love to have flowers in the garden.

My most frightening time was at Pocklington where we often had air raids. My husband had a rough time in North Africa and at the D-Day landings.

I am fortunate to have many friends in Northern Ireland, Southern Ireland and England.

S. Coburn (née Molloy)
Belfast, N. Ireland

BLACK BOOTS BY THE PILLOW

Margaret and friend decided to have a wee nap on the floor when things were quiet. For that they were given fourteen days confined to camp:

I was most interested in your letter in the *Press-Journal*. I was stationed at Binbrook and I was there when the RAAF arrived. I was a Teleprinter Operator and spent many happy hours in the Signals Section. They were a grand crowd in there.

The WAAF site was at the bottom of a field more or less and we were issued with bicycles which had to have some identification painted on. Many weird and wonderful things appeared on mudguards.

The night watch dropped a bit when there were no ops. One night, two of us on watch decided to have a wee nap so we got onto the floor with our respirators as pillows. We had a rude awakening I'm afraid. I opened my eyes to see a pair of very large, black, shiny boots by my pillow. One very angry SP occupied the boots. Enough said! We got fourteen days confined to camp.

On one night watch, I received a signal telling that seventy enemy aircraft were approaching north of the River Humber and the same number south of the river. We immediately informed Operations who would hardly believe us. Later on I tannoyed instructions to all Duty Crews. An Officer from Operations came through to us asking for an NCO and the Senior LACW. I was the LACW, so off I went. We were each given a pair of earphones. Neither of us had a clue what we were supposed to do. Eventually, the NCO said, 'Just repeat everything you hear.' We were beside the plotters; I think we were giving the positions of the enemy aircraft to someone somewhere.

At one time we had an Admin. Officer who decided we made the hut untidy by sleeping during the day. We were told to sleep in a hut which was another field away and on the other side of the fence. We had to take bedding with us, except for the biscuits. My pal and I went once. We had come off duty at 0800 hours and were due back at 1700 hours. It was not worth all the hassle for a few hours' sleep. The next time we waited until the hut inspection was over and then got into our own beds. The whole thing soon fizzled out.

I can't picture Binbrook village now, but I do remember going to the canteen to play table tennis. The woman in charge took our caps until we returned the bats and balls. I do remember too climbing up the hill to return to camp.

Margaret Knight
Turriff, Scotland

A GHOST STORY

No doubt there are many airfields and former airfields throughout Britain where stories are told of lost airmen or airwomen appearing as ghosts, but this is the first I have heard. It comes from Jack Paylor who now lives in Hull. Jack and his wife Doreen met under the wing of a Lancaster at Binbrook. Ever since they have shared continued interest in the Binbrook Station. Jack tells:

Binbrook has even found its way into ghost stories. A ghostly figure has been seen many times at dawn at the end of the main runway. All sightings report him as signalling frantically as if to an aircraft. It is thought to be a Sergeant who, realizing a Lancaster was taking off with bombs accidentally armed, was trying to stop it. It exploded just as it was airborne and, passing over him, killed him and the crew.

A TALL STORY

In July 1943, an electrical short circuit on a Lancaster caused an entire bomb load to drop onto the tarmac and explode. The CO at the time at Binbrook, where this occurred, was G/Cpt. Edwards, who said that while he was driving from one aircraft to another at 50 m.p.h. he was passed by an 'erk' running from the danger area.

Jack Paylor
Hull

BOMBS ON THE DECK

At the end of June in 1943, Lancasters at Binbrook, Lincs., were bombed up ready for a raid on Cologne. In one aircraft two ground staff were working when a short circuit caused a 'Cookie', a 4,000 lb. bomb, to drop from the aircraft onto the tarmac. The two airmen tried to roll the bomb away from the aircraft, but saw that it was hopeless. They ran and very soon the bomb exploded and with it two 1,000 lb. bombs, and incendiaries were scattered in all directions. A nearby aircraft started to burn and then its bomb load exploded.

W/C Martin with the fire tender was able to extinguish incendiaries and later, with Sgt. Kan, entered yet another aircraft to use hand extinguishers to put out flames. In spite of this, with runways torn and holed and damaged bombers, seventeen took off for the raid on Cologne. It was yet another example of the 'Press on Regardless' outlook of the 460 Squadron.

Norah Thomson, who now lives in Aberdeen, was at Binbrook when this happened. She wrote me two letters and in the second mentions the bomb drop. Here is her story:

I am at present living in Aberdeen. I was born here and have left for war service and holidays only.

I remember the bomb incident at Binbrook very well. My friend Fife and I were on our way out of camp by the back route as it was our day off and we were going for a cycle run into the country. All at once, a crowd of men came running past us saying that a bomb had dropped on the tarmac and that if it went off, it would probably take the camp with it. They ran as far as possible. We went on our way, had our run and when we came back the camp was still intact and that was all we heard of it. I remember G/Cpt. Edwards but the CO when I first went to Binbrook was Air Commodore Wry.

As you know, we were paid every two weeks. For the first week, we lived like lords, but the second week it took us all our time to get tea and a bun at the NAAFI. I remember once we were sitting in the NAAFI and we had one cigarette between six of us. We passed it under the table and had a puff each in turn.

One of my friends was a farmer's daughter and when she came back from leave she sometimes brought two or three eggs with her. They were kept in a box which we called 'the Ovary' and we would fry them in a tin lid on top of the stove.

Another girl in our hut was a small, fussy person – a bit religious. We called her 'Bossie'. One night, she was out on a late pass and someone put a thistle under her sheet. We were all lying in the dark when she came in, waiting to see the reaction. There was none! The next morning as she was making her bed the thistle came out squashed flat. She had not felt it.

Then there was Vera, a stoutish, Welsh girl with a heart of gold – always good for a sub in hard up times. When things went wrong, her expression was, 'Damn, Damn, Double Damn, Two Bloody Hells and a Bugger!' All that certainly relieved the tension.

I was very sorry to leave my friends at Binbrook but I had a hankering for overseas and was lucky enough to be chosen. On the ship to Cairo, we sang, 'For those in peril on the sea', and now every time I hear that hymn my thoughts go back to the deck of that ship, surrounded by water, nothing else in sight.

I went on from Egypt to Palestine and saw the biblical places and had a swim in the Dead Sea. What stands out in memories of Palestine was singing carols in Bethlehem round a blazing fire in the Fields of the Shepherds.

I have enjoyed writing about my memories. They say that dwelling on the past is a sign of old age.

Norah Thomson
Aberdeen, Scotland

AMONG MY SOUVENIRS

Margaret still has a gladstone bag which her grandmother gave her while she was in the WAAF. She called it her 'WAAF case', and it contains many precious souvenirs. Here is Margaret's story:

I was in the WAAF from 1942–7 and became a Teleprinter, to serve in twelve or more places, all in Britain. I too still have my cap badge upstairs in what I call my WAAF case, a leather gladstone bag given to me by my grandmother during my service. It contains stripes, buttons, various shoulder flashes and sailors' hat bands.

I did my Signals Training at Cranwell and was then attached to 3 Group at Netheraron. I was there when D-Day came, and as we came off night duty across the perimeter to our billets, the Horsa Gliders were there. These had just had the roundels painted on, so we knew it was for something big.

A few weeks before, King George had visited and the 6th Airborne Paratroops carried out a practice drop.

I went to Fighter Command HQ at Bentley Priory Stanmore for a few months. I was there at the time of the Japanese surrender and a few of us went on the underground to Piccadilly, Hyde Park, Buckingham Palace and the Nuffield Centre for Forces in the Leicester Square area. We had a mad time along with the thousands jammed in the streets. The last train went but we stayed on until the first one next morning about 6.30 a.m.

I finished my service at the Underground Signals Centre which ran along beside the Box Tunnel in Wiltshire. I was then not far from home. Today it is the RAF Police Unit, Rudloe Manor.

My late husband had been in the Middle East as an RAF Airframe Fitter and it was while I was on a weekend pass to my home that I met him in a pub where my father worked.

Margaret Griffiths
Swindon, Wiltshire

FORTY-SEVEN YEARS ON

Frederick Walker and his wife Nancy, both ex RAF, came to Australia in 1964. They now live at Warragul in Victoria. Some say the best way to win a man is to cook for him. Here is Frederick's story:

I joined the RAF early 1942 as a Motor Transport Driver and went to India and Burma in 1943. I was almost taken prisoner but luckily escaped. I had done three years in India and came back to England in 1946 for the Victory Parade. I still had another six months to complete my service in the RAF. I was posted to 222 Squadron in Somerset.

It was there that I met my future wife Nancy, who was twenty-two while I was twenty-three. It was strange that we were demobbed in the same week at West Kirby in December 1946, and we were married in June 1947.

Nancy tells me how emotional she became when she had to drive aircrews to the aircraft to find that some never returned. Often there were dogs which belonged to aircrew.

In your article you mentioned how you had met Elizabeth in quite dramatic circumstances. Well, I met Nancy while I was at Pay Accounts trying to sort out back pay from India. We eyed each other up. One night when I was duty driver and had received rations, the phone rang and a lovely voice asked if she could come and cook my supper. Nancy arrived with a friend and that supper led to forty-seven years of very happy married life.

Frederick Walker
Warragul, Australia

FROM TEARS TO SMILES

Kathleen was upset when tears flowed as her mother waved her goodbye as she went off to Innsworth but this emotional time was forgotten later:

I was a WAAF, LACW Equipment. My first posting after initial training was to RAF Sutton-Bridge, Lincs., which was a Central Gunnery School. I have happy memories of cycling to Kings Lynn to the dances in the Town Hall.

After two years there, I was posted to 16MU Stafford. This took me much nearer home, which was Stratford-upon-Avon. I stayed there until discharge. During those years in the WAAF, I had the happiest times of my life. There was one sad memory and that was when my mother and I were waiting for a train to take me off to Gloucester. I was going to Innsworth which was, and I believe still is, RAF Records. I remember waving goodbye to my mother and she was emotional and crying. This upset me although afterwards she said that Service life made me appreciate home more than I ever had.

Most of my thoughts of the WAAF were happy ones, some funny and we were all in the same boat, so we had to make the best of it. We had a Forces' nostalgia night recently and out came all the old photographs. Most of us could not recognize others but then it was a long time ago.

Kathleen Brassington
Derby

BOMBED OUT

Aileen was born in Greymouth, New Zealand and came to Britain when she was seven years old. While she was at Wethersfield in Essex, the camp was badly bombed and runways severely damaged. The whole camp was moved to Kievel in Wiltshire:

I saw your advertisement in the *Evening Herald* asking for WAAFs to write their experiences. I was in the WAAF from June 1942 until May 1946. I managed to get as far as Corporal and could have become a Sergeant but turned it down. Now, hundreds of times, I wish that I had taken that promotion.

I was a waitress in the Officers' mess on a Bomber Command Station – the last was at Shepherd's Grove near Bury St Edmunds. The men there were on operations to Berlin and the Rhine. I was often on night duty when crews went missing. It was very upsetting.

One station in Essex was bombed so badly that the camp was moved from Wethersfield to Kievel in Wiltshire. On another occasion, a doodle-bug came over the camp but missed us and fell in a field. We were told to go to the shelter and put on our tin hats. My friend and I decided to stay in bed but were eventually ordered out!

I was born in Greymouth, New Zealand and came to this country at the age of seven. I could never afford to go back but still have a sister, aged eighty-four, in New Zealand. I was allowed to wear a New Zealand flash on my tunic and great-coat.

If I was young again, I would go back in the WAAF as you learn so much and visit so many places. My maiden name was Peters, No. 2014319 and I still have my pay book.

Aileen Manning
Saltash, Cornwall

A CRASH ON THE WAAF SITE

F.D. Denby of Bradford, Yorkshire had a traumatic experience at Marston Moor. Here is her story:

Having read your letter in our paper, I was surprised to see that someone was thinking of the WAAFs who did their duty during World War II. I have often said that we were given little praise although I must say that we enjoyed the life. I was serving for five years.

I was stationed at Marston Moor between Wetherby and York where we had Halifax four-engined bombers as part of Bomber Command.

One night in 1943, we had a terrible time as we had a German plane crash on our WAAF site. We were under our beds with our helmets on and we thought that our number was up. I would love to go back to see the place again and have tried to get in touch with friends but have had no success. Many have moved and all like me have grown old. I am seventy-five this year. I have lost photographs of pals but still have my little Discharge Book.

F.D. Denby
Bradford

Perhaps 'Spit, Polish & Tears' will help ex WAAFs to find old friends. I have kept all letters and would like to help in tracing friends if you think you know and would like to contact a contributor.

LIKE MOTHER LIKE DAUGHTER

Dorothy of Sheffield passed on her love of Service life as her daughter left school at eighteen and joined the WAAF:

I was reading with interest your letter in the *Star.* I am an ex-wartime WAAF. I joined up in April 1943 and was demobbed in July 1946. I was trained as a Flight Mechanic Engines.

I went to Innsworth, Gloucestershire to do square bashing. I was then posted to Gosport to await training and had to return to Innsworth to start. The camps I was posted to were Hendon, Cottesnore, Lichfield, St Athan, Finningley and I finished at Swinderley in Lincolnshire.

When I was at Finningley, I worked on Wellingtons, Spitfires and Lancasters. As we finished working on a particular aircraft, we were allowed to fly in it. I have been taken up twice in a Wellington and three times in a Lancaster. On one occasion I sat in the mid-upper turret. We had some lovely times even though it was wartime.

I belong to Doncaster's Ex WAAF Association and have met one of the girls with whom I joined. My daughter is thirty-nine now and when she left school at eighteen, she joined the WAAF as a nurse. She went to Halton where she met her future husband. He is still in the RAF at St Athan and has become a Technical Sergeant working on Harriers.

Dorothy James (née Atkin)
No. 484604 LACW
Sheffield, S. Yorks

IT'S A SMALL WORLD

Doreen tells of her husband, an officer in the Somerset Light Infantry. His name was Jack Small and he and Doreen had been married less than three months when he was lost in action in Italy. In spite of this tragic loss, Doreen had what she describes as a happy time in the WAAF where she had many friends.

I joined the WAAF at Bridgnorth in November 1941, but I do not ever remember having the pleasure of meeting your Elizabeth. From Bridgnorth I was posted to Cranwell on a Radar Course and from there served at several Radar Stations, mostly on the south and east coasts. My happiest days were spent at Walton-on-the-Naze, Essex, where I stayed for almost two years. Whilst there, I met an officer in the Somerset Light Infantry. His name was Jack Small. We married in May 1944 and spent a week together. In June 1944, he came to Walton for the weekend and left at 6 a.m. on 6 June. That was D-Day, although we did not know it at the time.

Jack was posted to Italy and was killed in action on 19 July 1944. As you can imagine, I was absolutely devastated. I had been posted to Beachy Head and had left all my friends at Walton when I received this terrible news.

I must say that apart from this tragedy in my life, I can look back on some very happy memories and I never regret joining the WAAF. I made so many friends – some with whom I am still in touch.

Now that fifty years have passed, I find it a little difficult to remember a lot about my WAAF days except that they were happy ones. I do remember that once a friend and I were hitch-hiking home on leave and we were given a lift in a hearse. I also remember going to a dance at Cranwell when we saw a WAAF coming towards us, obviously on a date, and she still had the button stick in her cap badge.

When I was at Walton there was an air raid and we were in the WAAF hostel. We all dived under our beds and a bomb was dropped not far away, but apart from a lot of broken windows, there were no casualties.

I did not marry again until thirty-four years later, when I met Harold, whom I knew at school, but whom I had not seen since he was eighteen. He was widowed. He had served in the Palestine Police for ten years and later with the Metropolitan Police. We married on St Valentine's Day in 1978 and have been happy ever since.

Doreen Catten
West Sussex

MAYDAY MAYDAY

In her new billet, Joyce had quite a let-down but unexpectedly she became Queen of the May and was suitably bedecked:

On 1 May 1944, I arrived at my new billet which was in an upstairs flat over a gents' outfitters, in the main street of Pinner in Middlesex.

My new landlady informed me that she was going away for the weekend but I was welcome to make myself at home. I did this and as you will see was really let down.

I washed my WAAF shirt and proceeded to investigate the workings of the pulley clothes line. I opened the french window and found that a few feet below was what appeared to be a flat roofed concrete building. I assured myself that it would stand my seven stone weight and with a shirt in one hand and pegs in the other, I lowered myself down very gingerly and to my horror found that the roof was camouflaged glass, thickly pebble dashed.

As I didn't want to spoil my good looks, I stuck my elbows out, covered my face and very speedily descended to land in sand bags and fire buckets at the rear of the shop. I staggered into the shop and was quickly escorted out as blood from my numerous wounds started to drip on suiting material which was displayed nearby. I was transported to sick bay.

I fell asleep while waiting for the Medical Officer to examine me. In the meantime, the other WAAFs in the ward collected dandelions, buttercups and daisies and bedecked me with garlands.

By the time the MO arrived, I was beginning to wake. 'Ah,' he said, 'I see that we have the Queen of the May!' There I lay covered in wild flowers. I didn't qualify for sick leave and was given treatment and duty.

For a fortnight afterwards, I tried to avoid all contact with the shop keeper. Finally, he caught me. I was terrified that he was going to charge me for the glass I had broken. All he wanted was to ask me was if I had recovered.

Joyce Hughes

NIGHT DRIVING

Mary tells us of a very harrowing time when, after midnight, she was driving back to the WAAF site and was stopped and questioned by an American guard:

While I was on night duty at Moreton-in-the-Marsh, Gloucestershire, at about midnight, I had a call to take an RAF officer and his wife back to their hotel at Bourton-on-the-Hill. On my return journey, there were no street lights and my headlights were masked with small slits, and ahead of me on the road I saw a light flashing.

I approached it slowly and cautiously to find an American serviceman. He asked me where I had come from and where I was going. 'Back to the WAAF Site,' I said. He told me to lock all the doors and not to stop if anyone tried to flag me down, as a German prisoner had escaped.

My eyes were nearly popping out as I scanned the hedgerows back to camp. On arrival, I found that the WAAF Site was being guarded by American Servicemen who were still there in the morning. I never did know if the prisoner was found.

When prisoners were first brought to Moreton Station, they used to have to march past the WAAF site on their way to the Prison Camp and as we ate our breakfast we listened to their singing. It was a delight.

Mary Whitlam (née Mitchell)
Coventry

STUDY BY CANDLELIGHT

WAAFs were always keen to do well in courses which would have taken years in civilian life. They put up with all sorts of conditions which young people these days would not endure. Dilys tells of studying by candlelight after lights out. Landladies who provided billets were sometimes heartless: locked girls out; turned off lights; and did not always treat the girls as adults. Here is a story of hard work and danger:

I really was enthralled with your article in the *Argus* newspaper, concerning your wife Elizabeth. I may even have seen her at one station as I joined in the same year at Bridgnorth, Shropshire, in October 1941. I stayed there for six weeks and was posted to Bridlington in Yorkshire on an equipment course. Bridlington was a garrison town and we were billeted with landladies in guest houses. It was a time of heavy snow and we did PT on the beach front. I have never felt so cold!

We had to do a three-year course in six weeks so every minute was spent studying in our bedrooms; searching for candles so that we could still study after the landlady turned the lights out at 9 p.m.

We had a great many bombs dropped there. It was as though, if the Germans couldn't drop their bombs on land, they would drop them on the coast. We certainly had our share.

We had to take our exam in a large garage; the roof had been bombed so we sat in great-coats and gloves. We then had a two-day wait for results. I could not go home to Cardiff so went with a friend to Leeds. We had a couple of wonderful days. Her Dad was a butcher so we had some wonderful meals.

I passed and as my Dad had died put in for posting to Penarth, Glamorgan. Some WAAFs had been stationed there on barrage balloons but I would go as an Equipment Assistant.

Unfortunately there were no vacancies, so I was moved on to St Athan which was eighteen miles from Cardiff. At 6 a.m., up to my knees in snow, I arrived at the station. I arrived at St Athan frozen after travelling the last part in the back of a truck with a canvas hood. I wondered why I had joined!

I was given bedding and a meal after walking what seemed miles. The next morning I was sent to a hangar where over a hundred airmen were making tools. We were often bombed. The airmen looked after me and after night duty took me by torchlight to breakfast.

I was given a bicycle – most useful for going to the village for a coffee. I was then put in charge of a small clothing store near the edge of the airfield where Lancaster bombers landed and took off. It was mid-summer and through my open door I could see aircrew going to the aircraft. There was a Flight Engineer with lovely auburn hair and he used to wave to me.

The Admin. F/Sgt. managed to get me a living out pass so I travelled back and forth from Cardiff. An old RAF bus took me, the only girl, and the married men who lived in Cardiff. It was great to get into civvies and even risk going to local civilian dances.

On camp I managed to get a paraffin heater. With a saucepan I heated water to make tea for sergeants who came in to share the goodies my mother had made at the hotel she owned.

One day, when all leave was stopped, I met at a camp dance the handsome Flight Engineer. Three months later we decided to marry. I had decided to take a commission and passed the exam and interview, where I was told that I would have to leave St Athan. I gave up my chance and decided to get married. We had a guard of honour with airmen and WAAF and a reception at my Mum's hotel. In a quiet little country village in Pembrokeshire, we had seven days with walks along country lanes, no signs of war and all around us autumn's beauty.

When I became pregnant, I was able to leave the WAAF. We lived in Cardiff for a while and several other towns. In 1952, we had a second child. Unfortunately my first marriage did not last and when I married for the second time, I lost my husband in the following year. We had just planned to have a holiday together in Scotland.

Dilys Evans
Brighton, Sussex

FROM HALIFAX TO HEN COOP AND BACK

Dorothy, who lives in Bradford, Elvington where 77 Squadron was based tells how veterans and other volunteers have constructed a Halifax Bomber from bits and pieces. She calls it 'Our Halifax' and after hearing the trouble taken in the reconstruction, I feel sure that the Yorkshire people deserve to claim it as their own.

Dorothy acted as Hon. Sec. UK for a project to place a memorial for RAAF lost from 462/466 Squadrons. As you will see this was a successful endeavour. Well done!

I'm afraid that I did not serve on a RAF Station but was based at HQ 4

Group Bomber Command at Heslington, near York. This is now the home of the University of York. I served from July 1942 until I was demobbed in September 1945, as a Clerk, General Duties employed on the Signals Section of Air Staff. I was a qualified shorthand typist prior to enlisting. Our Signals Officer had worked with John Logie Baird before the war. He used to tell us that in a short time, every home would have a TV set. At the time I found that hard to believe.

Life at Heslington was pretty quiet but York, some 2½ miles away, was full of Servicemen and women of all nationalities. The nearest RAF Station was Elvington where 77 Squadron was based. Two French Squadrons, 346 and 347, followed. It is now the site of an Air Museum and well worth a visit; from being a derelict site ten years ago, it has now been transformed by veterans and others. The main exhibit is an almost completed Halifax Bomber, which has been constructed from bits and pieces, beginning with the fuselage which had been part of a hen coop used by a farmer in the north of Scotland. The engines were donated by the French Government. We are presently raising funds for a larger hangar to accommodate 'Our Halifax' – the only one in the world.

The 4 Group reunions are held every two years. In 1993 a Memorial Weekend for 462/466 Squadrons RAAF was held and a Memorial made in Australia was placed at Driffield. This beautiful stone now stands in the Memorial Gardens at Driffield as a lasting tribute to the airmen and airwomen who served with the two squadrons.

Dorothy Beasty
Bradford, Yorkshire

QUITE AN ATHLETE

Dorothy came to Australia in 1945 and she now lives in Ballarat, Victoria. At one of her stations she won silver spoons, cake forks and cups for athletics:

Thank you for your article in the *Weekly Times*. I was at Bridgnorth in 1941 and went to Bassingbourne, Bucks, 52 Squadron Bomber Command. If your Elizabeth had dark eyes and dark hair, I look a bit like her with the same kind of features. I had my cap tilted at a slight angle and we used to bend the brim a bit. I cried all the way through reading your article. Those wartime years were the best years.

My number was 2023149 and my rank LACW and I served for 4½ years. I was a star athlete at the station sports where I won the high and long jumps. I couldn't try them now as I am seventy-four.

I was a cook in the Airmen's mess and the WAAFs' mess. We cooked with large cauldrons on steam pipes for 3,000 men and 1,000 ATC boys.

I loved an arm around me in the local cinema, which was a white sheet set up in the recreation room where we lined up for our pay.

'White, 149, two pounds ten shillings.'

'Thank you, sir!'

It lasted us, too. Ten bob went home to my Mum in Romford, Essex.

I came to live in Australia in August 1945 on a cargo vessel which was used as a bride ship. I lived for a time on a sheep station. I lost my second husband Leslie on 2 August 1993.

Dorothy Holmes (née White)

Dorothy wrote a long letter and if space would allow I would have liked to include all of it. She now writes poetry and has had some published.

THE BEGINNING OF THE END

Pam Mulligan married an Aussie who was a POW for almost five years. She now lives in Heidelberg, a suburb of Melbourne. The story which follows was sent to me by one of Pam's friends who lives in Castlemaine, Victoria. Pam came to Australia in June 1946 on board the Stirling Castle. *I had returned to Australia in 1945 on just that ship.*

Pam is a very active member of the RAFA in Melbourne. I feel sure you will enjoy her story of the lead-up to D-Day and after:

As I went on evening duty it appeared to be like any other evening, the sun was still shining in June and the birds were singing happily overhead with an occasional cuckoo with its distinctive call. As I approached the sentry, he called, 'Halt, who goes there?' and I gave him the password of the day. I called, 'Goodnight' as I entered the Twelve Group Operations Room, continuing down the brightly lit stairs to the rest room. The building containing the heart of Fighter Control for that area was many feet underground for safety reasons.

Leaving my cap and gas mask I proceeded to open the Ops Room door. The warm filtered air assailed me as did the usual atmosphere of efficiency and purpose, telephones ringing and orders given. Joanne, the Ops Officer on duty, handed the signed log book over to me, alerting me to the situation before she happily went off duty.

The Controller had complete charge of the Ops Room, standing centre stage on a dais overlooking a large map of a slice of England. In this case it was Yorkshire, Lincolnshire, Nottinghamshire and down to the Wash. Fighters were stationed at aerodromes in the neighbourhood: Church Fenton, Digby, Wittering and so on, each having its own Sector Ops Room and also under (the control) of the Group Controller.

Airwomen sat around the map which was always 'manned', taking directions by telephone and placing the plots they received on the table to indicate all aircraft that were flying in the area and whether friendly, hostile or unidentified. The airwomen were called Plotters, mustered as Clerk SD or Special Duties. Women were very suited to this work. Not only were they quick and accurate but they coped well with long boring periods when there was no aircraft activity, or when bad weather closed down an aerodrome owing to frost, fog or other reasons. Then a few airwomen were released to go to the rest room to relax for a spell. If all was quiet they frequently knitted or sewed, even embroidered their trousseaux, read or wrote letters.

A section of fighters would be sent up to patrol the east coast when shipping was sailing north or south. The next sector would provide a section to relieve the first and so on.

The Ops Officer acted as a kind of Personal Assistant to the Controller, having a small switchboard for urgent calls which she could filter before passing them through to the Controller. She acted as a liaison between Army Intelligence and Sector Controllers.

The telephonist rattled on endlessly and it became certain that something important was about to happen. I collected the Field Orders for the next day from Intelligence and handed them to the Controller and other concerned people. The tension mounted. The Duty Orderlies handed around mugs of tea. This happened frequently as the dry air made everyone thirsty.

By this time senior officers were beginning to appear on the dais. The orders were for the invasion of Normandy, something we had expected, yet had had to wait for. Much activity would be going on around the south coast of England; landing craft would be at readiness to take the troops across the Channel. All the services would be alerted. Everyone had a job to do!

Signing off at 2359 hours I collected my gear, climbed the steps and slipped out into the blackout. Standing awhile to get used to the darkness I looked up into the heavens with its myriad of stars, pondering on the vast plan unfolding. It crossed my mind that one day in the future I would recall that night when history was happening, yet all around me airmen and airwomen were sleeping.

The civilians would be delighted to read in the papers that the Second Front had happened. They were so tired of bombing and strafing, doodle bugs and rockets. They were heavily rationed, getting little sleep and separated from their children who were evacuated, some overseas. This was the tonic they needed; it would be like a shot in the arm.

Searchlights swept over the sky, as often happened, though there was no outward sign of the invasion. I kept the secret close to me as I made my way back to the WAAF Officers' mess, a big old condemned house covered with ivy, where I would join the filter officers as they returned from duty, for supper and bed.

Quite soon after D-Day, as the front progressed, we heard that airwomen could at last apply for overseas posting. The Allies were moving quickly, leaving spaces for women to fill. It was great news to hear that I had been accepted as one of them. Things began to happen with speed after D-Day. I didn't know of anyone else who was going overseas; it would soon be goodbye to my many friends but for certain the new crew would produce many more friends.

We had a short leave to see our families, wondering how they would react. It was all very positive. I was the third member of the family to be in the RAF, so no explanations were necessary. On returning to Watnall we had medicals, injections and some battle dress kit to obtain. It proved to be very comfortable, jackets with trousers, so suitable for many reasons.

At the beginning of October eighty airwomen from all parts of Britain were sent by rail to Northolt, to the aerodrome. We had to carry our great-coats, gas masks and tin helmets, but our kit bags were stored in the 'plane. All were Clerk Special Duties. The average age was early twenties, most of us having already done several years in Fighter Sector Ops or Group Ops. We were almost top heavy with the loads we carried, causing jokes and laughter between the WAAFs, a good start to getting to know each other. Four Dakotas carried, in addition to crew, at least one officer and several NCOs and twenty airwomen, each having to add a parachute to the load. Included were two Administrative Officers with a few women clerks.

Most of the girls had never been in an aeroplane before, and here they were leaving their country for the first time and crossing the English Channel. It was a great experience! Their main question was, 'Where are we going?' but there was no answer given. Not much could be seen down on the ocean as the windows were so small. All of us were very excited, laughing and chattering and filled with anticipation.

It seemed no time at all before the 'plane was descending. We managed to survive quite well and were so eager to know our destination. 'France!' The word was passed back to the others. Well, that was what we had expected. We had landed near Amiens in the Somme, names we recalled from World War I.

The trucks were there to meet us and we were quickly whisked away, driving through flat country with small farms dotted around. It was too late to see the poppies as it was approaching dusk and already mid autumn. Being driven to our billet, I could see a majestic avenue of poplars which had recently lost their leaves but were making a wonderful picture that appeared to be very French. We drove under the trees until the lane opened and there was the 'Trouterie'. There were several ponds which were empty and I wondered what they were there for. Before the war the complex had been a trout farm. Trout were spawned in the ponds then transferred to other ponds as they grew bigger. Eventually, when they reached maturity, they were released into the rivers.

The connected buildings were very attractive with gable roofs and large picture windows overlooking the interesting grounds. Inside the building there was a huge central hall with a fireplace of grand proportions where I could well imagine an ox being roasted on a spit. A gallery on three sides had small rooms leading off for WAAF officers' quarters with bathrooms and a sitting room.

The next building was the Mess Hall where all ranks ate together, using our own mess tins and tools, and washing them up afterwards. The food was boring but there was always plenty of it. The other ranks slept in a separate building.

Eileen, the Senior Ops Officer, shared a room with me. We had stretchers issued to us, with just a sling to lie on. It was bitterly cold in those rooms with no mattresses and no heating. Eileen and I were on different shifts making it impossible to sleep well. Joan and Hope, the other two Ops Officers, also shared a room.

When we were told that the last tenants had been Germans there was no problem getting volunteers for a working bee! Out with the disinfectant, soap and scrubbing brushes. Everywhere became spotless. Soap was very hard to obtain on the Continent, though. The civilians had been through a bad time with many shortages.

The village where we were living was called Fouencamp. The Plotters were divided into three shifts which was one off, one on and one for sleeping or having some exercise. Stan was the Corporal who drove the truck. He drove us on duty to the village of Boves. The officer sat up front and the airwomen piled in the back, so battle dress was more comfortable.

The 34 Sector Ops Room had been hastily put together and was now operational. We were a happy, cheerful group working well together. We were specialist officers so the authority was not so strong between us and the other ranks. We would on occasions sit side by side throughout the night trying to keep awake, so it would have been odd not to build up a certain amount of interest in the other person just because she was a Sergeant or Corporal.

Off duty, two of us would go for long walks around the country. The locals were friendly and it was good to practise our schoolgirl French so we could communicate with them. Being in pairs we had a bit of confidence to barter with the farmer or his wife. We offered cigarettes in exchange for eggs. It was usually a successful swap.

Joan and I were invited by villagers to their small cottage for Sunday dinner. They had a nice fire going and pictures of the Royal Family. We arrived bearing gifts of the usual chocolates and cigarettes. Joan knew even less French than I did. It was difficult to communicate but we did our best. There were two small children who sat down with us. The daughter made it easier for us, with a few words of English. The goodwill was obvious. I didn't know what I was eating so I was glad there was wine to wash it down.

The airwomen had a good time visiting the shops in Amiens, an interesting town. Make-up and perfume were always popular buys as there was no tax on them. In England they were very expensive. Glass of all kinds was very reasonable too, but difficult to transport with care.

Christmas was on the horizon and we needed to find a tree and piles of greenery. This was of great interest to everyone. Many times we were exhausted from lack of sleep. If a few girls went sick it put a heavy burden on the others. We all needed cheering up. It was cold, with snow on the ground. The very fit ones would have a snowball fight, make a snowman or try to skate.

A Christmas tree was miraculously found and there were many willing hands to decorate it. Holly and ivy appeared, then the laurel and mistletoe – it was beginning to look a bit like Christmas. In the Ops Room there was only a skeleton staff on duty. The aerodrome was unserviceable owing to poor visibility so there was no flying expected. It seemed necessary to keep everyone cheerful in case they thought too much of home and families and became morbid, which could be catching.

The cooks excelled themselves making an excellent Christmas dinner which was served up by the officers as the tradition goes. It was a great team effort which was greatly appreciated. There was dancing to a radio, and carols sung around the huge fire.

Flying went on night and day and kept the Plotters very busy. The Allies were advancing through France. It seemed that before long we would not be needed in Boves. The rumour was that we should return to the UK.

Joan and I were invited to a lunch at the home of the local doctor. Other RAF people were there too. He spoke English very well but his wife understood not a word of our language. When we arrived, the bottles of red wine were standing in the hearth and the corks removed to allow the wine to breathe and reach room temperature. Courses continued to appear. The used plates were removed, while the cutlery was placed on a stand to be used again for the next course, as is the custom in France.

Madame smiled and kept the food coming. No doubt other members of the family helped in the background. Wine kept appearing too. The cheese course was served before the dessert which included champagne. I wondered what some of the food was. Raw ham, pigs entrails and horse were quite likely. The meal took the whole afternoon and was a great compliment to us, for this was our farewell dinner.

Early in January 1945 we returned to England. We had another flight across the Channel, landing at Digby, Lincolnshire. This was a coincidence as my first posting as an ACW2 had been to Digby in January 1940. Five years later I was returning to the same aerodrome! Again the snow was banked up everywhere. It was bitterly cold too. This was a short visit for 34 Sector airwomen to reform. I knew Lincoln well from my two and a half years there as an airwoman so I went visiting my very good friends whom I knew from my first posting.

Two weeks later we again flew the Channel to Belgium to work in the Ops Room at 85 Group HQ 2nd TAF in Ghent. The WAAF officers had a mess in the suburbs and the airwomen were billeted in a convent. Work became very hectic as March approached. The Americans were doing their daylight raids while at night the RAF was sending out its heavy bombers.

The markets of Ghent were full of spring flowers with exotic perfumes. The sight of them was a delight. Eileen and I still shared a room in which we kept pots of azaleas. They were such a joy to us: with the variety of colours and sweet smells they brightened up our windowsills. Off duty it was easy to catch a tram into town. The rattle of its progress is imprinted in my mind and so is the rotten smell of the cigarettes the Belgians smoked. Most times we would sit down at a street café to have an ice cream and to watch the passing parade. As it got warmer a few of us entered the local lido for swimming and sun bathing; it was a treat to be out of uniform and to be able to be anonymous. 'April in Paris' was the popular song of the day.

At last it was Victory in Europe. It came as no surprise. The crowds went crazy, with parties held everywhere. On 8 May 1945, there was singing and dancing in the streets. On the following day there was a dignified march through the streets of Ghent with many of the troops participating. A.V.M. Boyle took the salute with other dignitaries and officers standing beside him. An impressive number of WAAF marched past followed by Belgian widows and mothers carrying banners and armfuls of flowers as they sadly remembered their dead.

I received a telephone call from England from my fiancé to tell me he had arrived back safely from POW camp Stalag Luft 3, where he had been held for nearly five years. Compassionate leave was given to me at once and a flight back on an aircraft to Gatwick. I knew I should have to return to Ghent for a brief visit, to collect my gear. Everything was beginning to turn out all right at last.

Pam Mulligan

TEARS AND MUFFLED CRYING

Sheila loved dancing and would often skip a meal, even at midnight, to go dancing. I wonder if there was some great attraction at the camp dance. She does not tell us but leaves us thinking:

I started off my service at Gloucester in 1942. It was cold, dark and miserable. I was so homesick and could hear muffled cries under the old grey blankets from other new recruits.

I moved on from there within days to Weeton, Lancashire where I did my Physical Training. Boy, was it cold marching along Blackpool promenade in the depths of winter.

I then moved to Ringway, Lancashire, where the paratroops did their training. I remember waiting to see the dentist with some of the men. They were scared stiff. I just pretended to be brave.

After moving to Henlow, Bedfordshire, I remained there until 1946 when I was demobbed. I started to repair parachutes because I could use a sewing machine. Later, I was making harnesses which were made on a large industrial machine. I used to work on two-week shifts, two on and two off, with twelve hours each day.

We used to march to work singing all the way. What the heck for, I do not know. When it came time for dinner around midnight, I used to skip it and go dancing to have half an hour on the dance floor as there was dancing most nights on the camp.

I joined the camp cricket team but the least said about that the better. I also joined the camp concert party and became a Starlight Girl.

Sheila Orrell
Lancashire

LETTERS IN THE SAND

The letters of Corporal Mollie Wilson, aged nineteen, a WAAF from Northern Ireland, will not be washed away by time. Written as a young member of the Women's Auxiliary Air Force to her parents in County Tyrone, they give me an intimate, eye witness account of life in Britain with its tragedies and hardships. In these, Mollie's compassion and love of her fellows shine through and they have now been published and will live on in the hearts not only of her family but of many others.

Mollie, as a one-woman advice centre and letter writer for her WAAF friends, became a go-between for many who were courting and some who were married. In her own words she tells us:

If I couldn't tell them myself, I would find out. And I wrote their letters for them. You see, our girls were getting married and their husbands might be killed next week. And of course you could have married a hundred times in the war. I had my share of proposals, some from young men who never even held my hand, because they thought they were going to be killed.

One of our girls lost two husbands that way. As I was the best educated in our lot, I wrote all the letters. I wrote all the 'lovey-dovey' bits and became very good at writing love letters.

When I had time to think about it later I thought those girls were wonderful. I wanted to marry for life. I never thought, 'This young man might be killed next week and I can give him a bit of happiness.' I was of course so innocent and maybe a bit narrow.

Mollie had this great feeling of responsibility for others around her and at the same time had a strong commitment to her country. She continues:

I wanted to help the country but I didn't want to desert my parents. I always thought of them at home with two sons training as pilots and their home empty. So I wrote two or three times a week. and I said that I would tell them everything then they'd know there was nothing worse to tell. Those letters went around the village and everybody read them.

Then my brother Andrew was shot down over Europe in 1943 on his third mission. Three of the bodies were burned beyond recognition and one crew member survived. He was smuggled through Holland, Belgium and France by the Underground. It took months for him to reach the

Mollie Whiteside, 'The Little Corporal' with a friend celebrating VE Day.

Pyrenees where he was betrayed for money and taken prisoner. It was only then that my parents knew that their son had been killed.

My father had the most terrible heart attack. They said his heart just broke. I had to keep in touch even more to make up for that, and I would tell them funny things that happened to make them laugh. And I could always make my father laugh, even in the most difficult of times.

Mollie Whiteside
Northern Ireland

Mollie Wilson is now Mollie Whiteside and lives at Dungannon, Co. Tyrone where she is a very keen gardener who can have loads of people at her door looking for cuttings.

The four children in Mollie's family, two brothers and one sister, were all in the RAF. What a wonderful contribution this family gave to Britain in wartime. She will live in the hearts of her fellow WAAFs and I feel sure her letters in the sands of time will never fade.

THE SOUND OF BOMBS

A number who have written have memories of the time bombs fell from an aircraft at Binbrook and exploded. Just a few miles from Binbrook, Lincolnshire was an RAF Station, Ludford Magna. Mary, once stationed at Ludford, remembers the explosion and saw flashes:

What memories your article in tonight's *Evening Argus* brought back. I was a WAAF stationed at Ludford Magna from 1943–6. One night as we were walking back to our hut, we heard a terrific explosion and saw a flash which we guessed was at Binbrook. I wonder if it was the one you mentioned.

Tealby brings back happy memories. We sometimes walked through the fields to get to the 'tea-room' for poached eggs. What a treat! I can still see the polished table which always seemed to have a dish with sweet smelling roses.

Working as waitress in the Officers' mess we had so many sad times, seeing the aircrew off after their 'ops' meal and then to find that they had not returned. Some came back from prison camps after VE Day and were pleased to find some of the same staff. You can guess just how well they were received.

We all went to the air-field to see the Squadron off when they left Ludford to go to Binbrook. I think it was in October 1945. What a send off and what a flood of tears!

I belong to the 101 Association and keep up with their news. I also went to Brize Norten when 101 Squadron was welcomed back from the Gulf War. We had a lovely day.

Mary Barber (née Bennett)
West Sussex

GETTING DOWN TO IT

There are some of us who are destined to reach the heights. We who stand against the wall and find that we are still under five feet must remember that it is not all who fly with the eagles but some must run with the turkeys. Keeping up the bird metaphor, we could say that they are the ones who have got down to it for they have ducks' disease. They are the ones with brains even if those have settled into the nether regions.

This long introduction leads to a delightful letter from Mary Allwright of Bradford. Although Mary had all of five feet four she was among those of a lower order as you will see:

My length of service was from 1941–5 and I served as a nursing orderly in the UK. I reached the rank of Sergeant but before I could wear that distinguished rank my demob came through. I wished with all my heart that I had signed on and stayed for more years.

My first station for square bashing and being kitted out was Bridgnorth. I will never forget our passing out parade in front of the Station WO.

It was unfortunate for us that at first we had four squads but a WAAF Sergeant decided to make us into five squads, taking out the centre of each. This meant the smaller ones.

Being five feet four, I was the marker. We all smartly marched onto the parade ground feeling the bees' knees. Can you imagine our horror as we were brought to attention and the WO marched up and down and gave a disparaging shout, 'My God! What's this, the Ducks' Disease

Squadron?' We were suddenly deflated. [*Little rubber Duckies – Ed.*] That was just one of my experiences.

Mary Allwright
Bradford

BOUNCING MONSTERS
AND TOPPLING AIRMEN

We've all seen those big brave airmen topple over at the sight of a drop of blood or a needle. Not so the girls – they not only took it but had the last laugh as you will see from Lavinia Nind's story:

I was in the WAAF from 1941–5 and for most of that time was on barrage balloon sites. We took over from the men and were trained at Cardington.

After that we were on balloon sites all over the country. One I particularly remember was the one inside Woolwich Arsenal, where I was stationed during the doodle-bug raids. I remember an unexploded bomb falling close to us within the Arsenal and very close to a bomb dump.

I was also on sites around the coast. I think I can honestly say that we coped quite well with those old barrage balloons though there were twice as many WAAF – say sixteen girls to replace a crew of eight RAF. The weather was our biggest worry – I mean high winds and rain. We often had to work out in this trying to man-handle a veering, bouncing monster – getting soaked and very sore hands into the bargain!

When you remember our ages of nineteen to twenty years old – twenty-five seemed old then – we didn't do so badly. I am still in touch with two ex balloon girls, but, dare I say it, we are now in our seventies. Where have the years gone?

In the last year of my service life, I had to remuster as they did away with the balloons and I became a Teleprinter Operator. I worked in Signals on a camp at Weston-super-Mare. I left the WAAF as a Flight Sergeant which was not bad for a country girl who had never been away from home before – at least not alone.

I remember trying to find my way on the Underground in London. It was a nerve-racking experience to begin with but not a bad place to be when the bombs were falling.

When Jerry bombed Coventry, there was a call put out for blood donors; about two dozen WAAF offered our services and one or two RAF bods – they fainted before their turn came. How we pulled their legs afterwards.

Lavinia Nind
Malvern, Worcs

LOST ONES

While receiving letters from ex WAAFs, I found that there were many who moved me deeply by telling about lost ones. Behind their letters, there was a longing for loved ones who became husbands and then all too quickly were lost, never to return. Hope went on and on. That old saying, 'It is better to have loved and lost than never to have loved at all,' rings down the years and those so very short moments of love have become more and more precious and more and more beautiful with the passing of time.

Anne Toole of Belfast writes:

I was so sorry that you lost your beloved wife, Elizabeth, but you both had all those lovely years. I'm sorry to say that I didn't but I still have my memories.

My WAAF number was 2099057. I joined up as a cook. I remember that cold dark night I left Belfast. My Mum came with me to the boat for it was the first time I had left home – so many, many tears.

A German plane kept following the boat and shooting now and again but we all arrived safely. I was going to Morecambe for training in cooking and then Melksham and a lot more camps. I was like a gypsy.

Then, I got a posting to St Athan, South Wales. What an experience – a couple of other WAAF and I were given train tickets. We looked at these and found that we were all going to different places, so they all got off the train before me. I hadn't a clue where I was going, only a name on a ticket. I watched each station as it went by. It was getting dark and the next thing the train shunted into a dead end. I was the only one on it. I threw my kit bag onto the line. Luckily the driver saw me and and after a lot of aggro I arrived in St Athan.

Because I didn't arrive on time I was put on jankers peeling spuds and doing odd jobs. About six Canadian airmen had left camp without permission and so they also were on jankers. We all had a good laugh and one in particular kept smiling at me. He asked me for a loan of my knife and fork. He had his lunch and came back. We started dating and we went to see the film, *Me and My Gal.* In a short while we both knew that we had found real love.

We were married in St Anne's Cathedral, Belfast on 22 June 1943, then we got posted – Joe overseas, me elsewhere. He was posted to North Africa and did ops from there. Then came the biggest blow of all – that fateful telegram. They were shot down over Yugoslavia on 3 November 1943.

I never saw him again but kept hoping over the years that he would turn up. He told me that no matter what, I was to wait for him. I stayed in the WAAF until demob and then went back to work and looked after Mum. She left me in 1977 and I have been on my own ever since.

Anne Toole
Belfast

There are so many brave and lonely people such as Anne who have been dealt cruel blows by war. When war brings so much suffering, the words of that song come to me, 'When will they ever learn?' Man's inhumanity to man and to woman is past our understanding.

MESSING ABOUT ON MOTOR BIKES

Pat Mason, now Pat Becker, of Swindon recalls riotous times at 460 Squadron, Binbrook, Lincs., and backs up the stories told to me in my wife's letters while I was away from the Squadron. Here are Pat's own words:

You awoke many memories of my stay with 460 Squadron. I was serving in the Catering Office as a Sergeant Catering Clerk, one of the fifteen WAAF Sergeants.

I arrived at Binbrook in 1942 and served there until 460's disbandment in 1945. I recall Christmas '44 when a crew (Smith, Q for Queenie) took me for a ride around the mess on a motor bike and side car combination, and when homesick Aussies, remembering their sheep station life, drove a few sheep into the mess. Happy, if somewhat riotous days!

I spent a lot of time with one crew and their Scottish Flight Engineer. It was they who nicknamed me 'Moggie' because of my green eyes. This was a title that I was to receive again when I met my husband to be in the post-war RAF at Henlow, Bedfordshire.

I used to issue the flying rations and often served coffee in the debriefing room to the returning crews. I remembered many of the faces if not the names.

We wish you success with *Spit, Polish & Tears* and hope that it will redress the balance of criticism from latter day historians who attempt to diminish our efforts in Bomber Command.

Pat Becker
Swindon

DON'T BRING LOO LOO

Do you remember the old song, 'You can bring Kate and leave her at the gate, But don't bring Lulu?' It was a different sort of loo which came to Christine's camp. She was the only WAAF there so she had her own private loo. The arrival of this loo and the placement of it led to great amusement as you shall see:

I was in the WAAF from October 1941 till January 1946. I certainly couldn't manage that sort of life now, walking 100 yards outside on concrete paths to the ablutions – hard luck if you had to go in the middle of the night and it was snowing.

At one camp we had no drains, just buckets for four hundred WAAFs, emptied once a day by a man with a lorry with a white alsatian. It's funny how you remember those small details. We worked sixty hours a week for one pound and only two days off in three weeks.

My favourite anecdote is about my private loo. I was stationed at Buntwaters and for some reason attached to No. 64 Squadron, the only WAAF. All the rest were in HQ. There

Christine Simpson, 64 Squadron.

were six squadrons and our dispersal was the furthest away. I used to have a bicycle all the way around the perimeter, sometimes in snow.

One day I was in the dispersal hut being taught how to play crap, I think. There was no flying owing to bad weather. Suddenly, in came a very high ranking WAAF Officer who had apparently asked to see the girls who were scattered and further away than any others, to see if they were happy. In she sailed and saw all of these men and me. 'Oh rather,' I answered, when she asked if I was happy, but then she enquired as to what I did if I wanted to spend a penny. I replied that I seldom needed to and the interview ended.

That afternoon there came into the hut three men, two carrying a sort of corrugated sentry box and one an elsan.

'Are you the WAAF what works here?' they asked. 'We've brought your lavatory and have been told to put it where you want it!'

Whereupon every pilot, groundcrew, the lot, rose and set about suggesting impossible places to put it. Eventually a spot was chosen and 'Chris Only' written on the door. I would never use it because every time I wandered in that direction, there would be a shout, 'She's going to christen it!' I would be followed so I was much too embarrassed to use it.

I eventually married someone in the army and in 1948 he did a tour of that camp and went to look for my private loo but it was gone. Little did I think that one day I would be living as a widow not far from that camp.

Christine A. Simpson
Suffolk

IF IT HAD WHEELS WE DROVE IT

Betty Sara who has lived in Australia since 1946 was an MT driver, firstly at Lichfield and then at Church Broughton, a satellite. 'Holmsie' as she was affectionately known tells of her life on an OTU and of meeting and marrying an Aussie. Here is her story:

I was twenty years old when I volunteered and was advised to report – for the life of me I cannot recall where the recruiting centre was!

However, I can recall my original choice of a trade within the WAAF.

'Instrument Repair' was ignored however and I was directed into Motor Transport.

Initial training was at Blackpool – unhappy days as our RAF instructors bullied us mercilessly; I was constantly told, 'You'll never make a bloody driver!'

I battled on and eventually passed out as an MT driver.

So 2024034 ACW Holmes was posted to an OTU, Lichfield and thence to Tatenhill, a satellite of Lichfield, in February 1942. We were billeted in a lovely old manor house and the MT personnel were a great bunch of men and women. I formed a friendship with four girls there and that has endured to this day – in fact, I met up with all of them while in England in 1992.

We drove all types of vehicle – Fordson lorries, Hillman saloons, 3-ton Bedford trucks and a Dennis ambulance.

Towards the end of 1942, I was posted to another satellite of Lichfield, Church Broughton, and to my delight my four 'buddies' were posted with me.

Australians were training at Church Broughton on Wellington bombers and, apart from the tragedy of the war, I spent nearly three happy years there.

Sanitation was primitive around the flights and one of my jobs was driving the 'san wagon', collecting pans. We'd arrive at the NAAFI and the boys would jump off and call out, 'Holmsie, a cup of tea and a wad?' I tended to refuse because I was suspicious that they had not washed their hands! My closest pal, Alison, was on this run and one day when she went careering around the perimeter came disaster – some of the pans flew off the wagon. [*'High fliers' perhaps? Ed.*]

I found ambulance driving somewhat distressing; a crash would occur while returning from training exercises and the victims were boys of whom one had become fond.

We also drove the crew buses, taking the lads to the aircraft for night flying exercises, then waiting for the call to pick them up when they returned. I guess we all had a favourite crew and that was when I first met my future intended!

I found the Aussies a great bunch of fellows – they always treated us with respect and they usually curbed their language when they realized that a WAAF was driving the bus.

I lost my heart to an Australian from Bondi, Percy Hart Sara, known to me always as 'Pip'. He was eventually posted to 460 Squadron as rear gunner, but he was shot down over Germany on their second op in 1943. He was a prisoner in Stalag Luft 3 until released May 1945.

We corresponded during the years and when he returned to England we decided to marry. He was a hefty fourteen stone when he was shot down and weighed well under ten stone when he returned to England.

We were married on 4 July 1945 and he returned to Australia in August that year. I followed him out in January 1946, travelling on a 'bride ship', the *Rangitata*, in the company of many other English brides.

I remember that when we arrived in Melbourne it was very cool and I wore an English tweed suit for the journey by train to Sydney. So did Chris Murray, another English war bride with whom I still correspond. When we arrived at Sydney Central Railway Station, the temperature had soared to 106°F – boy, did I feel the heat!

So here I am, nearly fifty years down the track and I have never regretted for one minute my decision to join the WAAF and thus have my destiny planned for me.

Betty Sara
Toormina, NSW, Australia

HAVE A LOOK AT THIS, WILL YU!

My greatest mate both in Britain and then later in Australia was, of course Elizabeth. However, we Aussies used the word 'mate' when the British would have said 'comrade' or 'pal' or even 'chum'.

One of my Aussie mates, God knows how I ever put up with him, was John D. Bryant, an Aussie Bomb Aimer of sorts and known to all who had the misfortune to run across him as simply JD. Let me tell you about him.

JD would have made a wonderful Pope if he had set his mind to it. Thick-set, round-faced, erect, he had a dignity and presence almost majestic at times. His hair was neither dark nor fair and he kept it in the short-back-and-sides style. Cornflower blue eyes, bullet like, fairly sparkled, especially when he told one of his stories.

His smooth talk could have charmed the knickers off a virgin, but he didn't bother with the ladies. His interests were in spirits rather than the spiritual. Since JD had no religion other than the whisky bottle, we'll have to leave his chances of being Pope, and since he was in his late twenties,

age if nothing else would have ruled him out. He could have been a Pooh
Bear, a diplomat or even an Air Commodore, if he had put his mind to
it. However, JD seldom did that and so he was just a sergeant in the
RAAF. How he reached that rank never ceased to amaze those who really
knew him.

This story could go on forever so I must tell you about JD at OTU
Seighford. For some reason or other everyone in our hut decided to have
an early night except JD. We were glad to miss him.

'Did I ever tell you about the time at Yakandandah that we sold the
publican some of his own whisky that we had rescued from the back of
his pub?' This of course was the beginning of one of JD's yarns and they
were great yarns that kept you enthralled until the last line. However,
they became boring when you heard them over and over again.

Everyone in the hut was in bed. Lights had been put out and the fire
in the potbelly had died down. An occasional snore came from here and
then another one from over there. Outside, not a sound. Inside, peace –
s-l-ee-p. Hush.

Suddenly the door was flung open. It crashed back. Clang! went an
empty bucket near the door. Bash! went a figure over a chair. Hey! What
the bloody hell? Everyone suddenly awake. Then a voice out of the
darkness. A drunken slurred voice that came with a blast from the depths
of a large-chested man.

'Will yu have a look at me, will yu?'

There in all his green glory, looking like Neptune with great slimy
festoons of green hanging from his shoulders, his face, his arms, his knees
and his waist, there stood JD. He put back his head and bellowed again.

'Have a look at me, mates!'

The startled curses that rang out from almost everyone had to be heard
to be believed.

'You stupid bastard, JD. Where the bloody hell have you been?'

It gurgled out of him as he spat green, waved those green ribbons of
slime around. He had been in the Sergeants' mess and had, as usual, gone
for the top shelf.

Well gone, full to the eyeballs, he had stumbled out into the outer
darkness, no lights around, no sense of direction; he had plunged on to
walk straight into a pond. It was one of those ancient ponds that had been
gathering a green carpet on its top for years. Undeterred, JD walked on,
and on, and on. The water rose higher but there was no going back. He
went on until the water became shallower and shallower. The carpet of

green wrapped around him. A little further and he walked out and onto firm ground.

Somehow, he found the hut and you know the rest.

'You stink, JD,' we all yelled.

The smell was like a broth of ten thousand stinking feet, dozens of old juicy pipes and the breath of a hundred-year-old cow, who had chewed the cud for a century and then belched millions of cubic feet of methane. It is said that the breath of a cow will bring tsetse flies from miles away. This stink would drive them away and kill them stone dead. It was so thick that you belted your head against it when you tried to sit up.

'Get out, JD! Get out, you're stinking the hut out. Look what you've done to the bloody floor!'

JD raised himself to his full height – majestic, wonderful, set in green. He had that wry half-amused smile. He had done it again. Somehow, I reckon he was almost proud of himself. The bloody idiot!

PARDON ME FOR BREATHING

Florence, who now lives in South Australia, was deliberately kept from joining the WAAF. When she overcame objections, she played a very active role as an MT driver on a bomber station. Her dread of dug-outs during enemy raids saved her life and on another occasion it was the toss of a coin that may have kept her from being lost yet again. Here is her story:

I wanted to join up to get away from my father. He was a possessive man, especially since my mother had died when I was thirteen. I was sixteen when the war started and he watched me like a hawk as most Italian fathers do. My brothers had all joined up and I was left to look after my father. I was the last of my crowd who had all been evacuated when the bombing started in Yarmouth when France fell in 1940. My back was up so I went to Norwich to enlist.

I wanted to be in Signals but the only two vacancies they had were for cooks and MT drivers. I had never driven myself but I said that I wanted to become a MT driver. Cooking was out, after looking after my father and brothers.

The chap said, 'I think you may be a bit short because the trucks need drivers of at least five feet three inches and you are just five feet two.' He said that he would give me a test on road rules and I passed. On the form I put, 'MT Driver'.

When I was travelling back in the train I noticed on the Enlistment Forms that I had to have my parents' signature as I was under age. I was just seventeen and I thought, how am I going to get my father to sign? I knew he wouldn't so I had to think of a plan.

At that time we still had a business and I used to do all of the tallying up. I folded this piece of paper which had the space for the signature at the top and I also had a plain piece. We had the same initials, FM, and he always had a funny way of writing the 'F'. When he had to sign the deposit form, I said, 'Gee, you make a funny 'F'.'

'No different to yours,' he said.

I said, 'You do. Look at mine,' and wrote mine on the plain sheet. 'Put yours underneath,' I said. He did of course and was signing the Enlistment Form.

The first place I was sent to was Morecambe, where we were given our uniform. We weren't measured as they just looked at us and said, 'This will fit . . . and this . . . and this.' The only things that did really fit were the shoes. The hat had to be lined with paper to keep it from falling over my ears. I hated that hat, for it gave me a headache every time I wore it.

We had to learn to march and how to attend Pay Parade, salute and say our last three numbers. We were sent to our first station, where I went for my trade test. At Northcoates, I advanced from ACW to ACW1. We were sent to Cawthellie to learn how to drive. It was before Christmas and freezing with snow and ice. Our instructor said, 'If you girls get through this course, you'll be bloody good drivers!'

The roads were treacherous near Snowdon and Little Snowdon. I'll always remember one girl who had been driving for years and she was a lot older than us. She thought it would be a piece of cake. She was the only girl who did not pass as she could not 'double de-clutch'.

I passed the course A1 on trucks and I loved to hear the sound as we changed down. They used to sing. I was put on trucks when I went to my first station at Northcoates.

The first accident I had was when we were on convoy near London. There were dispatch riders, one at the front and one at the back. The front rider used to see that there was no bomb damage on the road. If bombing was actually going on, he came tearing back waving his arms.

This meant that we were going to disperse. My co-driver said to me, 'God, they must have spotted us.' We went straight under a big oak tree by the road. I didn't smoke but she was a smoker and she became a bit shaken as we heard the tat-tat-tat-tat of the machine guns.

Foy said, 'Oh God, I'll have to have a smoke.'

I said, 'If you do, you'll have to open the door because I'm not having you smoking with the door shut.' She opened her door and I opened mine. She sat low in the seat as you could see a light for miles. She bent over and was lighting her cigarette and I felt as if someone was opening a huge oven door. Heat hit me and I knew no more until I woke up in hospital. I had hit the oak tree, split my head and had concussion. Foy had a broken collar-bone. The doctor said that if we had not had the doors open we both would have been killed. It wasn't my turn to go but I had a bad head for quite a while.

They sent me home on leave and when I got back, I was sent to take cars to Wales and bring back some armoured cars. In those days there were no trousers issued to women truck drivers and we met a blizzard as we returned. We were frost-bitten and I couldn't eat or drink as my mouth was so blown up. My hands didn't look like hands and my legs were swollen.

When we arrived at the 'drome, they had to carry us from the armoured cars as we couldn't walk. When the Medical Officer saw us, he hit the roof. He said, 'If my girls are going to do a man's work, they must have men's clothing.' He wrote to the Air Ministry and soon we were given what I think was the first issue of battle dress for WAAF.

In spring 1941, I was sent to St Ives, in Cornwall. I loved it. There, I went for a trade test and became LACW. We were still together, Foy and I. As we were living on the station we had our own dug-out. If there was a raid we were to go into that dug-out. Both of us disliked the dug-out for we felt trapped like rats.

We did have an air raid and a very bad one. Foy and I got into a chimney and sat there with our tin hats on. Sticks of bombs were dropped all around us and when we came out in the morning only one hangar was standing. The 'drome was flattened and our dug-out had had a direct hit. We went on duty again and didn't say anything. My father was notified that I had been killed in a raid. He just about had kittens. They asked him if he wanted my body sent home.

Our MT officer said, 'You two should be dead. You were supposed to be in that dug-out.' We had to go before our CO, a woman who told us off for disobeying orders and she gave us fatigues.

I said, 'This is bloody lovely. We're being punished for being alive!'

After fatigues, I was put on stand-by duty, night duty. This meant that I had to go to the MT office, sit there and wait for jobs to come in. This night I went to find that there was also a new girl who had been there just three weeks. She and I were on and two calls came through. Our Flight Sergeant, whom we called 'Chiefy', said that one job was for an ambulance and the other for delivering cameras. The new girl said that she didn't want to go on the ambulance as she would pass out at the sight of blood. Chiefy said that there was no flying as there was ground fog. One aircraft from 502 Squadron was out on circuits and bumps. We tossed a coin and I lost so I had to take the ambulance.

I reported to the ambulance office to be told that it was an easy night and I should get myself a book as we were not allowed to sleep. I lay there reading when all of a sudden a buzzer went. I said, 'What's happened?' The MO said, 'That silly blighter on circuits and bumps must have crashed.' He yelled, 'Come on, girl, let's go!'

When we got there, the plane had landed but there was a car used to take men around to put cameras in aircraft for early morning take off. The new girl must have driven onto the runway by mistake. If he had been landing it could have been a different story.

The car was a soft-hood Vauxhall and the airmen were in the back. I think that what had happened was that she had panicked and stalled her engine as he came at her. They were sliced off from their eyebrows. The heads were taken off and it was a mess.

We had to put the bodies in the ambulance, and there was one young boy there. I liked him; he was called Wilfred. He still had a photo of my young nephew in his pocket. This had been enlarged for me. It was terrible when we had to take the bodies to the train as they were to be sent home. Wilfred was only twenty-three and the young driver just nineteen.

There is another thing I can remember about ambulance work at St Ives. I was taking Chiefy, one of the medical orderlies, off camp when we saw smoke. We crawled through a hedge to find an aircraft burning. I had hit high tension wires. We found the pilot still in his seat and then I found another body. Then the terrible smell of burnt flesh hit me. I was ill for weeks afterwards.

Florence Riddoch
Mount Gambier, South Australia

SIX AND A QUARTER YEARS
IN THE WAAF

Some experiences in the WAAF of Flight Officer E. Anne Skoulding (MID), written on her behalf by her husband, R.B. Osborn, DSO DFC.

Anne Skoulding, then aged nineteen, volunteered to join the newly-formed Women's Auxiliary Air Force sometime during those last hectic weeks before the Second World War was officially declared on 3 September 1939. At the time of signing up to serve, each volunteer was allowed to choose which trade she would like to enter in the event of being called upon to serve. The choice was limited to: cook, transport driver, clerk or telephone operator.

Being only slight of build, Anne decided to keep away from the obviously hard physical tasks of being either a cook or a transport driver, while to become a clerk did not interest her one bit so, by process of elimination, she decided to become a telephone operator. Anne, who had been an orphan since the age of four, had kept her decision to join the WAAF to herself, not even telling her guardian and his family what she had done. And so, when a telegram arrived for her a few days after the war had been declared, she had quite a bit of explaining to do before she could travel to RAF Martlesham Heath, a fighter station not far from her home in Suffolk, where she had been instructed to report to commence her service in the WAAF.

Another girl who arrived at Martlesham on that same day had chosen the same trade, and so in due course these two reported to the switchboard room to learn from scratch how to operate a telephone switchboard – one of those old-fashioned boards, with long cords to plug into a vast array of holes, and with a 'bird's eye' shutter that dropped open to signal whenever there was a call that needed their attention. Because of their 'golden' female voices, the two girls quickly became known to their unseen callers on the station as 'Tim One' and 'Tim Two' (after the TIM signal that one could dial to hear 'the girl with the golden voice' announce the time). To make a call, often unnecessarily, became quite a pastime for some callers on the station, men who often were bored silly with the long weeks and months of watching and waiting during the period of the so-called 'phoney war' when enemy activity over the British Isles was almost non-existent. However, once the Battle of Britain broke out in June 1940, the fighter boys had little time to spare for idle chatter.

Once the Battle of Britain came in mid-1940, things began to hot up all round. During what was later recognised as the second stage in the Battle of Britain, the stage when the Germans directed their attacks primarily at the RAF fighter stations, RAF Martlesham experienced its own blitz episodes. The telephone-switch building was heavily protected against such attacks by being surrounded by a high sandbag-wall; this soon proved its worth when several bombs exploded nearby one day. The girls were badly shaken, but luckily quite uninjured. Once the 'all-clear' had sounded, the switchboard immediately lit up like a Christmas tree as all their many unseen friends called in to check that the two 'Tims' were still all right.

Soon after this, Anne was ordered to attend an administrative training course. She vigorously protested that she was not interested in adminis- tration and wanted to continue as a telephone operator, but to no avail. So she went away to attend this course – and to her great surprise she soon found that what she was having to learn was really quite interesting after all. (During this enforced absence from Martlesham, Anne, who had become engaged to one of the fighter pilots ('Ham') shortly before going away, received a rather garbled account about 'Ham' having been killed on ops . . . She never did get a satisfactory explanation of just what happened to him.) However, despite her personal sorrow, Anne kept herself deeply engrossed in her course and, when it was time for her to return to Martlesham, she was quite content to quit her old switchboard for the wider fields of WAAF adminstration.

By this time the WAAF numbers at Martlesham had grown consider- ably, and very soon Anne found herself promoted to the rank of Corporal. Not long afterwards the WAAF Sergeant was posted to another station and Anne was promoted yet again, becoming the senior administrative NCO and assistant to the officer in command of the WAAF section at Martlesham Heath. This role appealed to her tremendously but, only a short while later, she was told this time that she had been selected for officer training! Once again she tried hard to refuse, saying that she did not want to be an officer and was very happy being an NCO.

Anne entered the WAAF officers' training school at Gerrards Cross, north-west of London, in late 1940 and about eight weeks later she gained her commission as an Assistant Section Officer (A/S/O). She was imme- diately posted to RAF Henlow, a huge complex of Maintenance Command units not far from Gerrards Cross, and became assistant to a more senior WAAF officer who was in command of a section in one of the many trade training schools there.

About the end of 1941, Anne was sent on a temporary posting to RAF Cottesmore, an advanced training school within No 5 Group, Bomber Command, for further experience. Later, after her return to Henlow, her WAAF commander asked her what kind of posting she hoped she might get now. Anne replied that she hoped to be given the chance to set up a new WAAF unit of her own somewhere. Such an opportunity came much sooner than expected, for, only a few weeks later, she was posted to join with a group of five RAF officers under the command of Group Captain 'Dinger' Bell; their combined task was to help bring to completion a new RAF station that was then under construction at Wymeswold, not far from Cottesmore.

During this long wintery period of 1941–2, Anne became very friendly with a young Squadron Leader pilot ('Barnie') on the staff at RAF Cottesmore, the parent station for Wymeswold. Towards the end of the winter, Anne and Barnie became unofficially engaged – but then the wheels of the juggernaut of war turned once again, and Barnie was posted to RAF Scampton to start his second tour of ops. By now the WAAF section at Wymeswold had grown to a size that required that a Flight Officer (Flt/O) should be in command. G/C 'Dinger' Bell tried all that he knew to persuade Group headquarters to give Anne accelerated promotion to Flt/O – he keenly wanted to have her remain as commander of 'his' WAAF section – but the authorities were adamant that Anne was ineligible for such promotion because it was only very recently that she had gained her routine promotion to Section Officer (S/O) rank. And so a Flight Officer was posted in to take command over Anne and 'her' WAAF unit while, sad to report, during the following summer Barnie was posted as 'missing on operations'. These two events occurring one on top of the other as they did, were bitter blows for Anne to sustain, but she put her head down and just got on with the job.

A complete change came for Anne towards the end of 1942 when, first, she learned that Barnie had been killed in action and, second, that she was to be posted to RAF Holme-on-Spalding-Moor in Yorkshire, a station in No. 1 Group. There was a satellite station close to Holme called RAF Breighton, the home of 460 (RAAF) Squadron, and the WAAF commander at Holme told Anne when she arrived that she would be going over to Breighton to command the small WAAF section there. On the very night of Anne's arrival at Holme the aircrew of the station were holding an end-of-year party for the ground-staffs of the station, and a few representatives from Breighton (including me) were invited to come to see how it was being done because we were intending to do just the same for our ground-staffs a week or so later. Some of the WAAF officers, including Anne, came along during the evening to watch the party, and the opportunity was taken to introduce Anne to some of the Aussie officers who were present. The first to whom she was introduced was myself!

A day or so later, the WAAF commander brought Anne over to see Breighton for herself. Breighton was just another wartime dispersed station, not unlike Wymeswold but somewhat smaller, and it was dependent on Holme for many services. There was only one other WAAF (Intelligence) officer at Breighton to share the tiny WAAF officers' quarters with Anne, and so it was something of an anticlimax for her to find herself in command of such a small section. During the period of Christmas/New Year 1942–3, Anne had time to get to know her new command properly while, owing to the rotten flying weather, it also gave me time to get to know Anne a little better for myself. However, on 23 January 1943, my Lancaster was shot down over Holland and I was taken POW – this was yet another personal shock for Anne to overcome.

Anne stayed at Ludford Magna for only a short time (still with only S/O rank) before a signal came in posting her to command the WAAF section at RAF Scampton, for which responsibility she would also become a Flying Officer at last.

It became clear to Anne, the moment that she arrived at Scampton, that everyone was 'over the moon' in their excitement and satisfaction following the successes of the Dams Raid, but when she, as commander of the over four hundred WAAFs on the station, sought to find out about their various duties so as to satisfy herself that these were reasonable, she was met with a complete wall of silence on all sides. She was quite taken aback by this, something that she had never experienced before. It took some days before the penny finally dropped – there was a complete acceptance by everyone on the station of the need for tight security. It was quite some time before Anne found herself being accepted as someone to whom they could talk freely about their work.

The period of 1943–4 was one of high-pressure activity throughout Bomber Command, from the time of the Battle of the Ruhr right through to the invasion of the Continent, and on throughout the bitter fighting that was finally to push the Germans back to their final defeat. The WAAF unit on a station such as Scampton was as deeply involved in this all-out effort as were all other units, and so it was to Anne's utter dismay that one day in April 1944 the station CO told her that he had noticed that the WAAF would be celebrating its fifth anniversary next month. He told her that he considered that this most important occasion ought to be recognised in a fit and proper manner – he had been Adjutant at the RAF College, Cranwell, before the war and so was well-versed in all manners of service etiquette! He said that he considered that the Scampton WAAF section should therefore hold a full ceremonial parade and march-past to mark the occasion.

'But, Sir! I don't know how to command such a parade!' pleaded Anne.

'Then the Station Warrant Officer shall teach you!' he replied. (The SWO had served at Cranwell at the same time as the CO.) And so it was ordained. The SWO took Anne out on the station parade ground on a number of occasions, marching her round and round to rehearse all the stages of a review parade, with her also having to learn how to overcome her normally gentle speaking voice and to bellow her commands out loudly enough for them to be heard in the furthest corners of the parade ground. On the appointed day, with the official guests all seated on the reviewing dais, a detachment from the RAF Central Band led the Scampton WAAF unit out onto the parade ground with Anne at their head. The full review and march-past ceremony was carried out with great precision – the first time that any WAAF unit had ever performed such an exercise. Anne carried out her unexpected ceremonial duties with commendable success, and the CO was well pleased with the whole occasion. (Actually, as the official photos show, only about half of the total of around 400 WAAFs at Scampton were on parade at that time – the other half of the unit were either busy with essential duties, or else were asleep after having been on night-shift.)

At a time unknown to me, the mayor of the north-eastern port of Sunderland presented to the RAF, in memory of his son who had been killed in action while flying in Bomber Command, a trophy that was to be available for competition within whatever area of RAF activities were considered to be worthy of receiving such a reward. It was finally decided at the highest level that it would be appropriate for the Sunderland Cup to be directed to a competition between all WAAF units throughout the RAF, with the award being made to that unit which scored the highest points following a most detailed assessment of every aspect of its normal service activities. Particular notice would be taken of the general morale within the unit – a matter which in the last resort depended very much on how effectively its commanding officer undertook her wide-ranging duties.

Preliminary assessments of all WAAF units were first to be made within each Group in all the various Commands of the RAF, with each top-scoring unit then being judged against those others which had been selected under the same criteria from all the other groups, but this time the judging was to be done by one central panel of judges. This was necessarily a slow and tedious process, and so was quite a long-drawn-out ordeal for those who had been selected to endure it. Anne, as commander of the unit judged to be the best within No. 1 Group, therefore had to present her Scampton section for judgement on that second occasion. Naturally, all the WAAF at Scampton were highly excited at how things had turned out for them, and hopes ran high within the unit.

At this point, I have to intrude myself with a personal explanation. I was repatriated from Germany to England in an exchange of wounded POWs in September 1944. After rehabilitation, and with a little bit of string-pulling on my part, I managed to be posted to Scampton early in 1945 as a supernumerary Intelligence Officer. But in April, just when the Sunderland Cup was about to commence its lengthy judging processes, I was given the chance to return to Europe to take part in a general POW recovery exercise called 'PWX'.

During my few months at Scampton before I had joined the PWX, I had taken pains to pursue my friendship with Anne to the extent that, on the very day before I was due to sail over to France, I felt that I just had to make a lightning dash back up to Scampton to see Anne once more, arriving in the evening. But, unknown to me, that day also happened to be the day for the preliminary Sunderland Cup inspection at Scampton. Anne's fellow officers, sensing that my sudden and dramatic return must have some special significance in relation to Anne, rallied around and put on a wonderful show of hospitality for the inspecting team by entertaining them in the officers' mess that evening! No one seemed to notice Anne's absence, and thus it was organised for the two of us to spent a very important and enjoyable few hours alone together. I asked Anne to marry me, and she accepted!

Incidentally the WAAF officer's batwoman, LACW Harrison, had been a seamstress in civil life. She insisted that she should be allowed to sew Anne's wedding gown – an excellent job she made of it too.

It was not long after our wedding that the final results of the Sunderland

Cup competition were announced. Scampton was placed third, with the WAAF unit based at an aerodrome with the delightful name of Little Snoring (in Yorkshire) coming first, and the WAAF section in another dispersed station coming second. But, at the same time as the official results were published, Anne received a kind and personal note from one member of the judging panel who confided to her that the panel had experienced great difficulty in determining the final result. Apparently they had all agreed that Scampton had been outstandingly the best WAAF unit overall but, when they came to consider how they should allow for the differences between life in a peacetime RAF station (such as Scampton with all its permanent brick buildings, etc.) as compared with life in a typical wartime, dispersed station (such as Little Snoring with its Nissen huts scattered all around the countryside), they had to agree that it would not be fair if a considerable bonus was not allowed to the latter kind of station – hence their final determination for the award of the Sunderland Cup.

Once procedures for general release from the Services were put in place, I found that I was due for my release a little before Christmas 1945, which happily meant that I could go back to my College in Cambridge in time to attend the term beginning early in January and so be able to complete my shortened war-service degree course by June 1946. I therefore returned to College to finish my course, but very soon after I had quit the RAF for my place in 'civvy street', Anne found that she could not stick the thought of staying in any longer by herself. She applied for an early release as a married woman, and was out not long after I was, even though she didn't apply until just after I had left the Service myself. Once again, we agreed that we should keep ourselves apart so that I could get down to the unfamiliar business of doing serious academic studies after over six years service in the RAF – but the strain soon became almost intolerable for us both. Luckily, halfway through my course, the Easter vacation came along just in time to save us and, incidentally, it gave us our very first experience of being together for two whole weeks at one time after the first nine months of our marriage.

Richard Osborn

AMONG THE TULIPS

Ruby didn't tip-toe through the tulips, she drove a coach through them. She seemed to have no trouble at all about getting herself on a charge but she recovered from these setbacks:

I cannot remember dates, but war was declared when I was fifteen years of age. I remember my father remarking what a serious thing this was; however, I still continued my career as a window-dresser in a large city store until eventually, after much bombing, the store was burnt to the ground, leaving me no alternative, at the age of seventeen, but to do something else.

I enlisted for the WAAF where I spent the next four years. After four months intensive training, we drove lorries up to three tons, six wheel coaches, night and day convoys, many vehicles. I personally drove the ambulance for at least two years on Mosquito Squadron No 85 and unfortunately had to sleep in a billet next to the mortuary. Not very inspiring.

I did not obtain any important rank, having been on three charges: first for driving a lorry with no hat on, secondly for being absent one night in London. The third occasion was when I attended a wedding and missed the train, horror of horrors, being confronted in one of the main streets in Norwich, with a nice green jumper tucked in my uniform, a beautiful red scarf and no identification whatsoever although I had been driving the ambulance all the previous night. I was brought before the WAAF Officer (Queen Bee) and received three days' pay stopped and confinement to camp (three days' pay was 3s. 0d., not a fortune). However, I recovered from all these unfortunate setbacks.

We had many humorous encounters, as, for instance, when on one long convoy we had to move all the squadron's pet rabbits and the lorry was absolutely full of caged rabbits, which necessitated stopping the whole convoy every few miles to feed and water the livestock. Also, one night we actually had American planes landing at our English aerodrome in Kent. I personally drove that night an RAF coach, conveying the American personnel to the officers' and sergeants' mess for 'Rest and Refreshment'. I know they were surprised to find a girl driving one of these coaches and the control tower the next morning was even more suprised to find someone had backed a coach over their prize tulips. 'Nuff said!

Well, a lot of RAF and WAAF personnel were killed which was extremely sad; for their sacrifice we really must be eternally grateful.

R.J. Stuttard, Ex WAAF
LACW 2035351

STUMPED

Isobel managed to stump the CO's Humber. Of course she was given considerable help by an airman, who was, very soon after the stumping, on his way to the Middle East:

I'm sure that some of the WAAF reminiscences will be quite fascinating. When we are fifty years on, our concept of situations change and some that filled us with fear and dread have now passed into nostalgic memories. I'm sure that all of us who are still here, now view the war as something that did not really exist.

I wonder how the young people of today could live without computers, video games etc. Life fifty years ago was not so complicated. Then, my name was Isobel Russell and my homeland Northern Ireland.

One of many incidents stands out in my mind. It happened at Killadeas about mid 1944. The MT Section was located in a wooded area, in which some of the trees had been felled to allow vehicles to be parked under the natural cover. The result was that here and there a few stumps remained a couple of feet above the ground.

To understand my story, it would help if I explained that some RAF drivers resented the WAAF taking over as this meant its airmen were released for overseas postings. This did not suit some, as they were living in civilian married quarters, on the cream of the land, as the border with the Republic was only a short distance away. There, they had no rationing or shortages.

Now to my story. I was detailed to drive the CO's Humber estate car which was always serviced and kept in pristine condition. I had to go to the officers' mess to pick up some very important VIPs and convey them to the HQ. Being naive and new, I was delighted when one airman driver offered to direct me out of the parking area. I cautiously reversed out, following his directions, only to hear a terrible crunching noise, and as horror swept through the yard, there was the Humber suspended two feet in the air on the top of a tree stump. Fortunately, a diplomatic Corporal saved the situation by taking a Bedford 15 cwt, used to take gear or crew to aircraft, to pick up the VIPs. I often wonder what their reaction was.

Before forty-eight hours were up, a very unhappy and regretful RAF driver was on his way to a Middle East posting. He had learned his lesson from a stumping and he was out!

Isobel Beattie
County Down, N. Ireland

MY LIFE IN THE WAAF

Kathleen was a Yorkshire girl and she now lives in Essex. Recently, she was asked to give a talk about her time in the WAAF to a Social Group. She really surprised herself once she started and I was delighted to receive from her a story of some 8,000 words. Now, all of this could not be included, for indeed it formed a little book of its own, but I have tried to pick out the highlights. Here are the parts that I have chosen from a very readable and moving story:

I think that I decided to join the WAAF because the uniform was better than the ones that WRENs wore at that time. They had an awful round hat and black stockings with their dark jacket and skirt and I wouldn't have liked all the khaki of the ATS. Air Force blue suited me best and so that was my decision. I went along to the Recruiting Office in York and, after an interview, they asked me which section I wanted to work in. I knew that my eyes weren't so good and that eyes had to be very good for radar work, which was my first choice, so I plumped for Signals. He said, 'How are your maths?' and I said, 'Oh! All right.' I had my medical by a doctor in York; at the time I had an awful cold and cough, which was on my chest, and I thought, 'Crumbs, this is going to fail me.' But it did not and I was passed A1.

My first posting was to Bridgnorth in Shropshire. On the first day there we collected our uniforms. We went into a very large hut, where there was an amazing amount of clothing and equipment. We were given plenty of time to choose our tunics and skirts to get the right length and fit; I was surprised how long they gave us. I felt fine in my jacket and the skirt was the right length. Even the shoes were better than anything I thought there could be in the Services – slim fitting for me and lace-ups, which were fine; after all, I was a country girl and used to such things. I quite liked the look of myself in my uniform except for the hat which looked very severe and proper at first. The pyjamas were awful: they were white and blue striped winceyette. I don't think anybody wore them unless it happened to be a very cold winter. We didn't wear vests and bras. The knickers were long, elastic-legged, in Air Force blue, known as passion-killers, of course. But really and truly, once you were in uniform, you felt like a WAAF and you sent home your civilian clothes and that was the end of civilian life.

The old crest of RAF Bridgnorth.

Also on that first day, we had an FFI (Free From Infection). About ten of us sat on a long bench and a medical orderly came along behind us and lifted our hair up, looking for nits behind our ears, which was amusing to some and appalling to others. Of course, these things were necessary because if somebody had nits, perhaps a lot of people would have them in the end. I can't remember anything else of that day.

The rest of the time at Bridgnorth was spent marching – which I quite enjoyed – drilling, and becoming a WAAF. The hut held about twenty girls and the girl in the bed opposite mine was not at all happy. She cried every night and was talking of going home. I said to her, 'I don't think that life here is at all like it will be on a station. When you get your trade and you are on a station, it will be different and you'll enjoy it.' But no, she was off and by the end of the week, on her way home.

The girl in the bed next to me was constipated and was amusing because she put one senna pod in half a glass of water the first night, two pods the next night and so on until she was taking six senna pods. I think that she was OK in the end!

It was quite difficult getting dressed in the morning because I was always losing my back-stud. The corporal came into the hut one morning as usual to get us out onto the parade ground saying, 'Quickly, quickly!' and I said, 'I can't find my back-stud – I've lost it.' She said, 'You haven't lost it, Airwoman, you have misplaced it.' I soon got used to my back-stud and used to leave it in my shirt. Tying a tie took a bit of getting used to, but it was second nature in the end.

The Corporal didn't have much to do with us and it was the Sergeant who drilled us all the time and at the end of a fortnight about a hundred of us were on passing-out parade – and it was quite well done. Some girls could not keep time and they, of course, were left out of the parade. After it, we waited to see where we were posted.

The Signals group were gathered together – I supposed that there were about ten of us – and we were put on a train for Harwell in Berkshire, where we were trained on Bomber Command receivers and transmitters and had to learn a bit of Morse, which was hilarious. We could send all right but receiving was something else! We used to go into shrieks of laughter, get about three words and then we were lost. We had to start again and do better next time. Morse took a lot of doing.

Part of the training was to receive calls from bombers in distress who used to call 'Darkie' on a frequency on which a watch was kept each night. There was a lot of receiving/transmitting equipment to learn about and we did all this in a hangar that smelt of dope which was used on the fabric of certain planes – it smelt like peardrops. It was warm in the hangar as it was summer. We felt that we were learning a lot about radio telephony.

Later I was posted to Portreath, Overseas Despatch Unit, with Wellington bombers flying out to the Middle East. It was there that I met my future husband Bill. On our off duty times, we enjoyed the beach very much as it was a beautiful summer and we swam and sunbathed and became as brown as berries. We used to go into Redruth, about four miles away, where there was a nice café, or further across the peninsula to Falmouth, where we enjoyed the harbour and some lovely bookshops.

I spent a lot of time writing letters home to Bill. I had often written to him and received many letters from him. As he was overseas, we had to use aerograms. There were normal size sheets of paper, bought for twopence from the Post Office, and when you posted them they were photographed and reduced in size to about 5″ × 4″. These letters were censored and one could not write about anything that happened on camp.

Bill and I got leave in March of 1943 and I took him home to meet all my folk; then we went across to Manchester so that I could meet all his

family. On our second leave together, around June, we got engaged. We
were very much in love and that summer, Bill came down to Harrowbeer
as often as he could and he stayed at a little guest house in Yelverton. He
had got his commission and was based at Wittering in Leicestershire,
training future pilots. We used to go to Plymouth often and in that lovely
summer, we thoroughly enjoyed being in Devon – life was wonderful.

In 1944 we were ready with plans for our wedding but, towards the end
of May, all leave was cancelled and no letters could be sent from camp,
so Bill had to phone everyone to tell them that our wedding was postponed
until June. Cycling back to camp on 5 June, we saw that all the planes
were being painted with black and white stripes on the underside of their
wings. The next day was D-Day. It was blowing a terrific gale and we
thought of all those boats on the rough sea; all we could do was wish
them well and God be with them. The next day, the radio news said that
the landings had been successful and that the troops had made some
progress, but we knew that there must have been heavy losses on both
sides.

Early in March, when Bill had gone on his second tour, five flights over
Germany, he flew despite having a cold and was quite deaf when he
landed and could not be interrogated. So he was given leave to get rid of
it and I rushed to get a leave pass. Bill called for me at the WAAF site.
The journey to my home near Thirsk was pretty adventurous in the dark
as there were no longer any road signs. They had been removed years
earlier when Britain was threatened with invasion. However, once we
reached the A1, there was no problem.

Three or four weeks after my leave, I knew that I was pregnant and
went along to the MO who told me that it was too soon to be sure and
told me to come back and see him in a month; meantime, I was to have
a pint of milk a day. I phoned Bill and he was ecstatic. I was resting in
the hut after duty, chatting to Marjorie Brown, when a corporal came in
and told me that I was to report to the picket post at once as the WAAF
Officer wanted to see me. I wondered what I had done wrong and as I
walked down to the picket post, I watched the smoke from the stove there
curling up into a blue sky. I felt a little uneasy. When I walked into the
picket post, the Officer asked me to sit down. She then told me that Bill
had not returned from the raid on Berlin the night before. I tried to stop
her as she was saying this. 'No, no,' I kept saying. I think you try to stop
people telling you shattering news, believing that by denying it, it will not
be so. I didn't know what to do or whom to turn to; then I thought of

Sgt. Wroughton, a lovely person whom I knew on camp and I went along to the Sergeants' quarters to find her. She was wonderfully comforting and told me not to despair because Bill might still be OK. But I was devastated and cried until there were no more tears.

I cleared camp after saying goodbye to everyone during the last week in May 1945. I hated giving up my uniform. I had grown so used to it and not having to think each morning what I should wear. I knew too that I was going to miss the comradeship that I had so enjoyed. My brother-in-law came to pick me up and take me home to Yorkshire.

That was the end of my life in the WAAF and the beginning of another life of having and raising our baby, another Bill, or, during the first year or so, 'Billums'.

Kathleen Boreham
Sussex

A WAAF FROM THE CHANNEL ISLANDS

I joined the WAAF in 1940 under my maiden name of Walker. At the time I was living in Jersey, Channel Islands, where I was born and brought up. I left home to join the WAAF and was posted to Innsworth Lane, Gloucestershire, for my initial training. On completion of training I was posted to Melksham, Wiltshire and was trained as an electrician and spark plug tester. At the time, I made a conscious decision to go into technical training as I felt I would be doing more towards the war effort. My home and the Channel Islands had recently come under German occupation.

At the end of my training, I was promoted to Corporal-Instructor and then later made up to Sergeant and I remained at Melksham until we had trained sufficient recruits in electrical trades. I was posted to Kenley, Greater London and then to Hurn near Bournemouth, to work on Typhoons and Spitfires as a technician. I was there when the D-Day Operations took place and remained working there until the squadrons became established in France.

All WAAF were posted to different stations and I was sent to Middle Wallop, near Salisbury. There I worked in the Motor Transport as an electrician. I remember well the happy days I spent there.

My next posting was to Acklington, Northumberland, where I worked on the Meteor aircraft, the first jets to be operational in the war. There

I met my husband, Warrant Officer Waye, then working in Flying Control. He had been posted home from Burma, having been operational as a rear gunner in Burma.

In the meantime, I was chosen to go on the Victory Parade and was sent for training for the event at Halton, Buckinghamshire. After an enjoyable training of several weeks, the parade was very moving and an enjoyable and extraordinary experience.

After the Victory Parade, as my home had been liberated, I was given leave to return home. On the journey from Southampton the ship was absolutely crowded with Service personnel. The experience was extremely moving and thinking of it still brings tears to my eyes. On board all was happy laughter and talk until we neared the islands, where everyone was so choked with emotion hardly a word was spoken. As we looked at the cliffs and the bays, at the beauty of the island, everyone was in tears.

Then as the ship arrived in the harbour, thousands of islanders were there to welcome us home. Everywhere you went whilst on leave you were treated like heroes, taken to parties and entertained.

On returning to the mainland and on completion of my service I was demobbed at Ormskirk, near Liverpool and got married.

Elizabeth (Betty) Waye
London

HEDGE HOPPING

I joined the WAAF in 1942 and did my training at Cranwell, as a teleprinter operator. I had been in the Post Office and they wanted me to stay as an Instructor, but I didn't fancy that so spent nine months in a photographic reconnaissance unit at Inverallochy near Fraserburgh.

We were completely spoiled as we were the first WAAFs on the camp. We were in Nissen huts on the beach and the rotten RAF Police woke us up each morning with a poker rattling along the corrugated iron. Our CO was Wing Commander Lord Malcolm Douglas Hamilton and he was really special. He cycled everywhere and told us not to salute him – just wave.

He arranged for us to have a flight in an Anson and he was the instructor with an Australian pupil. We did hedge-hopping and the girl who came with us was pea-green on landing and swore that she would never fly again, but I loved it.

Unfortunately, after nine happy months the unit was moved and we were all in tears when the Spitfires took off for RAF Benson. I was posted to RAF Turnberry and that was lovely but short lived. From there I went to Market Drayton and hated it, but again we were soon on the move to RAD Combined Ops., Pitreanie Castle near Dunfermline.

We worked one hundred feet underground and it was hectic. For medical reasons we were supposed to stay only eighteen months but it was two years before I was off to Leighton Buzzard – five thousand WAAFs and about six men. On the train home from Edinburgh to London, I had met an RAF pilot who was later to become my husband.

I was only a week at Leighton Buzzard and was then posted to Bush House, Kingsway, London. The World Service of the BBC were on the floor above us and behaved as if they were God's chosen people and didn't take on the lonely WAAF. We were billeted at Bentick Close, St John's Wood, luxury flats. They had removed the luxury but the bathrooms were great.

We used to walk from Bush House to St John's Wood through Piccadilly Circus and saw the seamy side of life, but when six blokes in a car stopped in an empty Oxford Street and made disgusting suggestions to us to join them, we fled and didn't walk at those early hours again. Prostitutes were everywhere and, being naive, we thought we were safer on the tube.

We had happy times in London with free tickets for shows and visits to the Stage Door Canteen. We saw many of the stars of that era and the plays we saw were very good. We visited the St Martin in the Fields' Crypt and had lovely cakes and coffee.

I was just twenty-two years old and was demobbed the following May and was married on 29 June 1946 to the charming pilot I met on the train. We had many happy years together and had two lovely sons. Sadly, he died three years ago after 6½ years in hospital with Altzheimers disease. I make the most of my life with my friends, golf and hill walking. I will be seventy-one in July and still enjoy my life.

Mrs A. Archibald
Aboyne, Aberdeenshire

WHEN IT'S LOVE, RANK MATTERS NOT

Margaret Lovell, a Yorkshire lass, spent a great deal of her service time in Scotland. She now writes from Dornoch, Sutherland to tell her story of meeting the CO of a Fighter Squadron and marrying him in Inverness Cathedral. Margaret was a LACW and as such could have been embarrassed from time to time.

I am not a Scot. I come from Yorkshire but I spent two years here during the war and then three more years during the 1960s and now I'm living almost as far north as possible.

However back to my story. I left England in 1944 after two very busy years as a fighter plotter. Actually I came up here because a friend who had been a naughty girl was posted here and was extremely cross, so I offered to take her place and I have loved every minute.

I went to the Orkneys to an underground ops room near Kirkwall. A year later, I moved to Dalcross near Inverness, where I met my husband who was commanding a Fighter Squadron there. As a very humble LACW, I was not up to Squadron Leader tricks and was very embarrassed from time to time.

For instance, my husband to be took an Anson up to the Orkneys to have lunch with a Group Captain who had been very strict with discipline. I can still see that G/C entering a hut on Domestic Night and telling us that it was a disgrace and that we would all stay in the next night and do it all again. As my host for lunch he was delightful and, knowing who I really was, ignored it completely, although he did suggest that I might like to see my old WAAF Sergeant in the orderly room.

Another time, I had a jaunt to an Officers' mess party at Wick. If the WAAF Corporal had known just who I was when she opened the door, I might have had it slammed in my face.

I was of course posted from Dalcross when the hierarchy knew of our liaison, but was not daunted. Peter brought his Spitfire down to Prestwick and parked it next to a large Atlantic plane.

We were married in Inverness Cathedral. It was noted in an Aberdeen paper that I did not notice there were thirteen people at the ceremony. It was actually the Squadron. One Flight Commander gave me away and the other was the best man.

We spent twenty more years in the RAF and after two thousand hours in the air, Peter was killed in a car accident in 1966.

I'm a keen member of the RAFA and have been chairman of a Branch at Morden in Surrey. Here in Dornoch, there are no clubs or branches within reach.

Margaret A. Lovell
Dornoch, Sutherland

OUR STATION AT BINBROOK

Mary Howden, who now lives in Sussex, has through all these fifty years maintained an interest in Binbrook and the staff who served with her. She has written about life in winter on that windy snow-filled camp, where for her the only comfort was the wonderful friendship she enjoyed. She has called her story, 'Memories of Winter'.

Early shifts for cooks in the Airmen's mess commenced at 6 a.m., and the winter months saw us walking along snow-filled hedgerows in the dark from our Nissen huts in Swinhope. Not for us the rattle of a typewriter in the comfort of a warm office, or the excitement and emotions involved in Flying Control. There was porridge to be stirred and eggs to be fried, bread to be sliced and buckets of tea to be brewed.

We made rissoles by the thousand and sausages by the mile and spent hours cleaning beetroot.

Something known as Domestic Night kept us busy on Wednesday evenings. There were buttons to be cleaned and bed spaces to be polished.

Personal hygiene meant a walk of some yards to the bath hut . . . not forgetting to take along one's own bath plug! Meantime the iron stove in the centre of the hut had been fed with coke until its chimney glowed red. Lucky those with a bed at the side of it!

Our early call was at 5 a.m., when once again to the wash room we dashed, cheerfully braving the gales and frosts of the Lincolnshire Wolds – this time using the water – still warm – from our hot water bottles for a quick wash.

Friendships were made, many of them lasting to this day. In 1977, I organised the first of many reunions for Binbrook ground staff. Many of those attending were WAAFs, and what wonderful occasions they were, with many people meeting each other for the first time since demob.

The heart with a Cupid's arrow and two initials carved on a tree one moonlit night in 1944 is still there. We all have personal memories – some happy, some sad.

Alas, RAF Binbrook is now derelict, but lives on in the hearts of us, for whom it was 'Our Station'.

Mary Howden
West Sussex

SO YOUNG

There were so many girls who left school to go straight into the WAAF. Whether they gave their age as eighteen or they managed to look older than they really were, it seems that they were accepted if they were medically fit. Marnie Moore, as she was then, tells her story. Marnie is from Annalong in Northern Ireland:

I served in the WAAF and joined in 1941 when I was just seventeen and had just left Grammar School. I was trained as one of the first RTOs – Radio Telephone Operators.

I don't suppose I need to explain what we did; enough to say that it was interesting, exciting and when I think of it now, it scares the wits out of me. Now I realise the enormous responsibility it entailed and yet the thought never crossed my mind at the time – youth and simplicity!

I was always with 11 Group, Fighter Command and at first at the Fighter Leaders' School at Milfield, Northumberland. We worked in RT cabins – Channels 1, 2 and 3. 'Take off' on Channel 1, then over to 2 and coming in to land on 3.

We also had to take turns on Flying Control on a Channel used solely for lost bomber planes. This was also used by the Flying Control Officer to bring the 'kites' in to land – which runway to use etc. At times this was scary for few of them came back unharmed and unfortunately some never returned.

After Milfield, I spent the rest of my service at Tangmere and this was wonderful all the time – both operationally and socially. Tangmere and Biggin Hill were the main stations when the invasion started. As we were at the RT main stations we worked on the 'Homer' D/F stations, giving directions to lost aircraft – not always our own. We used a thing called a goniometer to give the pilot his bearings and always lived in terror of passing a reciprocal. (A reciprocal is the opposite bearing, e.g. if the right bearing was 360°, the reciprocal would be 180°. This would send the pilot off in the direction opposite to the way he wanted to fly.)

We were fortunate enough, I think, in spite of the obvious danger, which at times we never thought about, to have been allowed to do this job.

At the end of hostilities, we at Tangmere received quite a number of prisoners of war, confused and bemused at the sight of us. Some of them had been prisoners since Dunkirk and had never seen a WAAF before.

So far, after re-reading, this letter sounds egotistical because I consider all WAAFs did an excellent and very important job – many of the jobs were a lot less glamorous, for example Flight Mechanics, a cold and dirty job; the Parachute Packers – very important; the Office Staff; and of course the 'Ops Rooms Plotters', the Cooks and the Cleaners. I think they all were wonderful. [*I am in total agreement. Ed.*] It was all wonderful team work.

I am still in touch with two friends – Frankie Kelly of Johannesburg, South Africa and Marie Kenyon of Cumbria, England.

Marnie Tosier
Northern Ireland
(Used to be 'Bubbles' Moore, RTO)

FORGET THE HORRID BITS

Although life in the WAAF had its horrid bits, Louise points out that there were plenty of good and exciting times. Louise was a WAAF who went overseas to the Far East, where she worked in Flying Control:

I was a Radio Telephonist and worked mainly in Flying Control. I was at RAF Duxford when the Americans took over. The airmen were posted but the WAAF stayed on for quite a while. Our food became much better and we had some wonderful shows on camp. Bob Hope and Frances Langford came and many of the good bands from America.

At Blakeney Hill, I worked in the cabins on a three watch system. It was very cold at night and I used to put my feet on a hot pipe running through the cabins. I burnt the soles of my shoes and was put on a charge for doing just that.

On 6 June 1944, I went south and then in December of that year went on a troop ship, *Ratmalana* to Ceylon, now Sri Lanka. There I worked in Flying Control and it was lovely to have Spitfire pilots from 81 Squadron come to thank us for bringing them home safely. After about twelve months, I was flown to Singapore when the Japanese surrendered. I was in transit for about six weeks and then went on to Hong Kong flying in a Sutherland aircraft. We lived about halfway up the Peak and had to go across to Kowloon each day. There I worked in a control tower.

I had such an exciting time as a WAAF and one forgets the horrid bits.

Louise Clare (née Restall)

SO MUCH TO TELL

One of the most prolific writers who answered the appeal for stories was Fay Martin-Smith of Suffolk. She was yet another who joined at a very early age. She tells us:

There were so many things that made my service life wonderful that I'd love to make it readable for others. I volunteered at sixteen, under age, in 1941 and served until 1946, finishing my time in Egypt.

For a number of years I was at Police HQ in Burnham, Buckinghamshire, but went on detachments to various places from there. I volunteered for overseas whilst at Bomber Command, High Wycombe and sailed in 1945 to the Middle East.

I did see Bomber Harris many times as my boss was Command Defence Officer and I had to take information to the bunker where I saw high ranking visitors. At first encounter, I was nervous but later got used to stopping and saluting as they passed.

I remember slipping on some ice in the winter and two officers helped me up before they got into their car. I was on my way for a meal and had my knife, fork and spoon plus my mug in my hand. They picked those up too and I wanted to hide. For ages I was teased at the Guardroom because those on duty watched it all happen. They knew me because of my work.

Three years ago I had a holiday in Egypt. My daughter who is a nurse and my husband arranged it as a surprise. I had always said that if I could afford it I would go back. I was being driven through Cairo when I saw the cinema 'Miami' still there.

Once, I was in that building when a hand grenade or some such was thrown through the exit door as the National Anthem was being played at the end of the show. Being a female, I was not allowed downstairs so it was mainly soldiers who were injured. We, the British, were not exactly welcomed at that time by a fanatical group of Arabs. There were armed guards on our transport to and from the billets and at weekends we had to be prepared to sleep at Group HQ, as we were surrounded by hundreds of shouting Arabs in the square outside an Army barracks opposite.

Fay Martin-Smith served at High Wycombe and in Egypt.

Early in 1945, I was lucky enough to be flown over Europe, a Cook's Tour, to see the results of the bombing by our planes. The RAF Station, Wichford, near Ely, had Lancasters, 115 Squadron. They dropped food to the starving people in Holland on our flight.

I can remember the meal before I flew. It was corned beef, tomatoes and new potatoes. I was the only female in the Sergeants' mess. What a fuss was made of me! Incidentally, I was air sick and that made me remember the meal even more.

The worst moment was when I jumped down from the crew truck to board the Lancaster. I reached for my parachute and to my horror, I pulled the rip cord. All the aircrew had a big laugh for I looked so frightened. I had to sign a chit to say that I had done it and I didn't have to pay for repacking. They said that they had never seen anyone use a parachute to jump off a lorry before.

Fay Martin-Smith
Suffolk

ANOTHER BINBROOK GIRL

Although my wife Elizabeth was a Scot, I regarded her as a Binbrook girl for it was there that we first met. I ask to be forgiven if I have a bias towards these lassies who served at Binbrook where there was an Aussie Squadron. Now, Doris Wilson of Grimsby was no Aussie but she was a Binbrook girl and she has maintained an interest in Binbrook ever since the war. Here is her story:

After reading in Grimsby *Evening Telegraph* about your wife Elizabeth, I must tell you that I too was at Binbrook. I also went to Bridgnorth at the start of my service, in 1942. My trade was a cook.

The ground staff used to meet at Binbrook until it closed. People have now bought the houses and it is called Brookenby.

I met my husband at Binbrook and he was a cook who came to Binbrook in 1944. Several other WAAFs and I were with 460 Squadron at Breighton and we came with the squadron to Binbrook in 1943.

A lot of men from the squadron used to go to the Marquis of Granby, a local pub, for a drink. It has now closed after all these years. I well remember the 'One thousand Op' party. There were so many having free beer that it was a job to lift your elbow to drink it. The Group Captain at the time was G/C Edwards, whom I met the last time the Aussies came back to an evening at the RAFA at Cleethorpes.

There is a memorial in Binbrook village for the Aussies who were lost. Also in the local church there is a memorial window to commemorate all RAF and RAAF who were at Binbrook.

As you know, the WAAFs were in Nissen huts at Swinhope. I can remember one very bad winter at Binbrook when it took all of us all our time to get to work on the early shift at 6.00 a.m.

We enjoyed some nice dances at Binbrook and we also went to the cinema. We have a 460 Squadron Association of WAAFs and airmen who every two years visit friends who live in Australia. It is organised by Peter Gibby of 10 Rydal Drive, Tunbridge Wells.

I was at Binbrook when Hull was bombed and also Grimsby. We had an idea that perhaps we at Binbrook would also be visited, but thank goodness that did not happen.

My home at the time was Sheffield and my name was Doris Callard. I still keep in touch with WAAF friends especially at Christmas time.

A sad sight – The Marquis of Granby, that famous pub at Binbrook – now closed.

Some of the cooks and I used to go by the bread lorry to Scunthorpe, then hitch-hike to Sheffield, a thing you could not do today. I spent most of my time as a cook in the Sergeants' mess at Binbrook. The mess has now been made into Brookenby Village Hall.

We went to a Memorial Service for the Dam Busters at Scampton. They had 'Songs of Praise' as it was fifty years ago. I met one of the aircrew from 460 Squadron and had an interesting chat. There is also a memorial at Kelstern for 627 Squadron. I go there to a service every year. To me it is like a service for all the aircrew who lost their lives.

I still have my old service book. In 1995 my husband and I will have been married fifty years. [*Congratulations to Doris and Eric. Ed.*]

Doris Wilson
Grimsby, Lincs

YOU'RE NOT ALLOWED TO LAUGH

I'm sure that all of us who joined the Services can remember our efforts in marching. Of course we were always in step and it was the others who just couldn't march. Perhaps it is just as well they learned. It is easy to imagine the giggles from girls who discovered they had two left feet, but they were told, 'There will be no laughter!' Christina tells of her first impressions in the WAAF:

On joining the WAAF in January 1942, I came down to earth with a jolt, after a sheltered life in Swindon, Wilts., my home town. The snow was falling, it was bitterly cold and my first station was in Gloucester, where I stayed for a week. This was where all the 'Rookies', as we were called, were kitted out.

We slept in a Nissen hut with beds on each side, and heating, such as it was, was two pot-bellied stoves. Across from our hut was a long low hut, with twenty wash basins on one side and twenty loos on the other. We had no privacy whatsoever!

After a good night's sleep, we were rudely awakened at 5.45 a.m., with a loud rendering of the Air Force March Past. We scrambled out of bed; we put the three 'biscuits', square cushions, on top of each other, with blankets and sheets folded in a uniform way. Then we had to polish our bed spaces, wash and be in time for breakfast at 7.00 a.m.

Now it was time to collect our clothes and other gear. This consisted of our full uniform, kitbag, polishing equipment, shoes and, most important of all, our respirator. This we had to carry at all times.

The next part was the medical where we were all examined and inoculated. At the end of our first day, tired and weary recruits, as we were, sat on beds, spitting and polishing buttons and shoes ready for our first parade on day number two. As you can imagine it was hilarious trying to get rookies to march in a line. And we were not allowed to laugh! The Corporal in charge was very tough and her voice – ugh!

At the end of the first week, half of us were posted to Morecambe in Lancashire, the other half to Kirkham. I was lucky enough to be in private billets at Morecambe, where for six weeks it was marching, lectures, more lectures and to add to those joys more inoculations. A few of us were lucky enough to see Adelaide Hall, who was a star at the Winter Gardens at the time.

My first course was in Devon, where I did training to be a nurse on Air Ambulance. I was very lucky to be billeted in the Victoria Hotel. During the war many hotels were taken over by the Services.

When exams were passed, it was another move to a hospital in Winslow. Here all the nursing staff worked very hard looking after sick and wounded. Even scrubbing floors in the wards was part of our work.

One of the stations at Downderry near Plymouth was continuously bombed and we had the ack-ack guns behind us on a hill. The noise and vibrations were such that if it was a night raid, we were shaken out of bed. Here, I would like to pay tribute to the people of Plymouth – their courage was outstanding. Amongst the rubble there were notices saying, 'We will rise again!' And now Plymouth is a super place.

I met some wonderful people during my days in the WAAF. Sadly, a lot that I inoculated were lost or never returned from the battle of Arnhem. My husband was due to go on that mission, but owing to his glider crashing in East Anglia, he was one of the lucky ones to be alive although seriously injured. Like many others, we count our blessings and wonder, 'What is war all about, as no-one ever wins?'

Christina Jenner-Akehurst
Totten Hill, Norfolk

COMING IN WITH A PRAYER
UNDER A WING

Elsa has for quite a time been writing about her experiences in the WAAF. She was for a time on No. 10 Squadron, a very famous Australian Squadron, of Coastal Command. She was on Flying Control and had some close encounters with a Halifax bomber:

I was very intrigued to read your article in Plymouth's *Evening Herald*, and I would like to add to your sentiments by telling you that I have been writing a book about my days in the WAAF. Because of certain circumstances I am still waiting for it to be compiled and printed. It had better be soon as I have turned sixty-seven. However my memory is still very vivid.

I served with Coastal Command and was stationed with No. 10 Australian Squadron at Mount Batten, Plymouth in 1943. I had finished the training at Gloucester and was waiting for a Driver's course. For six weeks, I acted as a 'Runner' and I went up and down a hill delivering messages to 10 Squadron and an RAF Squadron. I was absolutely worn out and looked forward to sitting behind a wheel. It was a good thing that I was only seventeen. I had put my age on to join, much to the regret of my mother. My older sister was in the WRNS, so after we were bombed out, I said, 'This is it!'

With all the past experiences, it is suprising how you remember more. I had an experience in Cornwall, where I was on night duty driving the 'Stop' and 'Go' van to direct aircraft to places around the perimeter. On this night the van engine was playing up and the officer told me to keep starting and stopping it as aircraft would be coming in soon.

The time was about 1 a.m., and a Halifax bomber was due to land, so I jumped into my van and watched the touch-down. I was ready to take it to Dispersal. I put on the 'Follow Me' light and the great aircraft was doing just that. All of a sudden, my light went out so I put on the 'Stop', but you know what aircrew are like; they wanted to get finished and off to bed. I was trying to compete with the speed of the Halifax but it was of no avail. Someone must have seen what was happening and called the pilot, 'Stop! Stop!' The aircraft slowed down and stopped. Where was I? My van was under the wing of the aircraft.

Elsa Halfyard (née Gore)
Plymouth, Devon

CIRCUITS AND BUMPS

Circuits and bumps were the first things which bomber aircrews did together at Operational Training Units. These could perhaps be called take-offs and land-ings, but circuits and bumps described the operation very well, as many a crew suffered the 'bumps' as their pilot felt for the runway in such aircraft as Wellingtons.

I well remember our crew nearly wiping off a control tower at Seighford, an OTU. We bounced about forty feet and went around again.

Margaret who was stationed at Lichfield OTU, tells us about Aussies doing circuits and bumps:

I read with interest in the *Worcester Evening News* how you would like to hear from ex WAAFs from the Worcester area. I joined at eighteen years in 1942 and after square bashing at one end of Morecambe, I went to the other end for driving tuition. After passing the course, I was posted to 27 OTU, Lichfield and then its satellite Church Broughton in Derbyshire. Although it was only an operational training unit, we had our share of trials and tragedies.

Aircrew members would recall that after learning to fly they were sent to an OTU where they started with circuits and bumps, moved on to cross country trips over Britain and then finally did a 'nickel', which was dropping leaflets over enemy territory. Sometimes OTU aircraft flew on diversion courses over the North Sea to spoof German fighters.

Our aircraft were Wellington bombers, the old 'Wimpies' as we called them. We had a large contingent of Aussies on our camp.

Among my duties was that of driving coaches which took crews to dispersals and then picked them up on the return. The crews often did not know whether the driver was male or female in the inky blackness after a night flight, so the language was enough to make your hair curl. A mortal sin perhaps in those days but it does not seem to be now.

I remember the night that I had to pick up the crew of O Orange. The pilot and I were friendly and the other MT drivers knew that O Orange was for Margaret. The other crews were back and I was waiting for O Orange. Then the message came to take the Rescue Squad to the local sewerage where Orange had crashed – no survivors. On Armistice Sunday, I always remember that young crew.

We did have our lighter moments. One day, I was allowed to drive a three-ton Bedford on the road. By that time I had my 'props' – I had been made LACW. My only passenger, a Warrant Officer, asked whether I was nervous the first time I took this huge thing out on the road. I was able to tell him, 'This is the first time!'

One of our drivers, Betty Holmes, married Pip, an Aussie, and gave Australia its first set of quads in 1950.

Margaret Atkins

Betty Holmes is now Betty Sara and she was asked to become a contributor to Spit, Polish & Tears. *She now lives in Torrmina, NSW.*

A CUDDLE ON THE WAY

Both Doreen and her husband Jack were on 460 Squadron Binbrook at one stage. They met under a wing and haven't parted since. Both have given me a great deal of information about Binbrook but we'll stick to the WAAF story:

Jack and I were delighted to receive your letter. We both wallow in nostalgia and we like to hear news of the old airfields in Lincolnshire.

I was often out of the camp so I didn't get to know a great deal about

'All for Joe'. The armourers at 460 Squadron prepare to load a 'Cookie' into the bomb bay of a Lancaster.

the activity of the airfield. I always say Jack and I met under the wings of a Lancaster. He was duty Sergeant one night and I was duty Driver. I had to take him around with the guards and from that first meeting we started going out into Grimsby as often as possible.

One night when Jack was on duty, he got someone to stand in for him and we went into Grimsby to the Palace Theatre. Suddenly, someone came on stage and said, 'Will Sgt. Paylor report back to camp immediately!' We nearly had a fit. It seemed that some planes had arrived and airmen needed billets. What to do! Well, it passed all right.

Another time, a Sergeant, a WAAF, Jack and I went to London to pick up two vans. Jack went along for the ride as he was not in MT. On the way back, we were speeding along the road to Binbrook when the bonnet of my van flew off. We had to go back and get it from the hedgerow and then hasten to catch the others. Of course when we did arrive they thought we had stopped for a snog.

One day I had to take a medical orderly to hospital. The roads were ice packed and there was a freezing fog. We had to push the window forward and drive with our heads peeping under the open windscreen.

This van was a Chev with a left hand drive ambulance and I hadn't been in it before. However, we got there and back. Perhaps these little things are nothing compared to what happened on operations but to us they were frightening.

I do remember Group Captain Edwards. He had his own driver. I don't remember her name but I can still picture her.

We certainly went to Smokey Joe's. I used to come home on leave and take back a dozen eggs. Then we would go to Smokey's and have beans on toast. They would poach the eggs for us and put an egg on the beans. What a treat for those days.

Doreen Paylor
Hull

The Group Captain Edwards mentioned in Doreen's story was CO of 460 Squadron and Smokey Joe's was a little hut just outside the camp. In that smoky little hut one could buy sandwiches, tea and baked beans. It was a great place for those who missed breakfast in the mess.

BABS FROM BRIGHTON

When Babs sent her story in she called it her 'Love Story'. She and her husband Philip will celebrate their golden wedding anniversary this year. Philip was in the Irish Guards and he was badly injured and lucky to survive when a bomb hit the Guards Chapel at the Palace in June 1944. Here is Babs' story:

I volunteered to join the WAAF and was called up in 1942. I reported to Gloucester where I was kitted out and stayed for three days. From there I was taken by train to Morecambe, Lancs., to be trained and inoculated. It was just before Christmas and it rained every day, but we were marched up and down the seafront and billeted in a boarding house – thirteen of us. We were not very happy on Christmas Day as the landlady locked us out in the evening as she was going to a party! Our great-coats never did get dry as they hung in the bathroom on top of each other. After three weeks, I was posted to 16MU at Stafford as a Clerk/Gd., where I stayed for about fifteen months and got used to service life and even started to enjoy it. My parents had moved to Stoke-on-Trent so I used to go home weekends to get my washing done.

On camp, I had a boyfriend who was in the RAF Police, so we used to go out of camp on Domestic Night. This was not really allowed but I used to have coffee in the guardroom which was very daring. I worked for the Commanding Officer for a while and then for the Admin. Officers. I shared an office with the Admin. Sergeant and Warrant Officer who were very nice. The Sergeant was a real cockney and talked about 'a ball of chalk down the frog and toad'. When he didn't get any letters, he used to say, 'It don't give you no bleedin' 'eart!' He had been in the First World War so was a real old timer.

A notice came out on orders asking for WAAFs to remuster to Clerk/Personnel selection so I applied and got selected. This meant going on a five-week intensive course in London, attached to Air Ministry, and we had to get an 80% pass. We were billeted in Regents Park but had to go to Bentink Court where there were flats in St John's Wood for meals. On the way we passed the London Zoo.

One evening a few of us went to Queensbury All Services Club which used to be the Old London Casino, where you could have food and watch a show at the same time. After that you could dance on the stage and Victor Sylvester was playing. A tall Irish Guards Corporal asked me to dance and he took me back to Regents Park afterwards. He was very polite and didn't try anything on which was a change for those days. As we were saying goodnight, the sirens went and he left to get back to Wellington Barracks. I could hear his footsteps running as the sirens died away and the guns started up. He asked me to meet him the following night and we would go dancing.

We went to Hammersmith Palais and Lou Prager was playing. We arranged to meet at Baker Street Station on Saturday but he didn't turn up. The night before I was posted to Padgate, Air Crew Selection Board, a few of us went again to the Queensberry Club and his friend spotted me and said he had been put on duty at Buckingham Palace that night and could not let me know. He took my home address in Stoke-on-Trent and I got frequent letters from him for a while and then they suddenly stopped. I thought he must have been killed in London and I would never know. This was nearly true for after a week or two I received a shaky note saying that he had been injured in the Guards Chapel, when it had had a direct hit on 18 June 1944, and was not able to walk owing to a spinal injury. He asked if I could go and see him in the West Middlesex Hospital so I dashed off without even getting a pass and hitch-hiked down to London.

I asked a policeman to direct me and he stopped a car and asked the driver if he could take me to Kew Bridge. It turned out to be Nat Allen who was a famous dance band leader and who had been in the Café de Paris the night it was bombed but he was not hurt. He took me into a hotel at Kew Bridge and bought me lunch. He gave me his card and said that he would like to see me at a BBC show in London and that I should ring him. My Corporal friend played in the Irish Guards Dance Band so he was very pleased when I told him that I had met Nat Allen.

It was sad to see a ward full of Guardsmen who had been in the Chapel, but they were the lucky ones – about 150 had been killed, and the Chapel had been razed to the ground. I went several times to see him and on 30 December 1944, we were married at St Paul's Church in Burselm, Stoke-on-Trent. We have a son and a daughter and five grandchildren. The daughter lives in Jersey and my son is in the licensed trade and is soon to move to Cobham in Surrey.

I went to ACSB in Doncaster then to RAF Pembrey, Wales. Then I was sent to Bridgnorth, Salop and, finally finished at Air Crew Selection Board at Euston House and billeted at St John's Wood. It was almost a complete circle.

After the initial training period, I loved it in the Air Force and made many friends. I am still in touch with one who was with me in the ACSB. I have been to a couple of WAAF reunions which were great and very nostalgic. I think that everyone should have some Service training, both boys and girls. It really sets you up for life and teaches you to live in Brighton.

Babs Barton
Brighton

A WORD OR TWO FROM OZ

Joan Armitage and her husband George came to Australia after the war and for many years lived at Kyneton in Victoria. When Joan first contacted me, I was surprised and delighted as Kyneton was my birth place and both Elizabeth and I lived there for a number of years. Unfortunately, we never met Joan but now I am delighted to be able to pass on her story:

It all began that summer of 1940, standing on the top of air raid shelters on a high vantage point watching the 'few' fight the Battle of Britain. From then on I was waiting to be old enough to join the WAAF. That day finally came in April 1942. A group of girls gathered on the Brighton Railway Station, probably all a bit scared. From there we went to Bridgnorth and then to Morecambe for square bashing. After that we came south to Chigwell in Essex to do balloon training. This was followed by a division of girls into groups of eight. Each group was put in charge of their balloon.

I spent the next year in parts of North London – Finsbury Park, Seven Sisters Road, and Manor Park. Back come memories of getting our balloon down safely in high winds – what a triumph! On one occasion the CO came personally to congratulate us.

One warm summer night I was sitting with my friend Jockie, back to back on a bench and singing all the latest hits. We each had a truncheon to fight off any enemy that might appear.

At last all of that was over and Britain was on the offensive. Then we were needed to do other jobs. Away we went to become flight mechanics. The hardest part then became getting used to a large station after being on small units. My first job was at an MU recycling Lancasters that had crashed. At last I had a chance to fly. I had passed my flight mechanic's course with good marks so after six months, I was posted to Halton to do a fitter's course.

It was here on 6 June 1944 that we were woken by the sounds of planes all going out. It was an unforgettable sight. The sky was filled with planes – a moving ceiling of planes, each with three broad stripes on each wing. We didn't know till later that we had witnessed the beginning of the invasion of Europe.

From Halton I went to Darlington, right up in the north-east, to 13 OTU and here once again I became part of a small group – one Corporal, four men and one WAAF. I was lucky as on the first day I was told, 'You've had the same training, so you do the same job!' Many WAAF were allowed to do only the simple uninteresting jobs and if anything unusual turned up men would take over. We were doing 'majors' on Mitchell bombers. As we were allowed to go up on test flights, I did a lot of flying. My favourite place was right in the nose. I had several flights in Mosquitoes.

It was while I was here that I met George who was to become my husband. We were still busy on VE Day and after as the Mitchell was to be used in the Pacific.

VJ Day came and it was all over. I was demobbed and George went overseas to Suez. Then we married and came to Australia. If you asked me was I ever scared I think I could honestly say, 'Not really.' I left school at the end of 1939 and for the next 2½ years lived on the south coast, right in the front line. We had at that time no concept of death or danger. We had grown up in a peaceful world and we were innocent. I had worked in a grocer's shop and one rainy night as we left we were machine gunned. Perhaps we had shown a glimmer of light. All that my friend Iris and I could talk about was the effect of the bullets hitting the wet road.

We did night duty twice a week at our local ARP as messengers delivering messages when the phones were out of action. We went on bikes. Later my friend Iris joined the WRNS.

I hope you have enjoyed my story as I have enjoyed writing it and reliving old memories.

Joan Armitage
Murchison, Victoria, Australia

ADMIN

Margaret Edwards was the daughter of a World War I airman. She married the CO of a 'Stringbag' Squadron – the Swordfish aircraft. Her husband's father was also an airman from World War I. Her story is short:

I joined up in 1941 as a clerk GD and then was commissioned to become an Admin. Officer. My first posted was to Bomber Command at Waddington and then to Scampton.

On a posting to the Outer Hebrides I met my husband who commanded 842 Squadron of the old 'Stringbags'. We married after the war in 1946 and as he was a Regular, we roamed the world for many years – a most enjoyable life.

We wish you well with *Spit, Polish & Tears* and look forward to seeing you on your visit to Britain.

Margaret Edwards
Norfolk

SPIT? WELL, PERHAPS NOT, JUST A BIT OF DRIBBLE!

Even before World War II, we had an expression such as, 'Wouldn't it make you spit!' There was a whole herd of 'Wouldn't it . . . ' Some even may have said, 'Wouldn't it make you spit blood!'

Then there were the rude ones. Most of these ended with the word, 'you'. The rest I leave to your RAF training.

There were all sorts of times that you felt like spitting. Weren't there times when you could have quite cheerfully killed the WAAF Officer? After all, the RAF did its level best to spoil your romance, your leave, your free time, your hopes and joys, your eating habits, your sleeping habits and perhaps even your drinking habits. Make you spit? Yes!

Churchill warned all of us. What did he say? 'Blood, sweat and tears.' There you are: Spit blood!

The sweat you got from polishing those brass buttons, cap badges and shoes. They wouldn't let you do anything without you having to sweat over it. Think of all that square bashing you did. The Sergeant yelling his head off. You bashing those feet up and down.

'Haybout turn!' and you went back to where you started. Silly! All that for nothing and the sweat underneath your arches and lots of other places too. You were so dry you couldn't spit. What did you do? Sweated it out.

Then to add to all your joys, you could have a good howl. Tears! Yes, tears of frustration, fear, sadness, loneliness and sheer bloody misery.

On the other side of the coin, there were tears of joy. There were tears when you just couldn't laugh any more. Your sides ached, your jaw was stuck, you gasped for breath and what happened? Tears. There was nothing else left to do. You were in a state of collapse. Please don't tell that story again.

Spit

Back to 'polish' for a while. Doesn't the Navy have a saying, 'If you can't move it, paint it!'? Well, I reckon the RAF had a saying, 'If it's made of metal, leather or wood, then polish it!' Ever tried polishing a bit of string or a slice of fried bread? Some of the cooks did, I'm sure. There were all sorts of shiny things dolloped into your mess tin. Some tasted like string, some I'm sure were fried in Brasso and they forgot to take the button stick and the rag out.

You looked in wonderment at a shiny dollop. Was it a bird? Was it a man? No, it was Superpolish. Guaranteed to make you shine inside and out. You would become a shining example to all your fellow sufferers.

Didn't you know that's why the Sergeant called you 'Sunshine'?

Did you know that all this polishing business was brought about by the top brass – those bods with scrambled eggs on their hats? They had to set the example – be a shining example. What did they do? In true gentlemanly style, they took their caps off. There they were – SHINING EGGHEADS! POLISHED CROWNS! BRIGHT, BALD BEACONS ALL LIT UP!

Time for me to shut up!

THE ROYAL VISIT

If you have ever been involved in the preparations for the visit of a Royal Personage, you will recall the atmosphere of excitement and anticipation which starts months before the day appointed.

I was a pioneer WAAF wireless operator during the time of the story, working with men only in the early days, but as the months of 1941 and '42 went by, more girls were trained to do the hush-hush job we were given. I was promoted to Sergeant and had about fifty girls in my squad by the time we had notification of the Royal Visit.

In those days, with our freedom involved, we worked a eight-hour shift, no tea-breaks, no lunch-breaks, and we were happy to take our sandwiches with us and eat them still with head-phones on and listening-in. If we needed to answer the call of nature we would request the RAF officer in charge to take over our wireless sets whilst we signed off and then signed back on again.

As anyone with any experience of the Services will know, orders are orders and they must be obeyed without question.

So when it was ordered that my squad were to stay after duty and scrub the watchroom floor, I was very indignant to say the least. I stormed into my CO's office, after of course putting in my application to see her. She was still my old friend and adversary, Margaret Rose, who by now had been promoted to the rank of Squadron Officer.

We were still on very good terms off-duty, so I simply pointed out that I would not let any of the girls under my command scrub floors as they were wireless operators. We saw ourselves as a cut above the average aircraft hands. There's never been anything like the Services for class distinction! After hearing what I had to say I was told in no uncertain terms that unless I obeyed orders, I would be put on a charge.

Dissatisfied, I returned to the hut full of rebellion and told my squad to refuse to do anything about preparations for the Royal Visit. They were, I insisted, to do only the job for which they had been trained, that of wireless operators.

There following the inevitable being on a charge, for me, but this time for inciting communism, a somewhat dramatic response, and I received the inevitable punishment, being confined to barracks for seven days. I spent those seven days very cosily in my own room, reading, writing and knitting.

I had always informed my artist husband of the circumstances of my everyday life and he in turn would send a small sketch back by return.

Bigger repercussions were to follow however as the day for the visit drew closer. It was my squad who were detailed to line the route and wave! It was my squad who, although on night-duty, had to get up, make their beds and stand beside them, as it was our sleeping quarter that had been designated for HRH to visit. The paths between my rooms and the CO's office were trodden many times as I made numerous protestations. Order is orders was the answer I received every time.

The final straw was when I was summoned to her office one morning and there faced a whole posse of high-ranking RAF officers, to be informed that along with other especially selected personnel I was to be presented to HRH the Duchess of Gloucester on 20 January 1943. As I was leaving the room, a little voice from the only WAAF officer present informed me that I would be wearing my best blues.

We had two uniforms, one for working, and one for walking-out. It was unheard of to wear our best blue on duty: that was for leave and dances with the newly arrived Americans.

So I bowed to the inevitable higher authority and wore my best blue to be presented to HRH in our newly scrubbed watchroom (but not my squad!) and escorted her through the long hut, telling her we were wireless operators, and trying to enlighten her as to what went on in the front of the enormous wireless sets.

I still remember the days that went before in preparation, with rest rooms made out of duty-rooms, carpets appearing as if by magic to transform concrete duty rooms, table and arm chairs though I don't know who they thought had time to sit in one.

Almost inevitably I suppose, it poured with rain and my section of girls, just aching to get to bed, with only about three hours sleep ahead before going on duty again, were forced to stand and wave to a diminutive figure in blue inside a limousine as she drove past.

As a PS I would like to point out that I have never considered myself a Communist, rather a staunch Anglophile, and I was discharged from the WAAF without a stain on my character . . . HAPPY DAYS!

Edith N. Francis
No. 426271

My sincere thanks to Edith Francis for her story of the Royal Visit when she tried to beat the system.

STOOD UP

It is always disappointing to be stood up. However, when you are literally stood up and for as long as fifteen hours, then that can be not only tiresome but tiring.

Just a few weeks after Elizabeth and I were married, we travelled from London to Edinburgh by train on the way to Carluke to see Liz's parents. The train was packed, stacked to the eyeballs. We had to stand not in a carriage but in a corridor where bodies were packed so tightly that to take a deep breath could really have got you into trouble for being just a little too familiar with someone who was trying desperately to hold in their tum and bum in case they went where they shouldn't.

The air was blue – not with language, for most soldiers and airmen were being restrained in more ways than one. Thick blue smoke, foul breaths, sweating armpits, unwashed socks and expelled air thickened the little air that was in the corridor.

When someone lit up another smoke, more blue, less oxygen and more coughing, gasping and spluttering began.

Of course this plot thickened even more when one of those oval pungent lung-gripping fags was lit. The flavour of the air changed yet again. On the Wolds of Lincolnshire, where great lungfuls of air belted you into a bent posture, there I enjoyed an oval fag. Here in that corridor no enjoyment came, only another stink.

The rearrangement that had to go on when someone just couldn't hold on any longer was really something. The eyeball to eyeball became kneecap to kneecap – exciting for some and embarrassing for others. Feet were stood on; shins barked; stockings holed; belts caught up where they ought not to have been and any protruding portions flattened. Little blokes and lassies tried to find more room by sinking downwards where they thought there would be space. There, they found no air at all. The space was filled with solid stink.

All of this of course was so that someone could go the lav. Those who did make it found that the lav was already full. Several hung from the walls where pegs for clothing were placed; more than several tried to share the seat, while four or five more did a knees up on the floor. One just had to grin and bear it. There wouldn't be room to really bare it. There was no room for WAAFs and Land Army girls to faint with fright at the sight or the might of an Aussie with a bare behind. After all, he was from down under but he couldn't show his down unders to all those lads and lassies. They might not understand.

All this of course went on for fifteen hours. The rumour was that the line ahead had been bombed. Impossible! The war was over. Perhaps someone had deliberately planned this. Someone who wanted to keep us together had diverted the train; caused constant delays; messed us around and was chuckling away while we bore it.

At last, at long last, we reached Edinburgh, and we poured out. Ulysses said, 'I am part of all that I have met.' I felt a part of half a dozen Scots, a couple of Poles, a few Czechs and a couple of dozen Sassenachs. They had all impressed me.

A wee Scot, trundling a trolley along the platform, said, 'It's a lang hurl they gin yu the day.'

'That's right mate,' I replied.

As we left, Liz said, 'What did he say?'

'I dunno,' I said, 'but he was bloody well right wasn't he?'

AFTER AN OP

Nowadays we often say, 'Thank God for the Salvos.'

I still want to say, 'Thank God for the WAAFs.' Even after nearly fifty years, 'Thank God for those lassies.'

When you stumbled out of a kite after hours, sometimes as many as nine or ten hours, most of us lit up a smoke, peered into the gloom with tired squinted eyes and looked for a crew truck. It was never a long wait.

Outside the Crew's billet, peacetime married quarters. (L to R) Bluey Quinn RAAF,
Norman Small RAAF, Les Lancaster RAF.

Those MT lassies were always there; always a smile and a wave; always welcoming. Often they didn't say much but I know now just how many of them felt. Perhaps we had been to hell and back but they faced hell over and over again when they went to pick up a crew returning from ops. Their biggest hell was when a crew didn't come back.

In the parachute room I often stood exhausted while a WAAF pulled zippers on a flying suit; picked up parachute, mae west, helmet, flying boots and gloves and carefully folded and stowed all that gear away in my locker. She did it with a smile and there were times when we often forgot to say, 'Thank you.'

Across to debriefing and just inside the door stood a couple of WAAFs. They handed you cigarettes, a tot of rum, a cup of tea and a biscuit. I reckon they always picked the prettiest for jobs like that.

LOOK OUT, HERE COMES BARBARA!

That cry of warning could really mean something when ACW Oliver rode a bike for she never learned to use the brakes. She had two ways to stop – over the handle bars or crash into something solid.

When I first read Barbara's story my reaction was disbelief which quickly turned to rocking with laughter. She is a natural story teller and I hope her story bring you as much enjoyment as I had.

So here I was fifteen years of age and a war going on around me. I had a brother in the Navy and another in the Army and so I was determined to enlist, but the voluntary joining age was 17½.

My mother always said that I had itchy feet and this proved to be true. Determined, I applied at the enlisting office, lying about my age. Details were taken and I indicated that I wanted to go into nursing. I had visions of being the Florence Nightingale of World War II. I was told that in due course I would be informed of my medical date and to bring my birth certificate with me.

I left devastated, my visions of collecting the Medal of Honour gone. My mother hit the roof when I told her, but after a few days she calmed down and told me that if I could get in she would sanction it. After a few weeks a letter arrived and with a heavy heart I stuffed my birth certificate into my bag and set off for the medical.

The Sergeant at the enlisting office beamed at me – I was a volunteer and didn't have to be dragged in. Grimly, I beamed back through clenched teeth. After a few more questions, I was asked, 'Did you bring your birth certificate?' Dolefully I started to take it out of my bag. 'Fine,' she said not even bothering to look at it. 'Now for your medical.' I could not believe it – not even a glance!

I passed my medical with flying colours and on 3 March I was on my way to Bridgnorth to be kitted out. I thought my uniform was great. After all, no one could see the shoulder seams of my shirts fitting snugly round my elbows. Next stop was Morecambe Bay for square bashing. My only problem was my knickers. Mrs Bloomer would have been proud of them – volumes of material ended somewhere below the knees. They became well known in the WAAF as 'passion-killers'. With my first pay I bought new knickers and did this every week until I had a good stock.

Then came the most desperate moment of my career. I was informed by the Sergeant that I had to see my Officer. She would not tell me what it was about. I stood outside the door with two escorts. The order, 'Hats Off,' was barked at me and I was marched in. My employment cards had arrived at the RAF. At work if you were under sixteen you were issued a blue card. My firm had sent in the blue card! The game was up!

My Officer was very understanding and she arranged for me to go home with an escorting officer to see my mother. My mother said that my home was there to go back to, but if I wished to stay in the Forces I could. I stayed in the WAAF, but I was told that I could never serve abroad.

Florence Nightingale the Second vanished. I went on to the Princess Mary's Hospital at Hulton in Buckinghamshire. It was an RAF Hospital and still is to this day, but is now known as RAF Hulton. It was a crash course. We could never become qualified nurses but I learned a lot. There was marvellous comradeship among the girls. I passed both oral and physical exams without any problems and was transferred to Filey in Yorkshire. The camp was a half built holiday camp. The RAF had taken it over but it wasn't deemed fit enough for the WAAF, so we were stationed in the village. I had to ride a bike to camp every day. I couldn't ride a bike then and I can't now.

No matter how the girls tried to show me how to brake, I still went over the handle bars. I wobbled all over the road but the worst thing was that I could not stop. The girls had to pedal like mad to get into the camp and open the garage doors so that I could fly in, hit the wall and fall off. I couldn't even stop to show my identity card to the guard at the gate. They got to know me and had the gate open ready for me to fly past.

Eventually we were transferred into the camp, fit or not, much to my relief. There were massive golf links behind the camp and a very large hotel. We got word that the Free French were coming in so the hotel was taken off the map and made into a military hospital. The French arrived emaciated, ragged, dirty and shocked. They had marched almost a thousand miles from Chad in Central Africa to the Middle East. There, they had been deemed unfit for service and sent to England.

Some of them were very ill – typhoid, malaria, pneumonia and lice. Our first job was to battle with the lice which were passing on infections. There were pubic lice, lice under the arms and head lice. One major problem was language as they couldn't speak English and we couldn't speak French. I will never forget those boys with their despair and shock miles from home. I didn't know it but I was growing up!

We were given special rations for them and with loving care they soon began a slow recovery. One very young boy had massive, painful quinsies. The doctor gave him a local anaesthetic which made him drowsy. The doctor then asked the sister if the boy knew that it was going to hurt. She shook her head – the language problem again. The doctor barked at me to hold his hands. In went the lance and in a split second I thought my hands were broken. I don't know which hurt the more, his quinsies or my hands.

As they slowly recovered a battle broke out in the wards – a Blanket Bath War! To give them privacy, we always drew curtains around the beds before starting a blanket bath. After bathing them, we handed them a sponge and a towel to finish off a vital part of their anatomy. We turned our backs to save them embarrassment, but, Oh no, they wanted us to finish. Many a tussle went on behind those curtains. We didn't save them all, but those we did passed out so proudly in their new blue uniforms with a badge.

The Cross of Lorraine was pinned on their caps. They were lovely boys and I was glad to be part of their lives.

Aerial combat was now in full force and volunteers to train on burns units were asked for so I volunteered. I was sent to Ludmouth in Devon, on a ten week course. It was there that I first encountered Americans. They were billeted in guest houses and hotels within a three mile radius. They were great fellows and full of fun with plenty of money. They were training to be marines. When I went to their dances they taught me how to jive – better than riding a bike!

Unfortunately we had to be in by 10.30 p.m., as we were on a training course. We were billeted in a quaint old hotel, the Victoria. The Yanks were devastated when we left them at 10.15, but we got around it. We'd book in at 10.30, then go upstairs to the bathroom and out onto the fire escape and away down the stairs where our American boyfriends were waiting for us. We got away with it for weeks until one night, creeping into the bathroom, early hours of the morning, shoes in our hands, we saw our Sergeant waiting for us. Ten days jankers I got for that – washing dishes, peeling vegetables and to finish it off, we were marched with full pack along the streets of Ludmouth. Of course we saw our American friends. At that time I did not know what was in store for these young marines.

I left that station and returned to Princess Mary's where a burns unit had been established. It wasn't until many years later that I went back to Sidmouth on a holiday and asked the manager of the hotel if I could look around. It is still the same today – time has not changed it. He told me that the young marines had been out on practice manoeuvres in the English Channel. German Intelligence got to know of it and the German E-Boats were waiting for them. It was a massacre, for over five hundred young lives were lost. Britain kept the details of their deaths a thirty-year secret. I did chat with the villagers who told me what they could about it.

I have been once more and I walked along the same corridor. The bathroom is no longer there as all the rooms are now en suite. The fire escape is still there and I stood – I could hear the muffled laughter, see faces and hear voices and I let the tears come. I will never go back again. There in that village is a memorial erected to honour those brave boys.

I was now back in Hulton where we received air crews. They were badly injured with cruel burns. We held them in transit for a few weeks, preventing infection and treating their burns, until they were ready to go to East Grinstead. There, they met Archibald McKindoe and they became known as 'The Guinea Pig Club'. I saw great horror but came to accept it. One of my saddest memories was of a young WAAF. The call came for a female orderly. I went into the Resuscitation Ward and had to cut away the uniform to try to find her identity discs but it was no use. They were also burned. Her death left a great sadness in me. A plane had crashed onto the hangar where she was working. She was identified as Alice Larenby – just eighteen years old.

I then married and was discharged eight months later as I was expecting my first child.

Barbara Noonan (née Oliver)
Hove, East Sussex

460 SQUADRON REUNIONS IN AUSTRALIA

Mention the 460 Squadron biennial reunions in Australia and somebody will almost immediately think of Betty Gardener. Very early after my initial appeal for WAAFs to write, Betty wrote and she has kept in touch since. She has attended reunions in Melbourne, Sydney, Brisbane and now this October 1994 in Perth, Western Australia.

While Peter Firkins, our 460 historian, was writing Strike & Return *she made a contribution to 460's history. She was a member of the team in the Control Tower at Binbrook and after being demobbed went into civil aviation, Air Traffic Control at Heathrow and then on to Filton, Bristol. The aircrew boys gather around her at reunions as she has so many stories to tell. Here is the story she passed on to me:*

Firstly, let me say how sorry I was to hear that you have lost Elizabeth. Her photograph is very familiar so perhaps we lived in the same Nissen hut. I was at Binbrook from late 1943 until 1945 when I had a brief spell at Hemswell.

I met my husband on my first station – RAF Watton, Norfolk. We married in 1950. He came from Bristol but I was a Londoner. We had two children and eleven years ago he collapsed and died while he was helping my daughter to move house. He was fifty-nine at the time and had not had a day's illness. Since then, with the wonderful friendship I have received from 460 Squadron, both British and Australian, I have picked myself up but of course one never forgets.

I have been fortunate enough to attend reunions in Melbourne, Sydney and Brisbane and this year I shall be going to Perth. Each time I have stayed with friends in Gosford, NSW, and Squadron friends in all other states.

After the reunion in 1992, four of us flew to Perth for a week and on one occasion Peter Firkins took us out for the day. I know Peter as I was able to give him a few thoughts when he was writing *Strike & Return*, the 460 Squadron history.

Now, what am I to say about life in the WAAF? We, like the men, came from all walks of life. During my stay at Binbrook we were of course billeted in Nissen huts which were very cold in winter, unless your bed happened to be near the stove in the middle. We all sat on beds nearest the stove to enjoy our tea and coffee. The ingredients for these were 'borrowed' from the cookhouse which happened to be next to our hut! We had two very lively WAAFs with us, one from Kent and the other from Scotland. Around 11.30 p.m., they would raid the cookhouse and return with a very large tin of jam or marmalade. Anyone like myself working shifts rarely attended CO's parades. We were either going on or coming off duty.

We wore thick stockings in the winter and most of us thought they looked better when worn inside out. This was a chargeable offence. I was caught by an SP on a London station and confined to camp for a week.

I very much enjoyed being a R/T Operator in Flying Control. We had extremes of work from circuits and bumps to bombing raids. During take-off there was supposed to be radio silence, but if someone had a problem or had left something behind, they did contact us and we had code words to say so that hopefully the problem could be sorted out.

Then there was the long wait for the return. This of course was very tense and could go on for hours. Oh! the joy of that first call and as others returned, maybe three or four at once, we stacked them in the circuit. Maybe No. 1 would tell No. 4 to 'get up them stairs'. Usually during the return the CO and Engineering Officer would be in the tower to advise if there was a tricky landing.

On the wall we had a huge blackboard on which was written the Aircraft Letter, Pilot's Name, Target, Time of Take-off and Time of Return. This was the responsibility of the airman of the watch, who during the time of waiting made numerous cups of tea for us.

The very worst time of all was when an aircraft was late in returning. This could be because it had been diverted elsewhere for all kinds of reasons but we would listen out for hours and if there was still no response we knew he had crashed or been shot down. What awful times those were!

On a lighter note, pilots would try to fool us and instead of the correct aircraft letter sign they would say such things as, 'R – for Mo,' instead of 'R – for Roger'. Bright sparks those Australians!

Speaking with former crew members since my visits to Oz, they have been surprised to learn that we wrote down, word for word, all air/ground communication. We had many abbreviations of course. Now, all conversation air/ground is recorded.

During our Oz visits we have gone to RAAF stations and so far on each occasion I have been allowed into the Holy of Holies – Air Traffic Control.

Betty Gardener
Nailsea, Bristol

A WONDERFUL BUNCH OF GIRLS

Rita of Hove in East Sussex described the WAAF as a 'wonderful bunch of girls'. I feel that I must agree wholeheartedly – the war brought tragic experiences to many, but there was a need for great efforts, for teamwork, for sacrifices, rising above one's own selfish pursuits and for sharing. The girls of the WAAF did all of those things and more to become a great bunch. Here is Rita's story:

I read your article which was printed in the *Evening Argus* with great interest. I joined the WAAF in December 1942 and was sent to Emsworth and then to Morecambe for square bashing. I went to Elsham Wolds as a trainee RT Operator.

My future husband was a Fitter Armourer stationed at Scampton with 100 Squadron and we met in Grimsby. I used to go to Binbrook quite often and your article brought back many memories.

In April 1942, I was posted to Cranwell where I did a Wireless Course. After being at Group HQ Bawtry, I was finally posted to St Eval in Cornwall. During all these transfers I kept writing to Sidney.

Yes, I did meet wonderful Australians, Canadians, New Zealanders, and South Africans and I did have some traumatic experiences. Aircrew often came into the Control Tower to have a laugh and a joke before going on operations. I would watch the blackboard throughout the night. The night duty I remember more because they came around more often, and then about 4 a.m., the first of the planes would return. We would hold our breath and then came the worst time when F Freddie or C Charlie did not return and the sadness was indescribable. The comradeship and the friendship was one of the most wonderful happenings and I shall never ever forget.

In December 1944 while I was still in the WAAF my husband and I were married and we had forty wonderful years. He died tragically in May 1985. I was very sorry to hear about Elizabeth and thank you for writing a book. We were a wonderful bunch of girls.

Rita Seltzer (née Noorden)
LACW 2077894

TENDER LOVING CARE

During World War II, tremendous strides forward were made in the treatment
of burns. This was due to the dedicated work of doctors and to that, we can add
the devotion of the WAAF who were responsible for the nursing, which was often
needed over long periods.

At Rauceby Hospital in South Lincolnshire, the RAF established a 'burns'
hospital. On 11 April 1990 a reunion was held at Rauceby to celebrate the 50th
anniversary of the establishment of an RAF Unit. Until 1940, Rauceby had been
used as a hospital for the mentally ill. F.M. Backhurst, who was stationed at
Rauceby, sent me quite an amount of material telling about Rauceby and I would
like to include some quotations from the booklet issued at the reunion:

A number of young men, who became legends in their own lifetime, had
occasion to be patients at Rauceby. For instance: W/C Guy Gibson VC
was there before he went on his fatal mission. F/Sgt. John Hannah who
won his VC at the age of eighteen in 1940 was a patient, but sadly he was
discharged from the RAF in 1942 and died in 1947. Air Chief Marshal Sir
Angus Walker, who was Commanding Officer at Syerston, lost an arm in
an airfield accident and was a patient.

Happy memories, albeit painful, abound from the most exalted rank
to the lowliest erk. Morale at the hospital was high and often spirits
lightened in the form of shows and dances which were held weekly. Many
famous names trod the boards of Rauceby's stage. At dances music was
provided by the hospital's own dance band 'The Medicos'.

The feeling of close companionship shared by the medical staff led to
the formation of a unique club simply known as, 'The Rauceby Club'. It
was formed by W/C Eric Jewesbury and included all medical staff who
had worked or had connections with RAF Hospital Rauceby. Its mem-
bership list reads as a *Who's Who* of the medical profession, as many of
these doctors and surgeons went on to achieve eminence in their particular
fields. The Club was unique in that it was the only one of its kind ever
formed.

Now to the letter I received telling of the work of a WAAF in the Medical
Branch:

I was in a branch of the Services which is not very often thought about – the Medical Branch of the Services. For the largest part of my service I was stationed at RAF Hospital, Rauceby, Lincolnshire.

We had quite a few of RAAF boys pass through. I was mainly on burns, Officer Ward, Surgical and finished up working in the Operating Theatre. I have many happy memories of the comradeship and of the thrill of seeing someone come in badly burned or injured and then go out looking well again. To know that you had a part in helping them gave you a great boost! This gave you the strength to go on when you saw others who did not make it. The hospital was a friendly and a happy place in spite of all the pain, the disappointment and sadness.

We did our best to cheer those who were far from home. The lads in the dark blue uniforms will always be remembered for the cheerfulness.

Some bad crash victims came to us. One I remember was G/C 'Gus' Walker who had an arm blown off when a plane blew up before take-off.

I saw your article in the *Leicester Mercury*. I hope you get a good response for *Spit, Polish & Tears*.

F.M. Backhurst
Hugglescote, Coalville

NIGHTMARES

Almost every WAAF who joined during World War II had to do things she would not have dreamed of doing in civvy life. Jeanne Williams, who went to boarding school before joining the WAAF, was not quite as shocked by the tedium of service life as many were, but she tells of tears, sadness and hardship. However, as you will see, her account ends with the words, 'I wouldn't have missed it for anything.' Here is her story:

One morning in 1941, when I became nineteen, I left Paddington Station for RAF Innsworth. With many others, I was given a meal. I'll never forget the greasy liver and bacon casserole, slabs of bread and margarine, a spoonful of jam and a mug of sweet hot tea. All this in a heat wave!

The second shock came when we queued for for FFI – i.e. head lice and scabies inspection. I had no idea what the medical assistants were looking for, but I did notice that more than half our group disappeared to another part of the camp.

Then we were marched – well, we tried didn't we – to our sleeping huts – twenty-four bedsteads, separated by lockers, mats, two large black stoves, a folding wooden table and two forms. On each bed were three 'biscuits' – straw squares which made up to a mattress – a straw filled bolster, four blankets, two sheets and a bolster case.

The NCO showed us where the ablution hut was – fifty yards away – and told us to sort ourselves out and she would see us in the morning, at 6.30 a.m. Eventually, we decided whom we wished to sleep near, made up our beds and turned in for the night. There was not much sleep that night what with the hard beds and the crying from most of the girls. One must realise that in those days few girls had ever slept away from home, or travelled so far from family. I was lucky for I had been to boarding school and was not homesick.

For the next three weeks, we were in a constant state of shock for it seemed that our feet never touched the ground. Starting at 6.30 in the morning and ending at 5.30, we were marched from pillar to post, kitted out, medically inspected, inoculated, drilled and lectured on all subjects in the RAF, drilled again, put through a gas chamber, more drill and of course numerous fatigues and daily physical training.

We didn't really mind the PT, it was the conditions under which we suffered it. We were marched into a large field with a nearby hedge and told to remove tunics, collars, ties, skirts, corsets and suspender belts and roll down our stockings. Our shirts were to be tucked into our navy bloomers – 'black-outs'. It was an airman's dream but our NIGHTMARE. Nowadays of course no-one would turn a hair but in the 1940s one didn't show the world one's underwear or undress in public.

As our Passing Out Parade came nearer, we polished our buttons and shoes all the harder, until the final day when we marched like guardsmen out onto the parade ground for inspection by the CO. Then came the march past by four hundred airwomen with not one making a mistake. How proud we were of ourselves, the WAAF and our uniform.

The next day at 5.30 a.m., we were sent to RAF Stations all over the UK. Fourteen of us were posted to Leighton Buzzard for trade training. We had kit bags almost as big as ourselves to carry as well as being festooned with gas masks, tin helmets, belts and a cloth bag containing our rations for the day – two dry cheese sandwiches and a piece of fruit cake. We had breakfasted at 4.45 a.m. and next sat down for a meal at 8.00 p.m. – more sandwiches.

We were billeted in an old workhouse and taken by truck each day to a section operations room for our training as Clerks/Special Duties – Fighter Plotters. We found the work hard but absorbing and after only ten days, we were posted to Fighter Ops Rooms owing to a shortage of plotters. Once again we parted company with our friends. Six of us went to Inverness. We thought it to be the end of the earth as we all came from the south of England. We were billeted in a hotel, minus all the comforts, and each day or night we travelled by truck to the Operations Room in the Dunrossie Hotel, some miles out of town. We worked three watches: Day One – 8 a.m. to 1 p.m.; Day two – midnight to 8 p.m., and Day Three 1 p.m. to 8 a.m. If we were lucky, we had one watch off per week.

In between duties, we had the usual domestic chores to do, kit inspection drill, PT. It was hard and tiring but in our free time, we enjoyed ourselves to the full. We explored the beautiful Scottish Highlands, cycling or hitch-hiking, played tennis, danced, gossiped and giggled in various service canteens and the cinema.

I spent two happy years at Inverness and was promoted to Corporal and posted to the Orkney Islands. I was among the first airwomen to be posted to RAF Kirkwall and we went to a newly built camp with ablution huts adjoining our quarters. It was alongside the RAF camp but separated by a bog and masses of barbed wire. Needless to say we were welcomed with open arms by the airmen who had even made up our beds, most of them apple-pied.

During summer, the Orkney Islands are beautiful but during winter, conditions are very harsh – almost continuous gale-force winds, horizontal rain, sleet and snow; few hours of daylight came our way. We were issued with 'Penguin Suits' – black oil-skins and sou'westers – one size only – Mens!

The Ops room was always very busy and we worked hard and played hard. I loved the Isles and enjoyed my twenty months there immensely. The duty tour for WAAF was nine months but I volunteered for a second tour. It may be of interest to know that for travel the majority of Service people caught the troop train known as the 'Jericho Express' from Euston at 10 a.m., the rest joined at Perth. All Servicewomen were put in one carriage which was locked. Food was always provided at approximately 4 p.m. by the Salvation Army – always a meat pie, questionable, bread and tea. Then, in the small hours of the morning when the train took on water, the splendid ladies of the WVS handed up scones and cakes and poured tea into our mugs which we held out of the train windows. We arrived at Thurso about 8 a.m. and were taken to a transit camp. Always there was a breakfast of fried spam and baked beans. We marched to a pier for the ferry, *Earl of Zetland*. The crossing through the Pentland Firth is well known for its roughness and so many breakfasts were lost before we docked at Stromness. Another truck transported us to Kirkwall where we arrived exhausted about 5 p.m.

From Kirkwall I was posted to RAF Exeter for a short while and then RAF North Weald – Blake Hall Ops Room, which was suffering from V1 bombs – buzz-bombs – and therefore casualties. It was odd how frightened of these bombs I was when taken away from camp and yet, whilst on duty, I can't remember feeling fear.

Soon, it was VE Day – how we celebrated that and then VJ Day and I was demobbed in February 1946. I was nearly five years in uniform and I would not have missed it for anything in spite of sadness, hardships and overwork but what companionship! I rejoined the WAAF in 1947 and went into Administration, to be promoted to Sergeant. I met my husband a year later. He was a Fighter Pilot and I was a RAF wife for eight more years.

I am still in touch with four WAAF who joined up that day in July 1941. Except for a few odd months we served together all of our Service life.

Jeanne Williams
Newark, Notts

A FAIR COW

I assume that the expression 'a fair cow' is Australian and it means that things are difficult. It was 'a fair cow' trying to get back to base when the fog clamped down. Possibly many an Aussie spoke in these terms while in the UK.

However, Muriel Lewis had a 'cow of a time' trying to get into camp by dodging the guard room. When she wrote her story for me, she did mix her genders and told me that the cow grunted disapproval – his disapproval! I wrote back and said, 'No Bull!'

During the war, my husband and I wrote to each other every day, time permitting, from 1940 until the end of the war. These letters have spent time in various attics as we have moved around and it is not until now, when I am on my own, that I have spent many hours reading and re-living the past. I think your plan to compile a book in Elizabeth's memory is a wonderful idea.

My husband was a W/O in 220 Squadron, Coastal Command, stationed in Scotland and Ireland. I'm afraid that I have never been mentioned in despatches or considered conspicuous where bravery is concerned, but those years in the Service were well spent as I am sure you will agree with me.

Of course, we remember only the good times. I joined the WAAF in 1941 and was issued with one uniform that fitted, my buttons were also nearly worn flat – what a swank when the new recruits arrived! I was stationed at Group HQ Worcester, in a stately home miles from anywhere, and life was never dull. There were some sad moments but good times too at the village pub getting into a happy state and then on to the village hop, running into competition with the local belles. This brings my memory to one occasion when I forgot to get a late pass. The HQ Hinslip Hall was set in very spacious grounds with the Guard Room at the entrance, and my companion at the dance assured me he could get me back into camp without passing the Guard Room. Well, he did! We had to go right around the estate through roughly ploughed fields and through hedges in the pitch darkness. In my happy state, I walloped, feet off the ground, slap on top of a sleeping cow who grunted his disapproval. Hysterics prevailed all the way to the billet. We made it!

Chris and I were married in 1942, and every three or four months excitement would mount as leave approached. We met 'under the clock' at Paddington Station. After the austere surroundings of a service hut, the wall to wall carpeting, silk bed-spreads, pink bath etc. were heaven in a posh hotel. It was a contrast that my grandchildren would never understand. I remember one evening after a day of sightseeing and a show, entering a lift to go up to our room, clutching bags of fruit and cake for a midnight feast and the sirens started to wail. People in night attire rushed past on their way down to the air raid shelters. We kept going. Love is blind. We were going to die together, if needs be, in Paradise!

The end of a leave and the parting of the ways from an outback railway station went something like this . . . One troop train, crammed to capacity, eye-ball to eye-ball in the corridor if you were unable to get a seat. In weariness after a long wait, we sank to the floor, sitting on our respirators, the light so dim you could hardly see the face next to you. The atmosphere was heavy with dejection and there was a lot of puffing on cigarettes to cover one's misery. Many was the time when 'Jerry' would be coasting around looking for a target. A sudden lurch as the train started would jerk thoughts and we would be on our way, only moments later to come to a grinding halt, and we would sit in suspense listening to 'Jerry's' engines that had also stopped for the moment. Everyone held his breath wondering if it would be his last. Sometimes, the little train would go backwards and then a great cheer and much laughter would roar through the corridors. None of the stations showed a name and one had to rely on the porter calling out the stops.

Upon return to camp with a heavy heart, we found that on such a small camp we were soon absorbed into the wise-cracking atmosphere, thanks to some wonderful friends. Of course, we must mention the hard bed, the cold and the tea made with powdered milk. Out would come the buns baked by every loving Mum.

I am still reading the letters and small anecdotes of Service life come up and I give a chuckle as my memory is prompted.

On one occasion, my husband came to stay in the village. He had more leave than me as he was aircrew, and we got an SOP – a sleeping out pass – for me. We booked to stay in one of the village cottages – real country folk – and we found, when we got there, that the loo was at the very bottom of the garden, all very dark and scary. I remember to this very day making my husband come with me, creeping like criminals, clutching a candle, smothering laughter as we crept along. We remembered this leave for a long time because Chris bumped on the end of the bed as he sat up to put his socks on, and yes, you guessed it – the bed leg broke! We propped the bed up and made a very hasty departure.

I think that it is a moving gesture to write in memory of your wife and in memory of all of us 'erks' who did our best to support the men who risked their lives.

Muriel Lewis
Bordon, Hampshire

AN EDUCATION FOR AUDREY

Audrey, a Yorkshire girl, had a load of Aussies on board when on her first trip as an MT Driver at Marston Moor she was nearly run over by a Halifax bomber taking off. She learned quickly that the ends of runways can be dangerous places and that Aussies have quite a vocabulary when you scratch them.

This is a true story which happened during the war at an airfield in Yorkshire called Marston Moor. Our RAF Station was known as a Conversion Unit which was used to train fighter pilots to fly Halifax bombers.

I was a new WAAF recruit who had been to Gloucester for my uniform, then to Morecambe for square bashing. At Morecambe I did a driving course. I had never travelled before except for a weekend to Leeds when I was nine years old. I hadn't a clue as to what an aerodrome was like. I had heard of runways, perimeters etc., but I had never made a mental picture of them, so you can understand how I felt at just eighteen years of age.

I arrived at this strange place and booked in at the Guard Room and a few other offices. I was given a bed in a Nissen hut and told to report to the Motor Transport Section after tea. There I was to be one of many male and female drivers. I was told to report to Flying Control in a 30 cwt. lorry with a material-covered top.

There I was, in pitch darkness, in a strange place, no lights to show the roads and just little slits of lights on the lorry and I had not the faintest idea where Flying Control was. However, after being given directions, I eventually found the airfield. I was told to join the other two lorries which would be parked opposite Flying Control. I travelled along this unlit 'road' until I made out the shape of two lorries and parked at the side of them. I was told by the other drivers that as soon as we saw a torch flashing at Flying Control, we had to go to see what was required. Sometimes we were sent to other parts of the camp and sometimes we had to transport crews to aircraft.

Suddenly, a light flashed and the other drivers said, 'You go and you will see what goes on.' I was told that a crew was in my lorry and I had to take them to 'A' Flight. I didn't know where that was so one of the other drivers volunteered to go with me for my first trip. We moved off to the right and seemed to go gradually round a bend to the left. We came to a point where I was told to stop and look, as we had arrived at the runway on our left. I stopped and raised myself off my seat to look along the runway. I could just manage to see lanes of tiny lights. 'OK, go across. It's clear.' said the other driver. So off I went. I got right into the middle of the runway, when suddenly there was a terrific noise and the lorry shook. There was a lot of angry shouting in the back of the lorry. I kept going, not knowing what had happened and at last arrived at 'A' Flight, but I needn't have worried. The crew, who were Australians, told me in no uncertain language that the Halifax bomber had taken off on top of the lorry and its wheels had scraped as it went over. The names I was called and the language used were quite an education.

Audrey Pickering
Scarborough, N. Yorks

THE GIRL WHO CAME TO AUSTRALIA

Patricia, the wife of Alan Young, an Australian, came across the world in June 1945 to meet her late husband's parents. Alan who operated from Binbrook, 460 Squadron, was lost on a raid in February 1944. Here is Patricia's story:

I was a WAAF stationed at Bournemouth with the Australian and New Zealand Air Force. There I met my husband, Alan Geoffrey Young. Alan was posted to Binbrook in August 1943. He was a Wireless/Air Gunner on 460 Squadron, flying with Lancasters.

He was on an operation to Germany on a raid to Stuttgart. On returning, there was an aircraft accident and a crash at Peterborough where all the crew were lost. They were laid to rest in the war cemetery at Cambridge.

Alan who came from West Ryde in New South Wales, asked me, if anything happened to him, would I go out and visit his Mum and Dad. I went to Australia in 1945 as a war widow. There I stayed for a year and had a wonderful time. His Mum and Dad and brothers were lovely people and made me so welcome. I liked Sydney very much.

I came home to England and met my second husband who had been in the Royal Air Force. Bertram Lloyd Hayes and I had two sons and one of my sons is named Alan. My eldest son, strangely enough, is living with his family just half an hour from Binbrook. I lost my second husband when he had a heart attack in 1983.

My husband's aircraft was 'G' George.

Patricia Lloyd Hayes
Southwick, Sussex

Another 'G' George was flown to Australia and now may be seen in the Canberra War Museum.

THOSE WHO CARED FOR POWS

Pat Whetton was one of the WAAFs who cared for POWs after the war was over. She also was present at the funeral of F/Sgt. Middleton who was one of the two RAAF airmen to receive the Victoria Cross in the European theatre during World War II. She points out that WAAF life is hardly mentioned in many war books and that young people are growing up now who have little or no idea what contribution women made.

I joined the WAAF in May 1942, volunteering and receiving the 'King's Shilling'. I went to Innsworth for kitting out, numerous injections, clothes that did not fit and a huge great-coat. Oh! those shoes were like iron cases and trying to break them in was murder which brought blisters galore. Trying to get them to shine meant hours of 'spit and polish' every evening. It was the same with the buttons and cap badge.

My square-bashing was done in Morecambe on the sea front in very cold and wet weather. It's a wonder that we all did not take off with the wind under those dreadful capes we wore – ground sheets. It was a very trying time and home sickness prevailed. My first station was in Lincoln Central Gunnery School for aircrew to attend and refresh.

At that time I was a waitress in the Sergeants' mess and we had to walk three miles to work along a large river in the pitch dark in order to serve breakfast. With our hair in curlers under our caps. the sentry always shone a torch in our faces on arrival at the main gate. I think he was lonely and just wanted to size us up perhaps with a date in mind. This of course was at six o'clock in the morning.

I told you that I attended F/Sgt. Middleton's funeral in Beck Row. It was very impressive indeed and I can still picture his girlfriend sobbing bitterly. She was a WAAF Corporal and was expecting his child at the time.

My dear husband died just a few months before you lost Elizabeth. We were married for forty-seven years after we met at Cosford. Will had returned from Burma with the RAF and was a Sergeant Cook i/c a large mess, where POWs were posted. By that time I was in a Medical Rehabilitation Unit to which POWs came after going on home leave.

When I arrived at Cosford, I wondered what was in store. By then I was a Senior NCO and had been told that people had been specially selected for the duty of caring for POWs who had returned from Germany. The slow trickle of lads arriving soon turned into a torrent as more prison camps were liberated by the Allies. Most of them were aircrew. On VE Day, when the news of peace came, the whole camp erupted. The chaps went wild and a huge bonfire was made on the road outside the WAAF huts. Chairs, tables and forms were taken outside to fuel the fire. Screaming WAAFs still in pyjamas were carried outside to join in the fun. The Air Ministry lost a lot of furniture that night. No charges were made and the Fire Brigade made only a half-hearted attempt to quell the fire.

Most of the POWs were not too bad physically but mentally they were scarred through internment. One W/O Pilot used to sit alone in the ante-room playing classical music. The chaps who had been in Jap hands were in a dreadful state, suffering from malnutrition, beri-beri, malaria, dysentery, and all sorts of dreadful things. They needed lots of care to build them up after their ordeal. It opened my eyes to the horrors of war.

Whilst at RAF Uxbridge, I hated having to go in the basement to shelter from bombs. These were the V1s and later the V2s – rockets. These would arrive on most nights as we were not far from London. With the vibration of bombs exploding, the blackouts used to fall down and so lights were extinguished and we sat in the dark calling Jerry a lot of nasty names. I never worried about dying but was annoyed at losing my beauty sleep.

At RAF St Athan in Wales, I was with a Squadron of Canadians who had never been in action. They had come to Britain for training. They were a lovely crowd. Their mothers would have been horrified to see the antics. This of course annoyed the 'armchair types' the permanent staff. On my day off, I used to hire a bicycle and ride miles exploring the lovely Welsh countryside. It was so beautiful. I went to church once but could not understand a word as the service was in Welsh.

Pat Whetton
Beck Rowe, Suffolk

D-DAY AT EASTBOURNE

Today, at Eastbourne, on the prom,
Day trippers take the air,
But only a half a century ago,
Things were much different there.

As a Radar Operator,
In the spring of '44,
I was stationed down at Wartling,
Right on the Sussex shore.

We were billeted at Eastbourne,
Where we really had it good,
With a landlady who excelled herself,
In the art of wholesome food.

The drone of aircraft engines,
Disturbed our sleep at night;
As our heavy bombers crossed the coast,
Returning at first light.

Side roads were packed with armoured trucks,
Tanks stood in full array,
Awaiting for the High Command,
To name the vital day.

Unknown to us that day had dawned,
The fleet was under way,
And Allied troops were landing,
On the shores of Normandy.

When we relieved the night bind watch,
It came as quite a shock,
As we stared down on the table,
In the Operations Block.

The plotters with their 'fishing lines',
Were deep in concentration,
As they kept the picture up to date,
From the latest information.

Although the tide of war had turned,
We kept a watchful eye,
On any object which appeared,
Within our range of sky.

The V1s – nicknamed buzz-bombs,
Took us somewhat by surprise,
But the ack-ack guns and fighters,
Soon dispersed them from the skies.

The V2s were most treacherous,
Causing widespread devastation,
And the capture of the launching sites
Brought relief throughout the nation.

The race was on, and in due course,
Hostilities did cease,
And the nations of the world returned
To sanity and peace.

The best of times, the worst of times,
The laughter, the despair,
When history was being made,
I'm proud that I was there.

Jenny Lindsay (née Hamilton)
RAF Wartling, 1944

POIGNANT MEMORIES OF
WATCHING TAKE OFF

Audrey Taylor, who now lives in Reading, occupied the next bed to Elizabeth. It amazes me that in all England I should find someone who not only knew Elizabeth but who slept in the next bed. Thousands of WAAFs must, with aching hearts, have watched take-off and then in the early hours counted the aircraft as they came back.

I certainly remember Elizabeth who occupied the next bed to me in the Nissen hut at Swinhope, the WAAF site at Binbrook. I cannot remember her trade but I have memories of a quiet, thoughtful girl – very methodical and good with her needle and so very much in love with an Aussie airman whom she was going to marry. Elizabeth was a Scot, dark-haired, about 5 feet 8 ins tall, probably about twenty-two years of age. We often had little chats and she was good company.

I recall so much about Binbrook – the most dramatic days of my life. I joined the WAAF in 1941 – just 17½. After my initial training, I was posted to RAF Duxford, an operational fighter station with Spitfires and Typhoons. The USAAF took over the station and all RAF were posted. I was drafted to Binbrook in 1943 and worked in the Accounts Section. The Accounts Offices occupied the married quarters houses at the rear of the base Commander's residence (Air Commodore Wray).

I left Binbrook in late 1945, was sent to RAF Rufforth, near York and later posted to HQFTC at Reading where I remained until demob in 1946.

For me, Binbrook was the most memorable time of my career. I can recall so much as though it was yesterday. I think the most poignant memories for me are – going up to the runway to watch evening take-off – waving good luck to my boyfriends – returning to our WAAF hut – then in the early hours hearing the drone of returning aircraft – others following – and then a voice in the darkness of our hut saying – 'Two more to come home.' These thoughts still bring tears to my eyes, fifty years on.

I have so many memories – bright young men from the other side of the world – wonderful company – and the girls I met and kept in touch with. Friendships in those days were so deep and meant so much. Sadly, in recent years a few have passed on but I am still in touch with others.

Audrey Taylor
Reading, Berkshire

IN TROUBLE? A SMILE HELPS

When you are broke and down on your luck, there is often something which gives you a lift. I suppose many a WAAF went on leave without a bean and I hope they met friends such as this story tells:

I was in the WAAF in the early part of the war but I was never really in the thick of it. I became a batwoman to W/C Thomas. My maiden name was Jackson and my number was 2055050.

We always had a routine – Monday night, kit inspection; Friday morning, pay parade; Sunday morning, church parade. I remember very well the Passing Out Parade at Cranwell. We stood in line for an hour waiting for the Big Shot. Buttons were shining; shoes were shining; hair was two inches above the coat collar and then the heavens opened and it poured and poured. I don't have to describe what we looked like but the blow came when we were described as the worst sight the Big Shot had ever seen. Down came the tears!

What sticks in my mind most was a particular pay parade. I saluted and was paid sixpence. Shoe repairs and the loss of stockings had been charged. I was just going on leave and had sixteen shillings and my railway ticket. My home was a long way away and it meant bus and taxi. I was waiting for the bus and as I felt hungry, I went into a café for a 'cuppa'. I was given a cooked meal and a cheery smile on the house!

At no time was I anything exciting in the WAAF but at times I felt important. Things were hard but I gritted my teeth and carried on. My last station was at Driffield. It took a lot of hammer from time to time, day and night raids but no lives were lost.

I am now seventy-seven years old and have a lovely family – ten grandchildren and two great-grandchildren, but sad to say I lost my husband eleven years ago.

G. Kilvington
North Yorkshire

D-DAY, 6 JUNE –
A NIGHT TO REMEMBER

In her story 'A Night to Remember', Winifred has captured the excitement which came on the evening of 5 June 1944, when a little group of WAAFs knew that 'something was up' as she puts it. She has caught the electric atmosphere of the ops room when the CO passed the message, 'This is IT!'

The day after war was declared, with youthful enthusiasm, my brother Stephen aged sixteen and I hastened to the recruiting office. Then, for some weeks we bit our finger nails – would it be over by Christmas?

Stephen, a Gordon Highlander, died of wounds at Monte Cassino in 1944, aged nineteen.

I found myself in a Fighter Operations room in time for the Battle of Britain. Looking back, I was thrilled that I was there but at that time, with nothing but childhood on Ditchling Common behind me, it was bewildering to say the least. I soon grew up.

During a quiet period later, I seem to have volunteered to become a Radar Operator. This was called in those days RDF – Radio Direction Finding – and we also had GCI – Ground Control Interception. Until this time, RDF looked only out to sea. Now there was a new venture.

Squadron Leader 'Willie' Wilson, a First World War pilot, and his five chosen WAAF were soon in the Hartlepool Docks working in a mobile Radar caravan. From there, I wended my way south from dock to dock, finding myself on the south coast sometime in the spring of 1944.

We lived in empty houses in a seaside town full of Canadians. The atmosphere was tense and the hours of duty long. I can't remember where we ate. We were sick of war.

On the evening of 5 June, we walked to the ops room – somewhere underground, not now to be found. We could see immediately something was up. The outgoing watch were seething with fury, almost begging us to let them stay on.

The ops room was electric – everyone who was anyone was there, strutting about in the upper gallery, all anxious to play a part. The CO gave a little homily – this was IT! We would of course be the first target. Squadrons of fighter planes were in readiness. We were all given a letter from Eisenhower. Five years of training for this very night. We clutched our tin hats. The crews settled down. The radar screens were blanketed out by gliders. We sat tense, not knowing what to expect. The hours passed. Some brave soul offered to make cocoa. The answer was withering. 'All those men out there and you can think only of cocoa!' The hours passed.

We were now drinking mugs of thick dark cocoa – our staple diet on night duty. Irate phone calls from anxious pilots broke the tension. Calls from other Groups – what were we doing? The night was dark and silent – no enemy plane was seen that night on a radar screen. Dawn came. We straightened our ties and stretched our stiff limbs. Ten hours of NOTHING!

We allowed the new watch to take over and emerged to the world, weary and disheartened, out into the dawn fresh air to walk down the sleeping streets. Suddenly, in unison, it hit us all. We let out a great HURRAY, flung our tin hats in the air and cheered again. We were alive and THEY had landed and we, a small gang of unruly WAAF, had been 'in on it'. We cheered again. A window opened, an angry voice silenced us, 'Shut up, you bloody WAAF.'

The days after were exhausting – Air Sea Rescue, Intruder Patrols, Squadrons coming and going. I wouldn't have missed it for the world.

Soon, there was another night to remember – the first V1 fell. I then found myself on the Fairlight Cliffs with doodlebugs – but that is another story.

Winifred Denyer (née Maxwell)
West Sussex

FEELING SHEEPISH?

Among my souvenirs I still have love letters which Elizabeth wrote me when I was in London doing a school and while I was at Gamston waiting to go to Brighton before sailing for Australia.

Just now, I have looked through them again and there has been something wrong with my eyes and I have had to keep blowing my nose. I did find the story which Elizabeth told me about the final break-up party of the Aussies at Binbrook. Phyl, whom Elizabeth mentions, was one of the lassies in the Tailors' Shop.

Here then are Elizabeth's own words:

Phyl has just told me something which is very typical and just what one might expect from Aussies. Here it is – on Sunday they all got drunk and brought back eighty-three sheep with them from the village and put them in the Sergeants' mess. They then proceeded to carry them upstairs to the bunks and put them in beside the boys in bed. When they woke up in the morning they were faced with sheep and the boys, who had been tight, opened their eyes and saw sheep staring at them. Can you imagine it, darling?

According to accounts received from a good source, the bleating was something awful, as they had separated them all.

They spent Sunday morning cleaning up the visiting cards. Also, the farmer kicked up such a row that they were all called up before the Wing Co. I'll bet he had a good laugh on his own just the same.

Well, Elizabeth had grown used to Aussies by the time she wrote this and as the years went by she was able to look back to the almost unbelievable pranks which Aussies dreamt up while at Binbrook.

THE WAAF FLIGHT MECHANIC

The lords of the air they call them,
They speak of their growing fame,
The front page of every paper,
Is adorned with a pilot's name.

In stories of deeds of valour,
Written up in the sky,
You read of the high speed battles,
Fought by the men who fly.

But there's one who gets no medals;
You never hear her name
She doesn't fly in the blueness of sky,
Nor pose for the news with a plane.

Her job can't be called romantic,
Nor one for the public gaze,
But the lords of the air respect her
And often give her praise.

Who inspects the kite each morning?
Who fills up the tanks each night?
Who keeps the engine nice and sweet?
Who keeps the pressure right?

Who is up at the crack of dawn?
Still there as twilight fades,
Pulling her weight a-keeping the crate
Ready to fly on a raid?

So next time you see a picture,
Of a plane and its smiling crew,
Remember the girl who keeps it aloft,
Who is only an AC2.

Next time you praise a pilot,
As the enemy falls a wreck,
Remember the WAAF who's not so daft –
The humble and proud Flight Mech.

Molly Woolnough
Newcombe, Victoria, Australia

Molly wrote this poem while sitting in a squadron rest room waiting for aircraft to return.

BLUE KNICKERS

Yes, this is a blue story – materially blue and if Elizabeth caught me writing this yarn, then there would be a fair dinkum blue.

I am not an authority of WAAFs' knickers, but I can tell you about how blue knickers were stitched up at Dyce RAF Station in 1942.

When Elizabeth, a fully fledged tailoress, was posted from Bridgnorth to Dyce, it would seem that the powers that were at Dyce did not really know much about how a tailoress should be employed on an Air Force Station.

Some bright bod, be it a WAAF Officer or RAF type, obtained yards and yards of blue material. I'm not sure just how blue it was but my imagination tells me it was pretty dark because dark deeds were about to be done.

The materials and a pattern, V shaped, long legged and most ample in all areas, were produced to Liz and other tailoresses. I can almost, even now, read the minds of those who planned this dark deed. They were saying, 'This'll keep them out of mischief.' Little did they know that anyone seen around or even suspected of wearing the final results would have little chance of mischief.

Elizabeth and others set to work and produced dozens and dozens of blue knickers. Imagine them piled up like great blue sacks in the equipment section. Perhaps eventually they were issued but to whom?

From Elizabeth's description of these dark blue sacks, I feel sure that anyone who actually wore them must have been in dire straits. Of course, one could never know – clothes rationing and wear and tear and pre-war knickers could have made many a WAAF blue. After all, the winters are cold in Britain.

As I said, I am no expert in knicker colours but I'll bet my socks that no one was tempted to nick those blue knickers from a clothes line.

RADAR REMINISCENCES

Sue tells of her wonderful experiences while working with boffins, training Americans and guarding crashed aircraft. She tells of a dog who drank 'charged' water just for kicks. At one time her little unit had to write down everything they ate – why? Here's her story:

I was at RAF Malvern at TRE. I lived in Malvern but we went out to man a little GCI station at Sledge Green, where we controlled the aircraft mainly from Defford. These were used for trying out the various types of equipment being developed. When we first went in early '43, 'we' were three WAAF operators. There were two mechanics, a 'flight' and a controller officer already there. SPs lived on the site.

Our CO when we were at Hack Green, Squadron Leader Kirby-James, moved down to Sledge Green at the same time and we were honoured to be picked to go with him to this secret, secret place. It was certainly a wonderful experience working with all those very clever RAF and boffins.

We worked most peculiar hours. When equipment needed testing quickly, we had little time off. At quiet times, we had a lovely life in the beautiful countryside of the Worcestershire/Gloucestershire borders.

Thinking about it now, the ops room was a hazardous place to work, with cables trailing around and about to the equipment being developed and/or tested. Factory inspectors of today would be horrified. I remember, particularly, one piece of equipment being developed had leads going outside through a window into a small bath of water. The water must have been 'live'. One of our dogs persistently went to drink from it. It gave him a kick over a ditch, but he must have enjoyed it because he came back repeatedly although he had water elsewhere.

We did much work when 'window' (now 'chaff', I think) was being developed. It was quite challenging to us. The aircraft went way out of our radar range so we had to do DR using our 'computer'. It was most pleasing when we were bang-on as the blip came up on the screen once more.

Not long before D-Day we had some new American equipment (584) to test and learn how it could be used. Our small team of Flt./Lt. Evans with Nan, Beth and Sue as operators had many practice runs with this equipment designed to control low flying 'planes behind enemy lines. We three WAAF had readings to do and report. The CO controlled the aircraft, giving vectors as it approached the target. He said in his rich tenor voice, 'Steady, Steady, Steady . . . Now', when the aircraft in action would drop a bomb.

Crews of Americans came straight from America to our small station. They listened to a couple of dummy runs, then the CO said, 'Would you like to try?' 'Gee,' they said, 'Say it all again. Your voices are so beautiful.' We did two more runs, then it was the GI's turn. Imagine our amazement when they did the exercise copying our voices.

After several trial runs, they left and soon afterwards went to France, I think, about D+1 Day. I must admit we were worried for they did not seem to treat it at all seriously. Fortunately, we learned later that they did very well but we often wondered if they were still mimicking our voices.

One afternoon, we were not 'manned up' but the RT was on in the ops room. I was dusting and having a tidy-up. The CO, Flt./Lt. Blunt, was in his office off the main room when over the RT came a pilot saying he was bailing out, giving a rough guide to where he was. The CO shot out of his office saying, 'Quick, come with me,' and we were in the 'tilly', out of the gate and on the lane in the direction of where we thought the 'plane would be. The CO said, 'Look for any smoke in the fields.' Being autumn, the farmers had been hedge trimming and plumes of smoke seemed everywhere rising in the clear blue sky. However, the pilot had given the grid reference so we kept going in that direction. About four to five miles on, we found the 'plane in the middle of a field. As it was felt that there were spies around the area and we did not know if there was any secret equipment on the crashed plane, Flt./Lt. Blunt more or less shoved me out of the 'tilly' saying, 'Don't let anybody near the 'plane. I will go and 'phone Defford.'

Always, when crashed aircraft are shown on TV these days, I recall that day. Fortunately, few people were around as everybody was busy in that farming area. There was no petrol to spare to chase around the countryside as there is today so anybody who came was on foot or on a bike. I do not know what I would have done if any persistent spy had turned up and I was certainly pleased to see the local policeman pedal up on his bike. In no particular hurry, he leaned his bike on the gatepost saying, 'What's up here then?' By this time, a few other folk on bikes had turned up. I was able to tell them that there were no aircrew on board to be rescued, so we all gazed at the smoke as it rose lazily up into the sky. Fortunately, quite soon RAF personnel turned up from Defford and I was relieved of my guard duties.

Strangely, that field was to be the scene of another drama a few months later when our duty bus ploughed its way through a hedge and ended up on the edge of a cutting for a local railway line.

Incidentally, at one time for three weeks we had to keep, for someone at the Air Ministry, a record of everything we ate. As you can imagine, it was quite a chore but we were interested to know what 'they' would say. Some weeks passed then came a letter saying we would be all right providing we ate plenty of carrots.

Sue Fisher
Norwich

INTRUDERS

As I write this, I feel that I am the intruder in this story. It should be all Elizabeth and all WAAFs. As Elizabeth is not here, you will forgive me for being the story-teller – the intruder.

During our time in the RAF, intruders were enemy aircraft which often mingled with a returning bomber stream, thus avoiding the British radar, and then waited for an opportunity to attack bombers returning from a raid. The bomber that was limping along on fewer than four engines, with perhaps some of its crew wounded or dead, became an easy target for the intruders.

Not long after our crew began ops, a 460 Squadron aircraft – F/O Warren was the skipper – was shot down over Britain by an intruder.

As a bomb aimer, I also had to act as a gunner from the front turret of the Lancaster. The rule was that all guns on the aircraft were to be put to 'safe' once the English Channel was crossed on the way home from a raid. After having heard of F/O Warren's loss over England, I purposely ignored orders and left the two front guns on 'fire'. Nobody would know.

Don't you believe it! As soon as our Lancaster landed, not over heavily as our Skipper was one of the best pilots, then the two front guns started to fire. A stream of tracers and armour piercing poured down the Binbrook runway. With a few short expletives I dived for the safety catches.

The next morning, I was up in front of the Bombing Leader.

'Was it you who shot up the camp when you landed?'

After a shamefaced admission and an assurance that I would never do it again, I was quietly and almost gently told, 'Don't do it again, laddie.'

To this day, I thank God that there was no one at the end of that runway.

HANG ON TO YOUR TROUSERS

Frances Walker who served at Dyce tells quite a story about the slipsteam of a Spitfire that de-trousered some erks sitting in a nearby latrine. She was neither flat-footed, knock-kneed nor colour blind, so they took her into the WAAF, where she loved it and it was with great regret she went back into civilian life. She tells me that she is not a Scot but was born in Edinburgh. Let us see about that:

I was born in Edinburgh but I am not a Scot. My husband died in 1981. He was a Scot from Aberdeenshire and I came up to Blairgowrie in 1985 nearer to in-laws.

In September of 1940, I walked in to Victory House in Kingsway, London. It was my lunch break and I worked for Smith's the booksellers. I had decided to join. A long line of women were snaking around from one official desk to another. You gave your name and particulars and then went for a medical.

'Are you flat-footed, knock-kneed, colour blind or deaf?' Then came FFI!

'Drop your knickers; lift your vest. Take this bottle and fill it!'

'Hurry along, please.'

Before my lunch break was over, I was a WAAF. I was given papers to proceed to the Grand Hotel, Harrogate for kitting out and basic training. It all happened at a bewildering speed and life was never the same again.

My first posting was to a Fighter Station in Essex where I worked in stores accounts. We had the American Eagle Squadron and the Canadian 242 Squadron on the station. North Weald was being hammered and the WAAF were in a country house called Blake Hall. Things were pretty primitive at that time. We were sleeping on the floor close together. Our kit was pilfered by some of the more dubious types. Eventually we were put into huts.

In a short time, I remustered into a mechanics' course at Hednesford,

Staffordshire. My friend went to Blackpool on a photographic course. Hednesford was a large camp with Fleet Air Arm and Navy, all under training as mechanics. We had a hard bleak winter in huts. The girls who grabbed the beds near the stove wished they hadn't because everybody draped wet washing over the bed ends. It was most unpleasant.

A few of us trainees, RAF and WAAF, were christened and confirmed at the Bishop's Palace, Lichfield. I suppose we all thought that in uncertain times we should be confirmed into a faith.

Early in 1941, I was posted to Tern Hill, Shropshire, an FTS with Miles Masters, Ansons, Gipsy and Tiger Moths and a sprinkling of others. It was easy work and I was quite thrilled when for the first time I swung a prop on a Gypsy Moth and the engine actually started.

We spent happy, sunny days on the hockey field where a hulking great blond NCO floored me every time the ball came anywhere near us. No quarter was given. I used to come off the field all battered and bruised but he didn't get off scot free either.

When I had a forty-eight hour pass, I used to go to Blackpool to see my friend who was doing the photographic course. Many types of training were done at Blackpool and on the promenade you could see troops marching up and down all day. The boarding houses were used as billets. My friend Rene was in one such house on Palatine Road which ran right down to the sea front. Rene used to smuggle me in and I would use the bed belonging to someone who was on leave. The landlady never seemed to be able to keep track of her lodgers, so if you were careful and kept your head down you had a bed and three square meals a day. It was a doddle.

Rene discovered there were bugs in her billet and she reported it to the WAAF Officer. She was told that she was talking rubbish and that all the houses had been vetted. She was not daunted. That night, armed with a torch and a voluptuous WAAF staked out as bait in the most likely place, she waited and watched. Hey presto, before long she had a glossy, fat bug held captive in a match box, and the poor WAAF covered in lumps. Off to the Admin. Officer went Rene. The Officer gave a sigh, 'You again, ACW Hurley!' Rene with a triumphant flourish opened the match box and out tumbled a very much alive bug. The Officer recoiled in horror and the upshot was that the girls were moved to another billet.

In late 1941, I went to Oxfordshire where Whitley bombers were being used to tow gliders. Glider pilots were being trained there. We lived in what had been married quarters – six to a house. I managed to get a bed in the sitting room next to the open fire. We took turns in nipping off just before pack-up time and taking a bundle of oily rags to light the fire and get the copper going for hot water. It was cosy in the winter. Life was busy and hectic.

One day, we pushed a kite out ready for an air test. Three of us mechanics were allowed to go up for a flip. Everything was fine and I was in the nose of a bomber in the bomb aimer's place, when suddenly a stupid clot decided that she would take over the controls and the pilot agreed. All hell broke loose and the plane went into a dive towards a farmhouse. I could see startled people running in all directions. I thought we had had it. Tiny, the pilot, who was a great big chap, managed to right the kite and get us safely back on terra firma. I felt very sorry for Tiny as he was in trouble for dangerous flying. Needless to say the WAAF was not popular and we were all grounded.

What an ugly kite the Whitley was. The song about it went as follows:

> I'll sing you a song of the Whitley one,
> The aeroplane that takes the bun.
> In the pale blue sky she stooges around,
> Until one day we'll all be bound.
> She'll come a blinking purler,
> She'll come a blinking purler,
> Oh, she'll come a blinking purler,
> Tra, la, la la, la, la la!

Early in 1942, I went to a Fitters' Course at Halton in Buckinghamshire. Things really began to get interesting. The practical side was fine but the theory and exams! I sat swotting in the Church Army Canteen every night drinking endless cups of coffee. It was pleasant countryside and we were comfortably housed in barrack blocks in dormitories. There was not much privacy.

Finally I was through and on my way to Dyce, a fully fledged fitter II Engines. With beret, battledress and boots I arrived in the hangar. This was a Photographic Reconnaissance Unit where pilots were trained for this work. My friend Rene was at Dyce in the Photography Section. I had caught up with her again, much to our delight.

The aircraft were Spitfires, Hurricanes and Ansons and other odds and ends, and my absolute favourite – the Mosquito. What a stir I caused that day. The Admin. Officer thought I was in the Observer Corps. The Wing Commander in the major servicing hangar was quite startled when I entered his office. He enquired as to what I was supposed to be, as I was, to him, a quite unknown species. It was decided that the monthly servicing hangar would be the place for me to start. The Wing Commander phoned the Squadron Leader and told him a WAAF fitter was about to join the work force. He was not impressed and a roar came over the phone. His reply was unprintable. The Wing/CO smiled and then said, 'Don't worry. His bark is worse than his bite.' This proved to be so and I was soon to be known with grudging pride as 'Our young Frankie'.

Quite rapid promotion came and I was a Corporal with my own gang, ground testing my own aircraft and sometimes going up with a pilot to air test.

It was on one of these tests on a very hot day that I had taken off my collar and tie, trousers also and was wearing only a tatty pair of oversized overalls and no beret. Suddenly, the oil pressure on the starboard engine went haywire and the pilot feathered the prop and requested permission to land at Kinloss as it was close by. He was told to return to Dyce where the visibility was better. I was glad because had we landed at Kinloss I would have been in deep trouble with no trousers – most improperly dressed. Over Dyce, the pilot could not get the undercarriage down. However, I managed to pump it down manually and thankfully the locking light came on. We left the aircraft at dispersal and got a lift back in a blood wagon which had come out to meet us. I dived into the crew room and on went the trousers, collar and tie in double quick time.

A funny thing happened one day when I was ground testing a Spitfire. Two mechanics were on the wings and two lying across the tail. I put the throttle through the gate for full boost and was a fraction slow taking it back. I switched off and got out of the cockpit to find two lads hanging on the tail gasping and dishevelled. Then I noticed that the tail of the aircraft was in line with the men's latrine. Several lads had been nonchantly going about their business when the slipstream of the Spit blew open the door and just about blasted them out of the other end of the latrine. It took a long time to live that one down. You can imagine the comments.

At times, life was great – breakfast in bed on days off. One of the girls, usually the hut orderly, would come back from the cookhouse with a pint mug of tea and a sausage and bacon sandwich stuffed down her battledress, all squashed and battered but it was eaten just the same. We went into Aberdeen where we had coffee at the Caledonian Hotel in Union

Terrace – a ritual to give the day a bit of class. We had dancing in the Palais or whooped it up in the Music Hall with an eightsome reel.

There was a bit of Gilbert and Sullivan at His Majesty's Theatre, then coffee at Herd's Café and on to the last bus back to camp. Great!

Break time was spent outside the hangars waiting for the NAAFI wagon to come along with the awful coffee tasting like anaesthetic and NAAFI wads like bricks. A mug of coffee was often shared with someone who had forgotten their own mug and several people took a puff of the last cigarette before the ration ran out. A WAAF who didn't smoke could always get a boyfriend! I spent a lot of time with civilian friends in Dyce village and they used to take me to a lot of functions in Aberdeen.

Rene and I parted company when the aircraft and ground crews were sent to South Wales near Haverford. I liked it there, but apart from the pubs, there was little to do. We got together a good entertainments committee and put on some very popular dances. Tickets were sought after by everyone on camp. The cookhouse provided the buffet. Local talent from the lads in the hangars provided a great band, including male and female vocalists. We planned and painted our own sets, mostly Hawaiian and other exotic scenes, and sometimes costumes were produced. Tradesmen, chippies and painters gave their time off willingly.

Clean, starched Van Heusen collars for any crisis could be bought at the Chinese laundry. They were unclaimed items from people who had been posted away. 'Velly handy, velly cheap,' at a tuppence a go.

We celebrated VE Day here before the ground crews were entrained and posted to East Fortune, near Edinburgh where I was born. I had come home so to speak. We had a great send-off from the Withybush Station. Even the Italian POWs were there to wave us off on what was a long, tedious train journey.

It was as I recall a long hot summer when we could cycle to Dunbar and North Berwick and swim in the sea on pleasant evenings. A fish and chip supper followed and we cycled back before dark.

Our gang was made up of two WAAFs, one airman and myself. Jocky King was a local who lived with his sister's family at Tranent. He was a nice chap but an awful scrounger who did the least work that he could. We had finished an inspection and had nothing to do on this hot sunny day. Jocky was tired after a heavy night before and said that he was going to take a nap until pack up time. He climbed into the fuselage of a Mosquito and asked me to lock the hatch. We three went off to do something else. Tea time came and we grabbed our bikes and hared off down to the cook-house, then off to the billet which was a mile away in an old disused building. It was almost dark when we remembered that Jocky was locked in the Mosquito. I had to cycle back to the airfield to get him out. He was very irate and thought that we had done it on purpose. He had missed his bus and had to hitch-hike to Tranent. Eventually, we were forgiven but it did cure Jocky of his disappearing acts.

Going on leave meant a three-mile hike to Drem, a Fleet Air 'drome, where the London train halted to pick up troops. It was a corridor train and was always packed. Once, I was lifted up onto the luggage rack and used my gas mask as a pillow. There I slept like a baby until we arrived in London the next morning.

It was with great regret that I took my demob in October 1945. I found it difficult to settle back into civvy life.

Frances Walker
Blairgowrie

Frances and I shared an interview with Nancy Nicolson of BBC Inverness. This was broadcast from BBC Radio Scotland and I have to thank Anne Bates, a producer, BBC Scotland for all the trouble she took to arrange this interview while I was in Britain in May 1994.

ALL COMRADES TOGETHER

As I read Muriel's letter, those words 'all comrades together' leapt out at me. Muriel was posted to an Australian Squadron 456 with which she stayed until they were disbanded. As a cook she worked in places where conditions were primitive certainly by today's standards. Here is her story:

Your article in the *Evening Argus* caught my eye because of the lovely picture of your wife wearing the same cap as I wore for nearly five years. My badge too is worn in many places through rubbing it to make it shine and pass muster. Buttons also had to have the same treatment.

I joined at Bridgnorth, Shropshire on 15 September 1941 for six weeks square bashing and choosing the trade we wished to follow. I chose to become a cook-butcher and was sent to Melksham Technical School for training. From there I went on to Cranwell until October and then to Bircham Newton in Norfolk. On that station we had Dutch personnel.

When I was asked where I would like to be stationed, I asked for London as I could get to my home in North London easily. However, the powers that be posted me to Pembroke Dock in Wales. I was now even further from home and on a Squadron. It was 119 Squadron and what a wonderful sight to see Sunderlands and Catalinas on the water. We used to prepare food and put it in insulated containers for the crews to take on the long flights. I stayed on that Squadron until it was disbanded in March 1944.

I was then posted to the Australian Squadron 456 and stayed with them until they were disbanded in February 1945. There were not many WAAF on the Squadron, a few MT drivers and seven cooks. We travelled in trains and went to Ford in Sussex and we were there for D-Day. It was there we had gliders.

D-Day was a great experience. The airmen's mess was lined with wounded and I was busy frying hundreds of eggs and chips. Most of the boys requested these. We worked for hours – non-stop.

The Squadron moved from Ford, much to my sorrow, because I had been able to get home on a twenty-four-hour pass, and we girls had semi-detached houses between us and not the usual Nissen huts. We made them like home and we would help ourselves to a few lumps of coal for a fire, putting it in our saddle bags, as we had almost three miles to cycle to work each day. Wherever we went cooks were issued with a bike because of the unsocial hours we had to work. I cannot imagine cycling along lonely country lanes at three in the morning. The very thought petrifies me. We had no fear in those days, all comrades together.

From Ford, we moved to Church Fenton, Yorkshire. It was a very bleak place and it was December. The kitchens were very primitive. I really don't know how today's girls would manage now they are used to better conditions. We had coal ranges and steam. I have visions now of standing on a box stirring porridge with a broom handle over a great steamer. There was never a can-opener to be found and we had to use a knife to open tins. If the Aussies came to us and asked to borrow a can-opener we couldn't supply one. They used to call themselves 'The Blue-eyed Killers'. The cinema was in a hangar on the airfield and we used to take a blanket as it was freezing. It all added to the fun of the evening.

The message came through that we were being posted to Bradwell Bay, Essex and we were very pleased to be leaving Yorkshire. We went on a twenty-four hour journey by train. Everywhere was blacked out as there were raids. When we reached Bradwell, we were told to return to Church Fenton. Once there, the order came to return to Sussex – altogether three days had been spent travelling and mucking about.

We were altogether once again, but not for long, as the Squadron was disbanded and we were split up into twos, never to meet again. I was demobbed at Stoke Heath in December 1945.

My husband was an Eighth Army soldier who had been my pen pal. We were married in November 1945 and we were together for almost forty years – just one month short as he died in 1984. When I was married, we came to live in Brighton and I love it here. I have three lovely daughters and eight grandchildren and I am content. I cannot get around as well as I used to do as I have arthritis and have had a replacement knee joint.

Muriel Summers (née Godden)
Brighton, Sussex

SALLY, WE CALLED HER

Most WAAF balloon operators had pet names for their balloon. No doubt they called those monsters a great many other names, when they had to be hauled down and 'bedded' in a raging gale. The little group in which Isobel from Belfast, Northern Ireland, found herself called their monster 'Sally'. Here is her story:

My sister who lives in Bangor, County Down, N. Ireland, sent me the cutting from *Sunday Life*, about your request in contacting ex members of the WAAF. I wish you good luck with *Spit, Polish & Tears*. The picture of Elizabeth is lovely and looking at it and the cap badge brings back many memories.

I joined the WAAF in the summer of 1942 and was demobbed in September 1945. I was born in Belfast on 19 August 1923.

One night, when I was at the cinema watching a film, suddenly it came up on the screen, 'Join the WAAF as a balloon operator and release an airman for flying duties'. The very next day, I did just that and a month later I sailed for England. I did my training at Gloucester and was posted to Liverpool, Bristol and Salisbury Plain.

The life of a balloon operator was tough; the work was hard – wire splicing, thick ropes to splice, patching balloons and pulling huge helium cylinders to inflate the balloon. Every night, we did guard duties, and she, 'Sally' had to be turned into the wind. Jerry took a delight in coming low to try to bomb us. Another thing which not many knew about was that we had to place a small bomb on the cable, so that if the balloon broke away the cable would break and not cause destruction over houses. We were bombed a lot and lost many pals.

When the balloons were eventually disbanded, I remustered to instrument repairer and was working out on flights on Lancasters, Liberators and Stirlings.

One day I was sent out to do a DI on the instrument panel of a Lancaster and there I met my future husband Bill. He came from Dorset and we were married on 23 March 1945 and that is how I happen to be living in England. We are still together and love each other dearly.

I loved the WAAF and made many friends and met many, many brave girls and sadly had to attend the funerals of girls like myself, only in their teens. I agree with you, the WAAF rarely got a mention. *Spit, Polish & Tears* sounds great, but there were also lots of laughs and smiles.

Isobel Lallemant (née Smyth)
Staines, Middlesex

RAWDON HUME MIDDLETON VC

In the European theatre of war, two members of the Royal Australian Air Force won the Victoria Cross. One was Group Captain Edwards and I have written about him in my Editorial. The other was Pilot Officer R.H. Middleton. Pilot Officer Middleton was a country boy from New South Wales. He had spent his early life on his father's sheep station. He was related to one of Australia's famous explorers – Hamilton Hume. He was quite a bloke, modest, but had a toughness that enabled him, in spite of dreadful wounds, to bring his aircraft back from a raid on Turin, bale out his crew and then go down with his own aircraft.

Pat Whetton, a WAAF who now lives in Suffolk, tells of a very special occasion when she was on leave:

When I was seventeen years of age, I joined the WAAF and served during the war for 4½ years. On my first leave, I came home to Beck Row and whilst there I attended the funeral of F/Sgt. Rawdon Middleton, an Australian who was awarded the Victoria Cross posthumously. He is buried in the RAF War Graves Cemetery at the little church in Beck Row.

It was a very impressive service, in the open air, attended by RAF and WAAF personnel. The Australian High Commissioner and his wife were at the graveside. Three boughs of wattle flowers were on the coffin. These had been flown from Australia for the occasion. British Gaumont had a film crew there and a film was made, but of course, it was all 'hush-hush'. As it was wartime Beck Row was not mentioned.

Pat Whetton
Beck Row, Suffolk

'THAT WON'T DO!'

Those are the very words used by Pamela when she returned to her old wartime haunts and found a plaque which gave no mention of the work done by the WAAF. This happened when she visited St Nicholas' Church in Poling where a secret Radar Station plotted the movements of enemy aircraft. As you will see, Pamela did something about ensuring the efforts of the WAAFs are remembered.

I joined up when I was seventeen years, in December 1943. I was told that radar was an exciting type of job but very secret. I was lucky enough to pass the entrance exam and went to Cranwell for three months' training. Getting the qualifications needed I became a radar operator, proudly now to wear the 'sparks' emblem on my sleeve. There were many types of radar equipment, and I was sent to Truleigh Hill, back of Shoreham by the sea, and into a private home for my billet.

This type of radar was called CHL, meaning plotting low flying aircraft. We were guarded by RAF Regiment personnel in case Germans tried to capture the equipment or us. If aircraft were in difficulty, we knew this by a signal on our screen and this meant that we had to go to man a search-light, set it up and then arc it towards a 'drome, this being Tangmere. It was very heavy to use, especially on a wet and snowy night. We got frozen!

Being on the south coast we were very busy on watch. After a few months I was moved to Poling CH Station near Arundel. CH meant that we tracked high flying aircraft. This equipment was very different to Truleigh Hill. On D-Day, we were hard at it and plotting of thousand-bomber raids went on at the same time. The bombers would go out *en masse* and we would give our plots to Fighter Command. They would tell us the targets that night.

In the early hours we would have them back on our screens not *en masse* but in groups and singles. We would be the first to know that some of our aircraft were missing. Very sad.

I stayed on radar until I was demobbed, with the exception of three months' rest. I was sent to RAF Membury, to work in the passenger section. There, the Dakotas were bringing our boys back from the Far East. They were very ill, weak and thin but in very good spirits. I would have to arrange transport for them. As I was at an airfield, I thought I should not leave the WAAF without having flown. I went to the CO and asked. His reply was, 'WAAF don't fly!' As I got to the door he said, 'I wouldn't know that, would I?' That did it. The next day I was off. I had no problems getting a trip as I was working with the pilots.

We were up for four hours. It was fantastic, beautiful. I was taken over to France, back along the coast and then back over the Channel. We landed at a couple of 'dromes and then back to Membury – a great memory for me!

At my time at Membury, I was back at Poling, my home ground and then to Bawdsay, where Watson–Watt invented radar. I go each year to a reunion. I enjoyed my time in the WAAF. I was lucky to have such an interesting job. Not many people knew of it because of the secrecy. Not even the WAAF Admin. were allowed to see the inside of our Ops Room.

Pamela M. Caley-Cullum
Worthing

As well as this story, Pamela enclosed a newspaper article from which this information is taken:

Visiting old haunts she and wartime friend Mrs Jose Rule found in St Nicholas' Church, Poling, a faded plaque with a few details of the base that once dominated the village. But, on that plaque, no mention was made of the part played by the WAAF. 'That won't do!' said Pamela who was in the WAAF until 1947. She decided to produce another plaque, telling the whole story. The framed text with pictures of the station was presented to the church and dedicated in a Remembrance Day Service in November 1993.

YOU'VE GOT ONE FOR THE LEFT FOOT
AND ONE FOR THE RIGHT!

Sergeants seemed to have a habit of bellowing. 'Got two left feet, have you?'
Well, the sergeant in this story was bellowing about shoes – those great heavy
thick things with which WAAFs were issued when they first joined. P. Bradshaw,
who did not give her first name, spent her war service in Flying Control, where
at times life would be very harrowing. She tells of her first firing of a Very
cartridge and of a gun which looked like a blunderbuss but it did not fire. Here
is her story:

I well remember Bridgnorth where your wife was kitted out. When I
received my uniform I was appalled at the shoes I was given and protested
that they were too heavy. 'You've got one for the left foot and one for the
right. Next!'

My war service from 1941–5 was spent in Flying Control at West Malling
as an RTO. I did hear the scream of a Polish pilot as he went down in
flames during a sweep and that was harrowing. Air crews and Flying
Control WAAFs used to meet at a nearby pub where the landlady kept
mugs belonging to aircrews on hooks above the bar. When someone came
in and said, 'James won't be needing his mug any more,' she knew what
it meant and removed it without comment. This I hated as we all did,
but the stiff upper lip was the only way to keep emotion in control.

When the Blind Approach system was required the pilot would ask if
Babs was well. On this occasion the answer from the FCO was, 'No, Babs
is unwell.' Any woman could have told them that that expression was
unfortunate to say the least. Over the intercom another voice boomed,
'Bang goes your dirty weekend, old boy!' I told the WAAF on that
frequency not to include the remark. Normally all speech had to be logged
either in code or plain language. All entries had to be accurate as the log
books had to be produced in the event of an inquiry and this had happened
previously. The hatch was flung back and an irate FCO asked if I had
heard this. I gave him a very bland look and said it hadn't been noted.
Later, the pilot concerned had a roasting from the FCO. (Well, it was the
1940s.)

After VE Day, the station was closed for flying but a watch kept in case
of emergency. I was alone in the watch tower with the Duty Officer in

Flying Control. He told me he was going to lunch and would be back later. To my horror he gave me a heavy pistol and said, 'If you see anything trying to land, point this in the air and press the trigger. The flare will warn them off.' My stomach churned as I listened to his footsteps as he clattered down the stairs. Nearly an hour later I heard the drone of aircraft and shot out to the balcony. A small aircraft was approaching and it began to circle and lose height. It was obviously going to land and as the grass runway was ploughed up it would probably have overturned. I snatched up the pistol and with both hands pressed the trigger. NOTHING HAPPENED. I kept on pressing and shouted to the aircraft to go away although I knew the pilot couldn't hear me. Suddenly, the pistol went off and I nearly fell over. I watched the flare and the plane veered away and went off to my intense relief. When the Duty Officer returned, I told him what had happened. His reply was, 'Jolly good, Corp. Have you got the kettle on?'

On another occasion I was on night duty in Fixed Receivers which was a hut with a bed in a clearing in a wood. It was surrounded by a heavy layer of pebbles so that anyone approaching could be heard easily. There was a heavy rifle like a blunderbuss which was for our protection. I asked, 'Who was the last owner, Cromwell?' It took two of us to lift it and when I asked for the ammunition, I was told it would be too dangerous as we might shoot ourselves! The reason we had the rifle was that a German aircraft had been seen going down in the wood. During the night the other WAAF woke me and said she could hear footsteps. I heard them too and immediately contacted the Control Room. They were very relaxed about it and said they'd probably get someone out there to search the surroundings. Again we heard the footsteps so I went to the door, unlocked it and called out in a loud voice, 'Come out, wherever you are!' The next moment a somewhat scared little black cat poked its head round the corner! Later the German aircraft was found and the crew arrested. It was taken to the airfield and visited by many RAF officers from other stations. Needless to say, no one asked how the WAAFs fared!

During an air raid, I was walking along with another WAAF to go on night watch. The RAF Regiment was blazing away with Bofors guns. Something hot scorched past my face and clanged on the iron roof of a nearby hut. That's the nearest I've come to losing my nose.

P. Bradshaw
London

WAAFS IN THE AIR

As a way of saying thank you to dedicated and long suffering ground staff some squadrons organised flights over Germany so that the effects of bombing could be seen. LACW Wattam, stationed at Wickenby, gives her account of a six-hour trip over the continent:

My story is from the time I was stationed at Wickenby in Lincolnshire. I remember very vividly going into the briefing room at Wickenby and being impressed with the enlarged maps of the Continent and the efficient way the duty officer went through the drill of explaining our route to Germany. The Met. Officer gave his up-to-date forecast and we were told the exact time to board the aircraft for what was to be the most memorable trip of my life.

The crew took every detail without comment, but this time it was different because the war was over and this was no bombing operation, but what could only be described as a leisure trip to inspect the bomb damage of Germany.

I was fortunate to be one of two WAAFs to be given the opportunity of going on this special operation.

We boarded our aircraft at midday and after a super take-off, I was then allowed to move from the body of the aircraft to the bomb aimer's hatch which gave me a bird's eye view of the journey.

We flew over Holland and saw the extent of the flooding. Only the roofs of the houses were visible. Then on to Germany we went where we saw the destruction of the industrial cities of the Rhine.

After six hours of flying, we arrived back at Wickenby, very elated and eager to tell our less fortunate friends all about our trip.

P.M. Leary (née Wattam)

DOODLEBUGS

What a descriptive name to give to a flying bomb which 'doodled' in the skies over southern England. My dictionary says that a doodlebug is the larva of an ant lion, or used in a slang sense, it means, 'a simple fellow' or the playing of bagpipes.

There was nothing simple about the doodlebugs which came flying towards Britain. Diana Lindo (LACW Tait), an MT driver, in her 'Wartime Jottings' gives us this wonderful story of the arrival of the first doodlebugs:

About a week after the invasion, we were wakened by a most peculiar noise, rather like an aircraft 'missing' on two engines, a sort of spluttering noise, followed by a terrific explosion.

Although there was no siren, we all leapt out of bed and donned our tin hats, putting forward the most amazing ideas as to what it was.

It wasn't until the next morning that we learnt that it was Hitler's first secret weapon – the V1 or 'Doodlebug' as it became universally known. Once more everything was in uproar. The places we had been to in Kent and Sussex became sites. Balloon operators were brought from all over the country and thousands of huge gas bottles travelled by rail and road down 'Doodlebug Alley'. Emergency hydrogen factories were set up. Miraculously, within a few days over seven hundred balloons were flying, stretched in a barrage from Gravesend to Redhill. The idea was to make a wall at different heights and so placed to make it as hard as possible for the bombs to get through to London. Soon the barrage was increased to over a thousand which was an amazing feat, as it was no easy job moving all the crews and their equipment when every available truck was heading for the coast with reinforcements for the forces in France.

Diana Lindo
Cirencester

I'VE BEEN SHOT AT!

If there was trouble around Isabel seemed to find it. When she was asked to clean shoes and make beds, she had a nightmare experience in a new hut where a cat had kittens and that wasn't all. Fed up, she just went home, but Dad was an old soldier and knew what the consequences would be so he wrote to Isabel's CO. Here's Isabel's story:

War was declared in 1939. What did that mean? We lived in a five-storey house on a hill. There was Mum, Dad and five kids and we didn't know anything about war. The council worker came and asked Mum could we move to somewhere safe as they were worried about the children. We had sirens, planes, bombs – the lot – on the East Coast. We had to move. It was terrible.

So we packed everything and moved to where Mum's Mum lived in Suffolk. Oh, the peace! There were no air raids and we had such peaceful sleeps. It was heaven! We all found jobs. I worked in a chemist's; sisters worked in a shoe shop, a printer's and the youngest in a milliner's. My brother was in the Navy.

Then our peace was shattered. Three Air Ministry letters on the mat! We had been conscripted for the Services. Rail tickets were enclosed for us to go to Colchester for a general knowledge test and a medical.

'Oh, well,' we said, 'if it will end this awful war! We don't mind!' Off we went – the three of us. My oldest sister failed the medical as she had a faulty heart valve; my youngest sister passed for the Army and I passed for the WAAF.

Rail pass again – this time to Gloucester for a month's square bashing. Oh, the marching! Sore heels, hard shoes, inoculations – I didn't like any of this. Then, a loud, shouting Sergeant Major! I don't think that he could talk softly. He shouted every day and all day. At last Passing Out Parade.

Then came postings and mine was to Blackpool to do a wireless operator's course. Oh, the thoughts of a cold seaside after just leaving the east coast. A long train ride tired me after all that marching. The Duty Officer met us at the station and took us to a boarding house. There were thirteen of us and two girls from Yarmouth – one with whom I went to school. But our joy was soon shattered. The owner didn't want WAAFs. He could get more money from tourists. It was November and nowhere to go! A lovely family further down the road took us all in. Six in one bedroom and the rest in other rooms. There were more parades, morse classes and engineering classes. I loved the engineering and passed that with flying colours but failed the morse. I couldn't bear it. I had to report to the CO who told me I had wasted the Government's money and so on.

So came another posting. This time it was to Nottingham to a Lancaster Bomber Station. Huge planes! What would I do there? I soon made new friends and was sent to Flying Control. At first, I was the tea girl, but then my job was to taxi the great planes out using a Tannoy. I had a call sign and a great chart in front of me all lit up with letters. As I sent the planes out I had to put the letter of the aircraft, e.g., 'O' for Orange, in a hole, until all the planes were on their way.

We worked all night waiting for the planes to come back. But of course some were missing and the letter buttons stayed where they were. I was not allowed to bring the planes down. The Duty Officer had to do that and it was very sad at times as we got to know the pilots.

From the huts to the aerodrome it was quite a way so we were allotted bicycles. When I went to pick up mine, I was told to be careful as one tyre was rather worn and they were waiting for new ones. The next day I went off on my bike down the long country lane when I heard the drone of a German aircraft. Forgetting the worn tyre, I pedalled like mad. Then there was a bang! It's the plane, I thought. They're shooting at me, and into the ditch I went, over a hedge and into a field. Just then, the Duty Officer passed and bellowed at me, 'What are you doing there?'

'I've been shot at!'

'Where's the blood?'

I never lived it down and gave up riding bikes. I had burst the inner tube and had a nettle rash to remember it all.

At last, another posting came through. This time it was to Medmenhem, Marlow, Buckinghamshire – the Photographic Section – instrument repairer and electrician. Another train ticket, another journey.

The Duty Officer met us at the station. It was Lady Sarah Churchill. What a lovely lady she was. She took us to the canteen and bought us scones and tea and then settled us in our huts. The next day breakfast was brought but I wasn't keen on devilled kidneys.

In a huge house, said to belong to the HP Sauce people, two officers worked. There were wonderful gardens, weeping willows and other huge trees. At the bottom of the garden was a private lake where we were allowed to swim on our days off.

I was taken to the Instrument Shop which was huge and attached to the Photographic Section. Here thirteen men worked and I was the only woman. The boys were so good and they all fathered me. What were we to do here? There were huge hypo tanks to keep clean, films to dry and repair, motors to overhaul, generators to refit with carbon brushes, huge bulbs to replace in cameras – I loved it all. I had new friends again. The Duty Sergeant let me help him in the camp cinema. The only trouble was that it was too far to go home on my weekends off.

My fiancé was in the RAF and was posted to Palestine. There was not a lot of mail from him as there was trouble out there. And then came the news that he would be home. We got married in the little country church where Mum lived. After that he was posted to Greece. We all lived from day to day.

Great celebrations came with D-Day. The war was coming to an end and there was a shock for me – no married women were allowed to work in the Instrument Section. I couldn't believe it! I had worked night and day and now was forbidden to enter the Shop. I had to report to the CO who told me to report to the officers' quarters to clean shoes and make their beds. 'No way!' I told myself. I had helped to develop reams and reams of film night and day and I simply was not going to clean shoes.

I had to go to another hut with the batwomen and the first night a cat had kittens in one bed and a child was born in another! I wasn't used to this so I waited until they had all gone to tea, packed my bag, got a lift to the railway station and I was on my way home.

What a long journey it seemed. I went through the London Underground to see people settling down for the night away from bombs. I waited for a train to Colchester and arrived there to find that the connecting train had gone so the station master locked me up in the waiting room for the night. In the morning I was to get a lift with the mail van. At four o'clock he woke me and asked the mail man to take me to Sudbury.

He said, 'Hop in!' and away we went with him chattering to me. I was so tired but I woke up when he said we were at Polstead. He pointed out the red barn of Maria Martin's house where her husband murdered her because she was unfaithful with the Squire. That really made me want to get home.

I knocked Dad up and told him that I had another weekend leave. 'But,' he said, 'you've just had one!' As he was an old soldier of the First War, he knew that something was wrong. So he wrote to the CO and said that I had been treated badly. By return post she said to send me back.

So off I went once more on the long train journey, so nervous, and eventually arrived at Medmenham Station. Two six-foot SPs were waiting for me with a van. They bundled me in and took me straight to the CO. She said that she was sorry but the job I had done was now done by men. I was given fourteen days CB and no pay for a month.

The next morning the Duty Officer collected me and took me to the cook house where I spent four days peeling spuds in the open in November. I pretended that I didn't care but my poor hands! The four days soon went and the cook was lovely. She gave me hot meals. Next came another four days on the fire engine. It didn't sound too bad. It was a large lorry with hoses and cylinders of water. As we sped around corners, I nearly fell off. For practice we set fire to haystacks. Then the men said that it was my turn to hold a hose. I was wearing battledress and they said to stand at ease and put the hose between my legs and wave my hands when I was ready. It was foam and of course over I went, smothered in foam. They hosed me off with water and fell about laughing. But I didn't care or did I?

Next, they said that I had been good and not complained so I was given just four more days. As a local farmer had let us use his farm, we had to help him in the orchard. So I was to spend my last four days picking fruit. Off I went with a packed lunch to the apple, pear and plum trees. There they had huge ladders, wide at the bottom and narrow at the top. A huge basket with a hook was hung on the ladder.

The farmer said, 'I will ring a bell at lunch time, so come to the cottage for a drink.' Well, four geese took a liking to me and hung around my ladder. I filled another basket and managed to get to the plum tree and started to pick. I ate one, then another. They were beautiful Victorias. I had left my lunch near the bottom of the ladder and the geese ate that. Then the farmer rang the bell and the geese wouldn't let me down. They hissed and hissed and I was so thirsty so I ate more plums. Oh, my poor tummy! The other WAAFs came back, 'Where were you?' they asked, 'we've had our drink.' I didn't answer. I couldn't; my tummy just ached.

The next day my demob letter came and yet another rail pass. This one was to Birmingham. My last day in the WAAF! Was it exciting! I was glad to be home!

Isabel Rudd
Gorleston-on-Sea

WAS HE A SPY?

Ex LACW Bradbury tells of a cold, tearful beginning to life in the WAAF. However, WVS ladies gave a warm welcome at Gloucester with steaming hot tea. So often when someone seemed a complete clot and quite out of touch with what was going on, we labelled them as spies. I wonder if they were? Here is LACW Bradbury's story:

I was called up two weeks before Christmas and reported to a camp near Gloucester. The first night was spent in a big hut with a large number of beds. At one end a group of girls were crying pitifully for home and family, especially as it was so near to Christmas, while at the other end a number of girls who seemed very hard-hearted addressed the others in a very unsympathetic way and in no uncertain language. This didn't help anyone as the new girls felt strange and homesick.

We stayed there for five days getting kitted up and the morning we left we had to be up at 5.00 a.m. It was a cold, dark December morning. The rain was falling and we splashed about the camp getting our gear together. We were taken in trucks to the railway station to catch a train to Morecambe. I will never forget the welcome sight on Gloucester station of the WVS ladies ready with steaming hot mugs of tea even at that hour of the morning. I did drilling at Morecambe, back and forth along the promenade.

I was posted to a bomber station near York. The WAAF camp was half-way between the main station and a big house where the bomber crews were billeted. Whenever they had been on a raid and were coming back in the early hours, we would be woken up with the singing and shouting to relieve the tension of those long hours on an operation.

As I had no trade as yet, one of my jobs was to get up early and light the fires under the big boilers so that the girls had hot water for washing when they got up later. The camp was in two parts, divided by a stream running from the River Ouse. So I had a boiler to light on each side. It was a cold, dark February morning and, being unfamiliar with the small bridge over the stream, instead of negotiating it, I fell in. This wasn't at all pleasant.

After a few weeks I went to Cranwell to do training as a RT operator. When I passed, I was off to RAF Patrington on the east coast. We were billeted with families at Withernsea and travelled by coach to duty. I was working on transmitting and receiving sets, one in the middle of one field and the other in the next field. The main operating base was about three miles away. We had to keep the sets spot on so that the RT Controller on duty could direct the fighter pilots to attack the enemy planes.

I've heard the pilots shouting, 'May Day! May Day!' also the crackle of gun fire and the sound of a plane crashing. One night, we had a picnic when the Controller could not transmit. I was at the receiving end and at the transmitting end was a temporary sergeant, a man we didn't know, as our sergeant was on leave. He wasn't answering the phone so they phoned me to go out and see what was wrong. I had to go down to the fields in the pitch dark. When I got there he had one of the transmitter doors open so it wouldn't make contact. He muttered something about being wrong but when I quickly shut the door everything was OK.

Rumour spread around that he was a spy. All I know is that he was quickly removed.

When the enemy had been over bombing we used to look out gingerly the next morning, after fifteen hours on duty, to see if any had baled out. We had a rifle but no ammunition. Luckily, we didn't ever need it. We used to get plenty of silver paper streamers around trying to stop our transmission. When I look back on those years in the WAAF, I seem to have spent most of my time in a concrete bunker in the middle of a field with a row of talking robots.

LACW Bradbury
South Humberside

BALLOONS OVER GLASGOW

Vi Spense from Northern Ireland was one of the WAAFs who worked on balloons which were protecting Glasgow. She tells of the hardships of balloon life:

Now I'll tell you something about the balloon site in Glasgow. You probably know that a balloon had to be bedded down and kept into the wind at all times, the same as when it was on a tail guy mooring. When the wind changed, regardless of the time of day or night, we had to get out and get it into the wind. Can you imagine what it was like on a cold, wet and windy winter's night? This would be in a blackout and we had to get the balloon bedded down and go up a ladder to furl the fins. Rain would run down your arms and your side as you wore big clumsy mackintoshes. A corporal would be panicking in case the balloon took off. Learning to splice wire and rope tried even the best of Irish tempers.

We also had to learn how to drive the Ford VE winch for paying out and hauling in the balloon. There was always a mad scramble to get on the winch on a wet night. We did night duty guarding our balloon – two hours on and four hours off. I was often following a hefty Scottish girl who rolled me on the deck if I wasn't up, fully clothed and ready to take over. We did this work in pairs and many a guard duty found us huddled in the air raid shelter praying that it would be a calm night. Then if the sirens went, it was out like mad to get the balloon up to keep the Germans high or maybe even bring one down if it flew into a cable. As I write this memories come back to me and I am eighteen again.

Vi Spense
County Londonderry, N. Ireland

BUZZ BOMBS FOR CHRISTMAS

Mary, who now lives in West Yorkshire, was woken early on Christmas morning of 1944 by the sound of buzz bombs overhead. I happened to be on the same station at Sturgate when this happened and we found it hard to believe that buzz bombs were being used so far north in England. It was known later that these bombs were carried by aircraft over the North Sea and then sent on their way to northern England. Here is Mary's story:

You say that Elizabeth did her initial training at Bridgnorth. Who knows, we may have met! My other stations were Melksham, Gloucester, Harrogate, where we had a Pilot Station, Leeds, Bradford, Morecambe and lastly RAF Station Sturgate near the village of Upton. We were near Scampton which was our parent station. At Sturgate, we did have FIDO but it was only a stopping place for Scampton if the fog became too thick. Pilots would land there instead of risking a further ten miles in the fog to reach Scampton.

The buzz bombs came over Sturgate on Christmas Day 1944. We were scared but they went on from us to Sheffield where they did a great deal of damage. A few years earlier I was on a train going into Sheffield station where there was an almighty air raid on. We were stuck outside the station for about two hours. This episode was the nearest I came to real danger during the war.

As a nursing orderly in Lincolnshire, I did have the nasty task of sorting out after an aircraft crash. Our place was for training pilots doing circuits and bumps. Sometimes, the bumps were for real!

Mary Allwright
Bradford, West Yorks

A BATH IN A BOWL

Violet Peapell, a west country girl, was one of the many WAAFs who lived with a small group of girls on a balloon site. On most of these sites the conditions were rather primitive. Baths were not always easy as no ablution blocks were provided, so all sorts of containers were used for a bath. I guess if it was big enough to stand in then the straight up and down bath had to do. Here is Violet's story:

I joined the WAAF on 12 June 1942, the day before my eighteenth birthday. When I enrolled at Bath, I met up with three other teenage girls also from the Wiltshire area. We became very friendly during our stay at RAF Innsworth, Gloucestershire. This was where we were kitted out and did our square bashing.

After eight weeks of learning general RAF rules and 'Spit and Polish', we were posted to our training stations for our trades. Thus, we all went our separate ways.

I wanted to be a parachute packer but was sent to become a balloon operator. However, I settled down and really enjoyed every minute at Pucklechurch RAF Station, Bristol. The course lasted three months and during that time we learned to splice wire and rope and the handling of a barrage balloon. This was all very interesting and hard and heavy work, especially when we had to bed down a balloon in storm force winds.

Before the course finished our entry was split into batches of fourteen girls, and the last three weeks we were sent to operational sites in the centre of Bristol. It was during that time we had our first experience of German warfare, when Bristol was bombed quite heavily. Of course this was our chance to put our training into use. Altogether, we had three raids on this site. This was something we shall never forget. Although we didn't have any casualties, there were two sites which did.

After taking an examination, we had to wait for results to come through. During this time, we were all put on general duties around the camp. If we passed, we were posted to operational sites. Our crew of fourteen was posted to Weston-super-Mare and it turned out that we were all west of England girls and we got on very well together. Even though we were classed as operational, there was never any real activity. Our air raid warnings went off quite often, especially at night when the German bombers were going to the Plymouth area.

The camp site was situated in a corner of a field on the outskirts of Weston-super-Mare. It consisted of two Nissen huts with concrete floors for sleeping quarters and a wooden hut divided for an office and mess room. Each week, two airwomen were detailed for kitchen duties. This meant that we had to wake everyone at 6.30 a.m., cook breakfast and prepare a midday meal for 12.30 p.m. There was no evening meal to prepare as everyone got whatever they wanted. The rest of our duties during that week were to keep the kitchen and mess area clean. We had a smoky old range which burnt coke.

Despite all of this, we were a happy crew and had some good laughs together. The only luxury we had was the lovely hot water which we had to fetch from the convent across the road. We were told that we could have as much as we wanted. This was a heavy task but we were pleased to get it especially when we had a 'bath in a bowl'. This was hilarious at times.

The daily duty list was put up each week and there was always one chore which everyone hated. This was cleaning all the boots and shoes. However I did not mind doing this and was often asked to change duties. It was a spit and polish duty and when I had finished the toe caps really shone.

One day, out of the blue, came a message that we had to attend a meeting at Headquarters. We were told that balloon sites manned by WAAFs were being made redundant, and we had to remuster to other trades. Within a few weeks we were all packing up to be posted. What a sad time it was for us all. Quite a few tears were shed as we went our separate ways.

My posting was to 24 MU at Ternhill, Shropshire to await an instrument repairers' course. This unit was responsible for stripping and repairing and rebuilding aircraft that had been on operational tours. Most of these were Lancaster bombers. It was during my stay there that I first flew in a Lancaster which had been put out for a test flight.

Eventually the posting came through for the instrument repairers' course and I was lucky enough to be sent to RAF Melksham, right on my home doorstep. This enabled me to spend my days off at home which was only three-quarters of an hour away by train. The course lasted three months and after passing my exams I was posted again to RAF Ternhill, but this time it was to the other side of the airfield at No 5 PAFU.

This flying unit was for training fighter pilots and we had all nationalities pass through. Of course this was different and much more interesting after barrage balloons. If we had done work on an aircraft and it was passed for flight, we could go up on the test flight if we wished.

Here, I must add that from time to time came the news of pilots who were lost on operations – either missing or killed. This of course was very upsetting as we had always found them such a happy crowd. I stayed at this station until the end of the war, when I was posted to Lulsgate Bottom which is now Bristol Airport. This posting was to await demob. I got married in October 1945 and was finally demobbed in December 1945.

Violet Harvey (née Peapell)
Wiltshire

PUT THAT LIGHT OUT!

Sergeant Jarman, as she was in 1945, was stationed at Binbrook. In her letter she didn't mention the Aussies. Perhaps her interest was a member of an Ack Ack Unit.

I was a serving member of the WAAF from 1942–8. I was stationed at Binbrook 1943–4 as far as I can recall as a Corporal Admin. I was put on a charge there for allowing a chink of light to show from the WAAF quarters. The culprit was my own WAAF sergeant.

Binbrook was a cold dreary part of Lincolnshire. I remember stumbling back to quarters in the dark and ending up in a ditch. One of the nice memories was going to a weekly dance and finding my partner was one of the Army crew of an Ack Ack Unit. He was the manager of a shoe shop I used to know when I lived in London. We certainly had a lot to talk about. Now in my mid seventies. I have some great memories of the comradeship in the WAAF – a sharing of anything that was going – even to the last Woodbine.

M. Underwood
Hove, East Sussex

LIKE TO SEE MY ETCHINGS?

Brenda, who now lives in Wakefield, West Yorkshire, writes of a cocktail of experiences from humour, horror and death, to camaraderie. Who would be next to be invited to see the Squadron Leader's etchings? This question had WAAFs rolling about with laughter.

Here is a rough outline of my years in the WAAF. I was born at Heathfield, Sussex on 23 March 1923. I volunteered for the WAAF in 1941 and had to wait until I was eighteen to join.

Square bashing was at Bridgnorth for six weeks and this was followed by a posting to 11 Group Fighter Command for training in Signals, RTO, then on to West Malling, Kent. We worked shifts in Flying Control, being in contact with our own squadrons, also taking on a rota basis to operate Mayday Channel to all aircraft, our own fighters and bombers limping home over the coast. All this work made a cocktail of humour, horror and death to comraderie.

Of the trauma of Maydays, one among many is permanently imprinted on my mind. He was on fire and when I requested that he transmit so that I could give him a fix, he said the Lord's Prayer. He landed most terribly burned and was transferred to the burns unit at East Grinstead.

Through working so closely with our own squadrons, I had a great admiration for all aircrew. The Beaufighters of 29 Squadron who did night flying flew from West Malling in 1941 and the crews to me were great unsung heroes. Before the Poles formed a squadron, we had two or three there in RAF squadrons. They seemed to take appalling risks, almost not caring. They had escaped from Poland leaving families, wives and girlfriends and the bitterness showed.

Incidentally, the last Beaufighter is now in the Museum Hedron. I saw it two years ago with my very interested sixteen-year-old grandson. Some RAF personnel were on duty and I had a wonderful two hours or so in conversation with one member who was so interested in my experiences. It was super to talk it through with someone who could understand.

The next posting was to Headquarters, Biggin Hill, when on my first day in Flying Control I took a lot of stick, good humoured of course, over the time a German aircraft had landed at West Malling.

We took turns at Flying Control, one week in three, the rest was at HQ

Towenfields, because of air attacks. I have a wonderful centre-fold from the *Tatler* of Towenfields ops room, artist's impression. It shows the door marked RTO at the back of the Controller's position. This was sent to me by my brother who was in the Army. One of the controllers was a Squadron Leader who had a reputation as a womaniser. One of our jokes was betting who would be next to be invited to see his etchings. He used to sketch! I can hear 'B' Watch even now as they roll about laughing.

For the invasion of France, I was at Tangmere Ops and Signals, housed at Bishop Otter College, Chichester. There again we did one week in three at Flying Control Tangmere and the other at Bishop Otter. I was actually on duty the night before D-Day – 2300 watch. An Air Vice Marshal came in at 2330 hours to speak to us. That was a long night with all our minds concentrating on the people who were over there in the Channel.

Later, I was sent to Pett, between Hastings and Rye, controlled by Tangmere, to operate one of the fixing stations on the cliff top. There I remember shouting a fix to Suzanne to pass on to Tangmere. During a raid a cannon shell zoomed through the upper tower. The noise from the low flying aircraft was incredible. I was there until the end of the European War when the women's services were demobbed.

Brenda S. Hodges
Wakefield, West Yorks

SNEAKING OUT IN CIVVIES

I wonder how many girls in the WAAF sneaked out of camp with their civilian clothes under a great-coat on their way to a village dance. Did they do it to compete with the local gals or did they feel they could look more appealing? Amy Pennock was one of those who did this. She worked in the Officers' mess at High Wycombe so took a bit of a risk. She has visited Germany since the war and was amazed at the rebuilding that has taken place. She now lives in a British Legion house in Tyne and Wear.

I served 4½ years at High Wycombe where the planning for the bomber raids over Germany was carried out. Sir Arthur Harris was of course one of those who did this. Not so long ago a statue of Sir Arthur was placed in London. This was not very well received by some who really did not understand the enormous contribution to the war effort made by the bombers.

When I visited Germany, I found it a lovely country but saw no destruction. They must have rebuilt. After all, it's fifty years ago.

I still remember going on leave and finding people who went into the underground to take shelter from the raids. There were many babies and small children. There never seemed to be any panic. I thought the Londoners were very brave. They had sleeping bags to stay all night and often I had to step over them to get to the train.

I was lucky to be posted right into the country, miles from High Wycombe. Our station was called Nap Hill.

I still remember my WAAF number – 2094435–and I shall be seventy-five this year. I could tell you more about Bomber Command but I was no heroine. I was looking at the photograph of Elizabeth and must say that mine is very similar. We had to wear our hair short, off the collar and of course the cap had to be worn. There were times when we were going dancing that we did not obey regulations as we sneaked out with 'civvies' under our great-coats. We kept them buttoned right up and no-one was any the wiser.

At present, I am living in a British Legion house for ex-service men and women. There are not many of us left now. Time has changed everything.

Amy Pennock
Tyne & Wear

SIX INCHES OF WATER – THAT'S YOUR LOT!

Many, many WAAFs had to march off to municipal baths several times a week, just to keep clean. This was especially true for 'balloon' girls who had to live in small groups in camps that were little more than a couple of Nissen huts. ACW Lewis, as she was in 1942, tells of the water allowance at the baths – 6 inches!

I am ex WAAF 2070756, ACW Lewis. I enlisted at Bath and joined the WAAF on 11 May 1942. I did my square bashing at Innsworth in Gloucestershire. I believe that camp no longer exists. From there, I went to Pucklechurch where I did my training as a balloon barrage operator. Then, we were sent to a couple of training sites in Bristol and later to a permanent site at the Eastville greyhound track, still in Bristol. This was before, a football ground, and I believe it still is.

Our living accommodation consisted of a Nissen hut where we slept, with a small kitchen where we ate and cooked and a small out-building where we did our laundry etc. We kept a boiler alight to heat the water and we had a row of galvanised bowls where we tried to keep ourselves clean. We were allowed to go into Old Town Bristol, where we could have two baths a week. There, the taps were controlled from the outside. Just as everyone else, we were rationed to six inches of water.

The site consisted of sixteen WAAFs – two crews of eight girls. We did all of our own catering and guard duty was done in rotation – two hours on and four off. We were given a truncheon – no rifles for the girls! We did our own repairs to the balloon. It was prone to break away and was once retrieved from a field of cabbages.

As you know, Bristol was badly bombed during the war but we managed to come through unscathed. When we were made redundant, we had to remuster into another trade, preferably into Group 1. After passing an aptitude test I remustered as a wireless operator and was posted for six months training.

Having passed, I then went to Grigwell and on to White Waltham which was an out-station. It was there that I met my husband who died sixteen years ago of a massive heart attack. He was a Yorkshireman. I believe you have been staying in Yorkshire during your visit to Britain.

B. J. Garbutt
Wiltshire

Yes, I had a number of stays in Yorkshire and found the people and the countryside really wonderful. I came away with many happy memories and a great determination to go back to Yorkshire.

SHE'LL BE WEARING PINK PYJAMAS

Flight Sergeant Harry Pashley met WAAF Dorothy Langdon at Binbrook in 1944. He and Dorothy were married just nine days before I married Elizabeth. I cannot remember Harry, but it is possible that we met at the Marquis of Granby, a local pub, or at Smokey Joe's which was just up the hill from where I found Elizabeth in a ditch. Now it appears that Dorothy knew Elizabeth quite well. These are Harry's words:

I met the WAAF who was to become my wife at Binbrook in 1944. She was 2009168 LACW Dorothy Langdon. She worked in Equipment, and of course would have frequently spoken with Elizabeth both there and in the Tailors' Shop. As our wedding day approached, 31 May 1945, Elizabeth offered to make Dorothy some pink pyjamas from a precious length of pure silk. These were duly beautifully made by Elizabeth and contributed to many a torrid night before they wore out years later.

Harry Pashley
Essex

JUST JACK

One of the Aussies who found a haven in the Tailors' Shop at Binbrook was Jack. He was a gunner in Titch Palmer's crew, a crew that survived the war.

Jack became a good friend of all the girls. He did not favour any particular lass, but provided a lot of fun as he had a wry wit and went along with quite a few gags and tricks played on others.

When someone was in trouble, Jack would be there to help. Of course there were times when he helped, when some may have wanted him to do otherwise.

One of the tailoresses, Joyce, aptly named Tiger, often boasted that she could take a piece out of an Aussie with one hand tied behind her back. I took up the challenge, having lined up Jack and a couple of lassies to back me. I grabbed Tiger, scuttled her on a heap of garments and while Jack and the girls held her, I bit her – no not there – on the tum! Tiger admitted defeat and took it all in great fun.

Jack's crew had done a couple of ops and he was becoming one of those whom sprog crews viewed with a little awe. He was even feeling a little cocky. Why shouldn't he? After all, before joining up, he was a Sydney taxi driver. If anyone takes risks it is a Sydney bloke who drives taxis through those tortuous streets.

His crew were on the Battle Order and the target was Potsdam. Now to get to Potsdam, the planned route was along the Berlin bombing alley – one of the most heavily defended areas in Germany.

Jack, who was always so reassuring to others, quickly said, 'She's apples! A piece of cake. It'll be bang on,' and all sort of RAF jargon. However, when Jack reappeared after Potsdam, he was a pale shade of green. Never again did Jack say, 'She's apples!' In fact, from that experience, we invented a new saying especially for Jack, who even took to using it himself. It was, 'She's right; don't be fright!'

MEMORIES

In World War II we joined the WAAF
To do our bit and help the RAF;
At first they didn't want to know,
They thought we'd just upset the show.

Gradually they began to heed,
The work we did fulfilled a need;
We fitted in and pulled our weight
And life on camp was really great.

The war dragged on with aches and sorrow,
One hardly dared to think of tomorrow;
But friendships were so very strong,
Always we helped each other along.

We often think of those bygone days,
Now all have gone their separate ways;
Thoughts of laughter and fun we made,
Such wonderful memories never fade.

So now once a month we meet,
Any ex-wartime WAAF to greet;
The spirit of friendship still exists.
Thoughts of happy service life persist.

So come on ex-WAAF of World War II,
Let's hear from many more of you;
Come and meet your friends of old,
Don't be left out in the cold.

May Brough

OVERSEAS

Many a WAAF dreamed of going overseas and a few achieved this hope. Some however were told that there was just no chance – they were too young; they were an only child; and there were many other reasons given. Myra was one of those chosen and she kept with photographs a marvellous record of her time in Sri Lanka and India.

While I was in London, Myra sent to me an album crammed with photographs of her time overseas. I feel sure that if she wished, with those photographs as an aid, she could write a book about her overseas service. Here is a brief account of her services.

I was in the WAAF from 1941 to 1946. I think that I was one of the first to join at 17½. I started off at Gloucester for my initial training and then as a Clerk GD, was posted to Biggin Hill – Operations. This was housed in a large building in Keston, Kent called The Towers. I believe it was moved from the Station after the Battle of Britain. I then went to Chigwell in Essex where they were training Signal Units for the Second Front.

I volunteered to go to the Far East and in December 1943 set sail from Liverpool and eventually landed in Ceylon, now Sri Lanka. I think that I am right in saying we were only the second batch to arrive there, the first having arrived in December. I was sent up to Kandy which was HQ Air Command – South-East Asia – Lord Mountbatten was Chief. I spent about a year there and was then posted to

Myra Irving served in Ceylon & India.

Bombay in India where I worked in Air Information. I was working mainly for A/C Leslie Kark who was writing the official history of the RAF. I don't know if it was ever published. It was there that I became a Corporal – Acting.

Eventually I returned home in 1946, only to be put in quarantine for two weeks as it was discovered one of the crew had yellow fever. You can imagine just how frustrating that was.

Myra Irving (née Manwaring)
Saltdean, Brighton

WHAT DID HE TELL YOU?

There will be many WAAFs who read this book and will not have known about it previously. To them I ask, 'Did you marry an Aussie, a Cannuck or a Yank?' If the answer is, 'Yes,' then the next question is:

'What did he tell you when he proposed?' Of course he may not have proposed but managed to get the message across in other ways.

Perhaps I was one of those. I'll tell you more later.

Aussies, like Yanks, were great at shooting a line. There may even have been talk of sheep stations, cattle stations, big houses, big businesses and many more promises. Many of these promises may have come true while others almost reached the mark.

The next question that comes to mind is, 'Where did he propose?'

Now here's where the interesting bits begin. I wonder how many of you were in a laundry at the time.

The laundry in the Tailors' Shop at Binbrook was where I said to Elizabeth, 'Would you please look after this six pounds and I'll start saving more so that we can buy a ring.' You see, I was the artful dodger. Not a direct proposal. There are many of us who find it hard to say the actual words, 'Will you marry me, sweetheart?'

Fortunately for me, Elizabeth got the message and we bought the ring in Grimsby and then the wedding ring in Reading, Berkshire.

Although I was a dodger, I did make a promise and that was, 'We'll never be rich, but there will always be roses around the door.' I kept both promises and there are still roses each week for where dear Elizabeth rests.

I must tell you more about that laundry at Binbrook but for the moment, that's another story.

BOMB SITES AND WAAF QUARTERS

I must admit that although I dropped bombs, I did not see many bomb sites. I mean places where bombs were stored on RAF camps, not the big holes in the ground where bombs had landed. In London and even in provincial cities of Britain there were plenty of those to see.

No, storage dumps of unfused bombs were not to be seen everywhere. In fact these were usually hidden, covered with camouflage nets or among trees. But of course trees lose their leaves in Britain in winter, so at least one bomb site that I saw at Seighford in Staffordshire had both trees and camouflage nets. This site was close to a beautiful old home known locally as Seighford House.

At Seighford our crew did an OTU. RAF types will recognise those letters as standing for Operational Training Unit. Since we were bound for four-engine bombers we trained on Wellingtons. Start at two and work up to four.

Earlier in the war, this camp must have been an operational one when Wimpies were used extensively in Bomber Command. Now, those bombs just sat there hidden away. We rode our bikes past them *en route* to tea and scones at Seighford House, where airmen and airwomen met and talked and drank tea.

Nearly every other bomb site that I heard about seemed to be on the outskirts of camps and quite often near the WAAF site. Binbrook was no exception: bombs – WAAF site. Scampton: Dam Buster territory – bombs – WAAF site.

Another arrangement that often happened: bomb dump – end of runway. Elizabeth, one of the many WAAFs who counted the Lancasters out at take-off and then lay in a Nissen hut praying for sleep, and still counting the kites, dreaded the roar of four engines over the arched roof of the Nissen hut.

An intruder usually waited until a Lancaster was approaching the runway before making an attack. If a kite was caught then and blew up, up would go the bomb dump, the WAAF site, many many WAAFs and Uncle Tom Cobley and all. Fortunately this never happened at Binbrook.

One lass who was at Scampton tells that no one would have known anything if the bomb dump there had gone up. Her estimation was that it would have taken the whole of Lincoln with it. Some bomb dump!

'O'

When we joined the Air Force we all had to learn to watch our 'Ps & Qs'. But, now many of us learned to watch our 'Os'.

You know, there were all sorts of 'Os'. I can't think of one for 'AO', except perhaps the 'Adults Only', which didn't apply to us because we were all adults. A few girls have admitted to me in their letters that they joined the WAAF at sixteen. I'm sure that didn't stop them appreciating stories that were 'AO'.

Now, there was 'BO', and we all know about that, on those long crowded train journeys when even the air became a little gritty. There were those hygiene lectures we received on first joining up. As a rookie airman, even with a few years of Army seasoning under my belt, I was a bit, well, what shall I say? I was given a bit of a body blow when the MO told us there were bods who needed to clean out their belly buttons.

Moving along, we come to 'CO'. Well, there were all types. Some were complete in their illegitimacy. Others were of doubtful origin. And there were those who were capable of improvement. Finally, there were good blokes – officers and gentlemen. I must quickly add that in the girls' stories written to me, the last lot were often found.

'DO' doesn't need much explaining. How often were you told? 'Just DO it!'

No 'EO'. Perhaps you can think of one.

Now 'FO'. They were the bods who had that one broad ring. Been around a bit, they had. The seats of their tailored trousers were getting a bit of a shine on.

What about 'GO'. Didn't you want to?

Poor old 'HO'! We'll leave him for Christmas and you can HO HO HO to the chimney pots and just slide down.

Of course, we've all heard of 'JO'. He's that bloke in Joe Blow, a well known Australian expression used for a bloke whose name you don't know.

'KO' comes next and that's what happens to you when because your undercart collapsed on the runway, you suddenly reduced speed from a hundred knots to nought knots and you are spread all over the front of the aircraft, just because you have a great urge to keep going.

Alphabetically speaking 'LO' is next. Leave that to the London bobbies – LO! LO! LO! What 'ave we 'ere?

Now 'MO', he's a bod we all got to know. Was yours an Aspro Joe?

'NO', that's the word all good WAAFs were supposed to say. There were a lot of airmen who were deaf!

'OO'. That's what you said when you were told that leave was cancelled. Of course you added a few thousand other words.

Am I boring you? Well, stick to it, we'll get to Z eventually.

'PO'. Well, here's an interesting bod. Remember PO Prune, that clot who could never do anything right? He, poor soul, was the lowest of the low, trying hard to be what he wasn't – tongue-tied, awkward and scorned by both ORs and officers, by gum!

'QO': haven't thought of one yet. Have you?

'ROs'. Army days tell you they were Routine Orders. Did they have ROs in the Air Force?

'SO'. So What?

'TO'. Not today, thank you.

'UO'. Not thought of then. UFOs have come along since.

'VO'. Not on this flight, Serg.

'WO2'. What's the '2' for? Well, of course there's a 'WO1', if you prefer. Another one of those bods of doubtful birth if you are thinking of SWOs. Not a bad rank really. The best of both worlds.

'XO'. Sounds like a disease. We'll leave it alone.

'YO'. Alas poor Yollicks. I didn't know him very well.

'ZO'. We got there, Undercart down. Full flap!

THE ROOKIE'S SALUTE

The response to my appeal for stories was most heartening and of course most came from the UK, but the news of the appeal spread far and wide. From New Zealand came a story after a brother in England had sent the article on. A WAAF who didn't give her Christian name tells of how she spent four years in Pay Accounts on various stations. Here is her story:

As you can see, I am in New Zealand. My brother in England sent me a paper cutting with your article in it telling of your plan to write *Spit, Polish & Tears* – an apt title, I think.

I was in the WAAF for four years working as a pay accounts clerk on various stations. This I really enjoyed. Of course, there were sad times but lots of fun times with great comradeship. There were tedious rules which we often broke – in at night by 2300 hours; no hair touching your collar; no long finger nails; no taking food out of the mess; all limited to a certain radius; booking out and in; marching to work in the snow on winters' mornings with a torch front and rear; button polishing every day. Of course there was always the rush to the ablutions in the hope that the water would be hot. Alas, wishful thinking, for so often the water was tepid. To cap all of this off some nameless girls put things down the loo and blocked it. No one owned up of course and we were all confined to camp for a week. Sure, there would have been murder if we could have found the guilty party.

Perhaps you are wanting to read the serious side of it all. At my age now, I look back and laugh at the tedium of it all – the 'Yes Sir and Madam', to the officers. One day when I was on an accounts course, real rookies, we saluted a Warrant Officer who of course did not respond, to our amazement. Later the CO walked past and we ignored him unwittingly. We were called back and reprimanded. He was a big man and I remember saying, 'Sorry, Sir, we did not see you!' He was not amused.

D.A. Williams
New Zealand

ARE THEY REALLY MARRIED?

When Elizabeth and I were married in the beautiful old church at Warfield in Berkshire, we had planned to spend our honeymoon in the Lake District. In fact, I still have the acknowledgement of the booking.

At the last minute we allowed my cousins to talk us into going to Fawley, a little place on an inlet called Southampton Water. There, they had a friend who would give us private accommodation.

We landed at Southampton and found that to get to Fawley required a taxi. Wonder of wonders, there was one available so we piled in, little knowing where we were going or how far it was. As we went on and on, I wondered if I was ever going to be able to afford the fare. At long last, we arrived and were not impressed with what looked like a very dull place.

A knock at the door and a long wait at last brought someone. No, they could not take us. I think we both said, 'Thank God.' However, now we had the journey back to Southampton and it was not going to be God who would pay the fare.

That night we stayed in a pub in Southampton and through the thin wall we could hear the drinkers at the bar. Breakfast of fried bread, bacon and eggs swimming in fat was shared with a large parrot who screeched from his cage on the kitchen table.

We beat a hasty retreat and began a nightmare journey towards Brokenhurst. On the way, we called in to at least a dozen guest houses to be greeted by stares from well to do retired couples, retired colonels, maiden aunts and proprietors, who had that question written in their eyes. 'Are they really married, or is this a young airman with a pretty girl looking for a dirty weekend?'

I kept saying to Elizabeth, 'Flash that ring!'

'Sorry, we have no vacancies.'

Late that afternoon, tired and digusted with suspicious people, we arrived at Lymington. Somehow, we found Lymington House to be surprised and elated. We were greeted with open arms. Yes, we might certainly book for four days but six days could not be done, unless we were prepared to give up our room on the fifth night and then return.

Believe it or not the lady in charge told a little old lady next door of our plight and she invited us into her home for that fifth night. She had lost a son in the RAF and greeted Elizabeth and me as if that son had come home with a wife. Beautiful bowls of roses were placed in our room. Her very best linen was laid out and we were treated like royalty. She was one of those loving mothers of England. She had given a son but she still had love left for another airman and his WAAF wife. God bless her.

The meals at Lymington House were quite unbelievable. There seemed to be plenty of everything. Quite often wild game was served. Morning and afternoon tea were always served, and great bowls of strawberries and cream often accompanied the tea and scones at afternoon tea.

Elizabeth was highly amused when she saw me leap out of bed and look very distraught at the sound of a church bell.

'Guilty conscience?' she asked.

'No, that blanketty bell sounds just like the fire bell at Kyneton, my home town in Australia.'

Many years later Elizabeth was to hear that Kyneton fire bell herself and be galvanised into action as the RSL Ladies Auxiliary were on duty. That is – they had to provide tea and sandwiches for firemen.

By that stage no one doubted that Elizabeth and I really were married.

She had become not only a great Aussie but one who was much respected even by maiden aunts and old colonels.

AUSSIE CHASES THE GIRLS IN BLUE

I had a good laugh when Iris wrote to tell me about the heading on my article published in the Plymouth Evening Herald. She says it was exciting to read, 'Ex Aussie Bomber Pilot Chases the Girls in Blue', for she thought those days were over. The first thing about this heading is that I was never a pilot but a bomb aimer, and the second thing is that I don't think I can run any more and I'm sure that in spite of it being fifty years on, some girls can still run.

Iris was with an Aussie Coastal Command Squadron and learned, as she says, some of the Aussie lingo. Here is her story:

I was deferred from call-up for service for two years and worked on night duty at an ARP Control Centre. In 1942 my call-up came and I went by train to Gloucester for a week to be fully kitted out. Next, I was off to Morecambe, Lancashire. It was winter and we marched along the sea front, sometimes in howling gales and pouring rain. It was always cold and no amount of marching could warm me up.

Two weeks were spent in Morecambe when it was considered that I was fully trained and was given seven days leave in Plymouth before taking up a posting as Clerk Secretarial at RAF Coastal Command, Mount Batten, Devon. Sunderlands and Catalinas were the aircraft used and the airmen consisted of RAF and No 10 Squadron RAAF, some Polish and other nationalities and of course the WAAFs.

I lived outside Plymouth, so when I first reported to Mount Batten, I had to catch an omnibus to Plymouth town centre, and then walk to Barbican, a small fishing harbour and fish market, to catch a ferry to a small village called Turnchapel. There was yet another walk, half of this up an almost vertical hill, before I finally arrived at Mount Batten.

I was given a post as a Clerk, Secretarial, to a Squadron Leader, who was the Chief Technical Officer. I was told to bring my kit the next day and to sleep in an old manor house. I found my way to a huge hangar-type building where aircraft repairs were being carried out on the ground floor – mostly by Australians with a few RAF and WAAF. The WAAFs were known as 'Sparkies' as they cleaned and tested spark plugs. Steps led to an upper floor where there were two offices, one for the CTO and his assistant, an RAF F/O, and the other for an RAF clerk and myself. A third room was for the 'Sparkies' for changing into their working clothes and making tea etc.

The CTO introduced me to the Aussies on the ground floor and a cheer went up! It took me a while to get used to the Australian lingo; some were more comprehensible than others. My work consisted of taking dictation for letters and reports, and a lot of typing returns etc.

The office had a peculiar fire with a large chimney going up through the room to the roof. It was fed with coke and had a voracious appetite – a lot of Aussies came to the office to have a quick warm-up. Well, that is what they said!

I grew to like the Aussies very much. They were always friendly and cheerful, despite the fact that they were so far away from their homes and families.

I slept at the manor house for three months; no food was available there, so it was a matter of getting up early to catch the RAF transport, which took us to the mess at Mount Batten for breakfast. However, I was eventually given a sleeping out pass and travelled to and from my home to Mount Batten each day. Of course there were air raids to contend with and many nights were spent in the air raid shelter. My parents and we three children had already lost one home with all our belongings and dreaded the thought of losing another.

The CTO said that he would like me to be a Corporal, so I took all of the tests with only one left to do – that was to drill a group of men for twenty minutes. I arrived at the appointed place on the cliffs where examiners were at the ready. I was confronted with thirty-six men of the RAF Regiment – giants they appeared to be! There was a very strong wind and my voice seemed to be carried away. However, I managed to drill them successfully, not marching them over the edge of the cliffs! So I became the proud owner of a Corporal's stripes.

I had one particular boyfriend and I was considering going to Australia, but fate took a hand in my future. I was taken ill with pleural effusion, spent three weeks in the camp sick bay and was then taken to a local hospital. When the fluid was drawn off from my lungs, it was found to be tubercular. After three months in hospital, I was taken to a sanatorium on the moors. I spent ten months there without a great deal of improvement, so I took the responsibility of discharging myself to go home with my parents, where I was sure that I would gradually improve. In this I

was right, although it took a long time. I had already been discharged
from the WAAF on medical grounds.

My boyfriend had gone back to Australia with all of the other Aussies
from Mount Batten. We corresponded for several years but I knew that
I would not be allowed to enter Australia with TB. It was very sad but I
knew it had to be faced. I later met a man who has been my husband
for forty-five years. We have a son and one grandson and have always
been ideally happy together. I will always remember meeting the Aussies.
Today it seems like a never to be forgotten dream.

Coastal Command played a vital part in keeping the sea lanes open.
No matter which RAF Command we were serving in, we all played our
part in the making of history.

Finally, I must commend you and thousands of other airmen for the
marvellous work you did during the war, in particular, taking your life in
your hands every time you took off on a bombing raid. We would never
have won the war without the gallant devotion of the men of the three
services.

On Plymouth Hoe, where Sir Francis Drake played bowls before
sighting the Spanish Armada, a memorial has recently been erected in
memory of those who lost their lives in various RAF services.

In conclusion I wish you luck with *Spit, Polish & Tears* and I do hope
that you receive many letters from girls in blue.

Iris Lewis
Plymton, Plymouth

*Thank you, Iris, for your kind words of appreciation. I am mindful of the fact
that WAAFs in every sphere worked as hard as the men and in some cases harder.
We Aussies came to Britain to help with the job that had to be done and we
were proud to share with both the men and the women of the RAF all of the
difficulties and also the joys of being in a team.*

THE TAILORS' SHOP IN BINBROOK

The Tailors' Shop at Binbrook was found in one of the cottages built as
married quarters during the early part of the war. All other cottages were
occupied by aircrew, with one crew having the use of a whole cottage –
up and down stairs.

A number of cottages adjoined and each had two rooms up and down with the laundry downstairs and a toilet and bathroom upstairs. They were built to last and now, some fifty years later, those cottages are still there.

The shop was found at the end of the first block which you found walking across from the Sergeants' mess. From the outside, nothing distinguished it from the rest. However, inside it was a different story.

Six WAAFs and one airman made up the tailoring team. They were Elizabeth, known then as Beth, Daisy, Phyllis, Renee, Marjory and Joyce known as Tiger. The one airman was Don, a quiet, gentle married man.

Daisy was a Corporal in charge. Several, including some girls and Don, had served their apprenticeship in civvy street. Elizabeth was a fully fledged tailoress when she entered the WAAF.

The team always welcomed aircrew and it became, against all rules, the custom for individuals to become honoured guests of the shop. I was one of these and of course had particular interest in being with Elizabeth. Others just spent some of their spare time hanging around, sharing food parcels, and eating toast made from bread spirited out of the WAAF mess and plastered with margarine. Some were there just to chat up the girls. Of course some were real customers, there for alterations to uniforms or to have repairs or stripes sewn on. These were mostly officers. The chatting up boys were in the main NCOs.

Fortunately for many of us the front window of the shop gave a very good view of the approaches. If the cry went up, 'Two Ton Tess!' there was instant action. Aussies vacated the building in all directions, some

The girls of the Tailors' Shop in Binbrook.
(L to R) Elizabeth, Daisy, Renee, Marjory, Joyce (Tiger), Phyllis.

even going down drainpipes at the back of the cottage, some through the back door, some through the laundry window, while some took refuge in the rag cupboard. This was one hell of a risk as you will see.

Two Ton Tess was a WAAF officer of rather large proportions and was aptly named after Tessie O'Shea, a well known British comedienne during the war. She had a habit of appearing like a will-o'-the-wisp from nowhere and then suddenly disappearing, suddenly to appear again. She made a habit of hunting in cupboards, pouncing into the toilet, looking in rag bags and many other places where God knows what might be hidden.

It is interesting to note that late in the war the ten ton bombs dropped on such places as Heligoland's submarine pens were also named 'Tessies'.

All sorts of clandestine operations were carried out by the girls in the Tailors' Shop. Pieces of parachute silk, airframe fabric and canvas were made into quite interesting articles. After all, anything was better than the blue knicker passion killers issued to WAAFs. Canvas would be a bit rough though, wouldn't it?

Not long after I had met Elizabeth, I drew on a piece of fabric the 460 Squadron crest – 'Strike & Return' with a rampant kangaroo as its centrepiece. With many coloured cottons Elizabeth stitched this and as I completed each operation, she worked the name of the target into the material, using red for night ops and yellow for daylights. I still have that piece of fancy work and it has graced many a table top. Some aircrew types preferred a silk scarf with the target names worked or stitched in.

Early in my visits, I noticed on the walls of the shop photographs of Aussie crews. I was told, and I didn't believe it at first, that crews with their picture on the wall always survived a tour of ops. This was really something as the survival rate in Bomber Command aircrews was about forty-four per cent.

To add to our joy, a month or two before the European war ended there was a shortage of aircrew coming to squadrons and so for a while each crew was expected to do not thirty ops but thirty-five for a tour.

We survived a tour with only once being hit by flak and that was on the last op over Berchesgarten. Yet, when I left the crew to go to a School in London, three of our crew were lost in training. It all makes you think, doesn't it?

There were probably many airmen who never once in their stay at Binbrook visited the Tailors' Shop – some may not have heard of it. I must say that my visits there smartened me up in more ways than one.

Not only a beautiful lass, Elizabeth contributed a great deal by taking my Aussie issue tunics, trousers and battle dress and making them fit me like a glove. No officer with his Bond Street tailored uniform had a better fitting outfit than I had. Also, I had little extras like a money pocket under the belt of a tunic.

The little club that formed of members of the Tailors' Shop and Aussie NCOs with all its romancing had only the one lasting partnership and that was Liz and Norm. We were a team for forty-eight wonderful years.

ALWAYS GOOD FOR A LAUGH

Joyce Morton, formerly Joyce Weaver, was a tall lass and her first pair of trousers were so large that she and her friend could have fitted into them. She kept these and from time to time wore them for they were always good for a laugh. After the war Joyce served in Paris. This posting, I am sure, would be envied by many a WAAF who stayed on.

I was seventeen when I joined the WAAF and it was not for any noble reason for I was coaxed into it by a friend who wanted to join. We were both enamoured with the battledress we had seen worn by WAAFs. We decided that was the style we wanted. We were both immature and opted for Balloon Operating when we learned that it ensured a battledress.

In October 1942, we were called to report to Adastral House from whence we journeyed by train to Innsworth, Gloucestershire. There we were kitted out. Being five feet ten, an unusual height for a girl, in order to provide length I received, you understand, an outsize uniform. Both my friend and I could have got into the trousers together. I wore them for years and they were always good for a laugh wherever I went. So wet behind the ears we were and so excited, our intake just could not wait to don the uniform, all crumpled and with tarnished buttons. We went swaggering around the camp and ran into an enraged WAAF officer, whom of course, we did not salute. I have not forgotten the wigging she gave us. On reflection, I wonder what kind of a person she was not to realise the situation.

Morecambe was our next venue and my pal was still with me for basic training. This involved marching up and down the promenade. We were put into requisitioned boarding houses. The landladies were pleased to get some cash – holidays here were out of fashion for the duration. I can remember my landlady still; her husband used to play the sergeant-major, making sure that we were not out after hours. She put on a high tea for us when she learned that it was my eighteenth birthday.

Some things were not so nice – inoculations. Some girls fainted; others had the collywobbles, while others were too paralysed with fear to do anything. The other trial we had to bear was the shortage of cash. We received ten shillings a fortnight. Yes, we had a roof over our heads and three meals a day but we were young and a healthy appetite went with that. We were unable to treat ourselves to the smallest things. By the second week we could not afford even a pennyworth of chips. What made it worse was that there were no young men who might want to entertain us. We had to pay for any entertainment ourselves. It being November, we could not just walk the streets and, sad to say, my pal was not in the same billet as myself. As a matter of interest all the lads were getting their training at the next resort along the coast. It was too far for us and no doubt they were in the same financial boat.

Then it was off to Cardington, Bedford, the two of us. We were thrilled to see the hangars where the R101 and other airships had their home. Now, the barrage balloons were housed in them and we were to commence our training as balloon operators. What with this knot and what else, the worse part was trying to understand the rudiments of the motor on the winch that controlled the balloon on that cold and windy airfield. We wore our pyjamas under our battledress. So much did we suffer from the cold, we broke the most serious rule of all and slept in the same bed to keep warm, not caring about discomfort. On reflection, it seems strange that we were not given away by anyone.

At weekends, we would sneak out of camp and, ticketless, ride the train home for the sake of some comfort and warmth. This was dishonest but we felt it was adventurous and necessary. In 1943, Balloon Command issued an order for all operator training to cease. The words used were that the future motherhood of Britain was being threatened as there were a large number of girls in hospital with prolapses of the womb due to constant heavy lifting of the heavy concrete blocks used to moor the balloons. We all had to remuster after spending so much time on the training. My friend and I plumped for a trade which required the least training and this was for telephonists who were given two weeks.

Here my friend and I split up to take separate postings. I was posted to RAF Bicester, Fighter Command. From there they were flying Blenheims which were called, morbidly, 'flying coffins'. I was pleasantly surprised to find how much leisure time I had and how the rules were relaxed. The NCOs spoke like human beings.

When I got my first forty-eight hour leave, it was then that I realised that going home was like being dropped from another planet. My life in the Air Force was so very different that it felt as if civvy street was not in the same world.

In camp I was billeted in what in peacetime had been married quarters. Now, each room was furnished with a double bunk. Four airwomen slept in each room. My allotted room had a built-in cupboard in which we kept our property, but it was not very satisfactory, as vital clothing would go missing. In order to bathe or do laundry a boiler had to be lit. To do this, some time had to be spent scouring the area for twigs of any kind and pieces of wood. If the wood was too big it had to be chopped laboriously with one of our dinner knives. There must have been a coal or a coke issue but I remember only wood which had been scrounged. There was a long wait and eventually a meagre amount of hot water was produced.

Eventually, a WAAF site was built about a mile from the main station and we were allowed to perform our ablutions and do our laundry there. Indeed, shortly thereafter, I moved into a Nissen hut on the site. Nissen huts I cannot recommend as they were ovens in summer and freezers in winter. We often went to bed with our clothes under our pyjamas. I wore a pair of long seaboot stockings.

During my service there, I was sent twice to satellite stations which were also OTUs. Here there was a new intake of aircrews every six weeks. I met socially men from all parts of the Empire as it was then. Our off duty evenings were spent getting to know one another at the local village pubs and occasional dances. There was a rule forbidding officers to fraternise with other ranks. This was often ignored. Didn't they know there was a war on?

I moved on again. 'Posted' was the term used for uprooting someone as soon as they were settled. Off I went, tearfully waving goodbye to all of my friends, to be landed in yet another strange place among strange people. My new station was Harwell. In the days leading up to D-Day it was a frantic time. All leave had been stopped for months.

After service on several other fighter stations, the most northern being near Nottingham, I fetched up at a Radar Station in Norfolk. This was a totally new experience as there were no planes. It was a secret operation about which I learned nothing, despite sharing a hut, going on duty and sharing rest periods with radar ops. We cycled to the operational unit, a mile or so from the domestic site. Once there, we parted company. Upon entering the building, I went to the PBX, my domain. Where the rest went, I never knew. The switchboard was a 'one position' so hours were spent in solitary.

While I was there peace came and when my colleagues were demobbed, I signed on for another two years. I must add here that my friend with whom I had joined left the WAAF in 1944. She sailed to join her husband's family, taking a new baby with her. In the meantime, her husband was in Italy with the Canadian Army. He survived and went home to Canada. My fiancé did not as he was killed in Italy in the aftermath of D-Day.

After signing on I volunteered for overseas service and to my delight was posted to Paris. It was now 1946 and I served in my usual capacity at the British Legation there. How overwhelmed I was after leaving dull drizzing austere England to find myself in sunny, hot, gay Paree. There just one year after liberation were the extravagant window displays. Paris was back to normal – swinging Paree. I was billeted in a chateau, Les Oeillets which stood next to the Chateau de Josephine. It stood in extensive grounds and had been occupied by the Wehrmacht. Such notices as *'Verboten'* still remained.

I spent a heavenly eight months there. It was not long enough. My application for a posting in Germany was not granted so I returned to the UK where, for my sins, I was sent on a drill course to RAF Hawkings. Returning to base, Middle Wallop, near Salisbury, I was detailed to drill the airwomen in the barrack square along with my normal duties. I was now a Corporal and I supervised the PBX. My pay was now a little more realistic. My final day in the Service came after another two years in autumn 1949. I was then stationed at Uxbridge Fighter Command. This time the billets were luxurious. We lived in a centrally heated block built to accommodate the Olympic contestants of 1948. There were three to a room with bedside lights and comfortable beds. Baths and toilets were in the same building. We thought we had died and gone to heaven.

I married a RAF W/O (Radar) whom I met after my discharge. At present, we enjoy ourselves by attending Radar reunions.

Joyce Morton
Essex

DRIVING THROUGH FLAMES

I have chosen Daphne's story as she writes about FIDO. At Binbrook, we did not have FIDO and several times I wished that we had for the fog clamped down almost on the deck and FIDO would have made landing so much easier as it lifted the fog some feet above the runway.

Daphne writes of driving down the runway in a jeep, going flat out, when the flames lit up each side of the runway – what an experience! Here in her own words is Daphne's story:

I joined the WAAF in 1941 as a raw eighteen-year-old, really unfamiliar with Service life. I knew that I would be expected to contribute something and didn't fancy munition factories. I soon settled down however and met many friends and now I don't regret having that experience.

I was at first based in Lincolnshire with Fighter 12 Group, stationed at RAF Wittering, near Stamford. As I was in the MT section I spent most of my time there driving around Lincolnshire in a Morris ambulance ferrying RAF personnel to various hospitals and doing standby in times of need with the Morris and the dreaded Albion.

My last year in 1945 was spent at a Bomber Station based at Pocklington, Yorkshire. This time I was ferrying pilots to aircraft and collecting them on return, with other jobs in between. I now find it hard to realise some of the things which were expected of us and it is amazing how we took it in our stride. As many of these things now come to mind, I have a giggle because I met some wonderful people from all walks of life. One rarely talks of them or those times for fear of being thought a little over the top and unbelievable.

What often comes back to me is the time I had a posting to Manston in Kent. It was here that there was a lot of action as paratroopers took off. At first, I was told to report to the water tower. This seemed a little odd for an MT driver. However I was on duty twenty-four hours on and twenty-four hours off with another WAAF, Phil Day. We were given a jeep and soon found that speed was essential with this task. The runway was huge, long and wide with FIDO lighting at each side. I had never heard of FIDO before that. I soon became used to tearing down the runway with the flames lighting up each side of me. It was like driving through fire. The aim was to lead incoming aircraft to the parking spots at the end of the runway. At the end was what was known as the 'loop' and planes would be parked there. I used to tear along this and with a plane following manage to make headway at the turn. This gave me time to stop, jump out and bring the aircraft to a stop with hand signals, telling them when to cut engines. I always felt wonderful to be given a wave and a thumbs up. Spitfires, Dakotas, Flying Fortresses, they all came. Looking back, I often wonder if it was all a dream. Many WAAFs did things which seemed minor at the time but now I am amazed.

Daphne Tuamy (née Rose)
Gosport, Hampshire

SMOKEY'S

The tucker in the airmen's mess was not always to Elizabeth's liking and quite frequently it meant a cook-up in the Tailors' Shop or a trip to Smokey Joe's.

Just down the hill towards Binbrook, on the right hand side, was Smokey Joe's. As the name indicates, it was quite often just that and one had to swim through a gloom of smoke to reach the counter.

However, the baked beans on toast or bonox spread sandwiches were often relished by hungry ground staff, aircrew or WAAFs. Quite often, the main customers were aircrew who, having found that they were not on the Battle Order for that day or night, would wander down to Smokey's for a snack and a yarn.

Elizabeth and I often met there and it was she who introduced me to yet greater culinary delights at the YM, in Binbrook village. There, the menu was slightly better and of course there was some seating. You could sit down in a civilised fashion and enjoy bacon and tomatoes.

Having been at Binbrook since 1942, Elizabeth had discovered most of the lurks and perks of the place and the best places to have a good cheap feed in Grimsby.

On our first outing to Grimsby, we also had Tiger – Joyce – come along. I remember feeling honoured to have not one girl but two with whom to link arms. At that stage, I had already made up my mind that Liz was the one for me. Tiger was great fun and one hell of a tease but she was to discover that two could play at that game as you will see in another part of this story.

Smokey Joe's on the hill going down to Binbrook. Norman and friend go for a Woodbine.

After we had been to a film and had seen once again the Inkspots we were ravenous and the girls took me along to a Grimsby fish shop. I remember being very amused about the sign outside, 'Frying Tonight'. What did they do on other nights? Boil or Roast?

I suppose fish shops, as with so many others, were rationed with fats, and fry-ups were not as frequent as pre-war. When one discovered that the ordinary rations were two ounces (60 grams) of butter, two ounces of margarine and two ounces of cooking fat per person, per week, it dawns that at home there could not be a lot of fry-ups. The usual eggs, bacon and fried bread for breakfast would have been restricted as the bacon ration was two ounces per week and eggs were one per fortnight. If you wanted to fill up on bread and jam, the bread was obtainable but the jam came at ½lb. once a month.

Back to the fish shop – we joined the queue which seemed endless but with two bright girls and plenty of banter from the locals, the time passed quickly.

'What'll you have?' I asked the girls.

There was no hesitation.

'Cod and chips, please,' said Tiger.

'Is that the best?' I asked.

'The best you'll get here and it's not bad really,' added Liz.

Cod and chips it was – all round. The best part was eating them out of the paper and licking the greasy fingers with no thought of cholesterol in those days. I doubt if any of us had heard of it then.

'Smashing!' I said as the tangy salt bit my lips.

I well remember being shocked when I first discovered that factory hands in places like Warrington practically lived on fish and chips. Perhaps we turn up our noses now but the fish was certainly one of the best foods then and probably still is.

All through the years, Elizabeth and I have enjoyed fish and chips. Our particular liking was for lemon sole and plaice. Even they have not made me forget the enjoyment of the salty, greasy but delicious taste of those fish and chips at Grimsby.

I enjoyed the feed and was beginning to appreciate the wonderful company of those two girls, Tiger and Liz. A small voice said, 'Take your pick.'

I did and chose Elizabeth, the quiet, shy one. Tiger was great fun while Elizabeth was wry; her wit was instantaneous, whip-like and showed that she had a deep and fine appreciation of the thoughts and feelings of others.

When she smiled, she had such an open friendly face that said to me, 'I'm coming to get you!'

She had a saying that puzzled me at first. It was, 'I'll get you at the corner.'

At first I thought, 'Look out, lad, you might not survive.'

Then she came out with, 'I'll push you up the lum!'

Now, years later, I understand a few Scottish expressions but she could still puzzle me with what I called daft expressions.

Well, our day in Grimsby came to an end at 2359 when we went through the camp gates, the girls to the WAAF site and Norm to the crew cottage. It was a great day and no more for a while but of course there was always Smokey Joe's, still smokey, still inviting, and I believe still there even years after the Aussies left Binbrook.

TALLEST ON THE RIGHT
AND SHORTEST ON THE LEFT

So many WAAFs and airmen have heard those words yelled across a RAF parade ground. Vivien who was barely five feet tall had no difficulty. She just went left and stood. Of all the WAAFs who wrote to me she was the only one who had been stationed on the Isle of Man.

I am an ex WAAF No. 2002741 and I joined in 1941 to do my square bashing and spit and polishing in Gloucestershire. It was not too frightening. When we had to fall in for parades, tallest on the right and shortest on the left, I just walked to the left end and stood there while all the others were sorting themselves out. I was barely five feet and lugging a kit bag was not too difficult – kind people lifted it for me! Though small, I was tough and strong. You needed to be!

After my training, I chose to be a radar operator as there was a shortage. I went to RAF Cranwell Radio School. After a course there, my first posting was to Rye near Hastings. We were bombed there but luckily no one was injured. Naturally, the enemy were trying to destroy us, our radar and our pylons. After a short leave, I was then posted to the Isle of Man where began another episode of my WAAF career.

On the Isle, our Radar Station was called RAF Bride; the Fighter Station and Bomber Station were near us. I was very happy there and we were a good team – full complement one hundred. It was near the sea which I loved and still do. At the time there was a Fighter Squadron over from Biggin Hill and, yes, Australians and New Zealanders amongst them. We spent many a happy time in the Imperial Hotel enlivened by rum and at times it lingered. I attended social evenings and dances and many a night wobbled home to my billet on a bike.

At that time, I had just become engaged to Flt/Lt. Jack Groves. We had known each other since 1938. He had joined the RAF as a Regular in 1939. Then he went to Egypt to earn his wings and the war broke out. With 112 Fighter Squadron he served in the Desert, then Greece, and finally escaped from Crete. He was awarded the DFC.

When I told him that I had joined the WAAF hoping to get out with him, he sent me a ring from Egypt. He didn't trust all of those dashing airmen! He eventually came home in 1942, posted to Carlisle, and we arranged to be married on the Isle of Man on 21 June 1942. Then he was to take over his own Squadron, again with the Aussies with whom he had flown out east. But it was not to be. He had flown in with his best man in two Hurricanes to arrange the last details of the wedding and, on taking off in June, they ran into fog and Jack was about to land when his mate tipped his wings and the plane landed in the sea and Jack was lost.

I tried to come to grips with myself. It was wartime and so many people went missing, died, were bombed, etc., but after such a flying career, it seemed tragic that such a brilliant pilot should lose his life that way. After a short leave, I was back at camp with the friends I worked and played with in the happy days. I will never forget the kindness shown by the Australians. I was posted with another WAAF, Kay; her fiancé had been killed in London by bombing so we were a good team.

We were to go to a Radio Operators' Mechanics' Course at Yatesbury in Wiltshire. I could barely pull a plug but I was a good radar operator on the screen.

Now for an amusing episode, We didn't want to leave RAF Bride, so on our last night before we boarded the ferry, we had a wonderful party and decided to bribe the sergeant in the guard room to give us the flag which was hoisted up every day. We put in its place our 'black-outs' – bloomers to you. He joined in the game and said not to worry as there was another flag he would hoist up before the CO took his inspection, if he did, that was. However, the sergeant did not get the black-outs down in time. You can imagine the scene. We were stopped boarding the ferry, and told to return the flag immediately or return to base. That was all we wanted, but there was to be a charge. We did as we were told and sailed away to a very different world at Yatesbury.

There we found hundreds of WAAFs and RAF, big Nissen huts, inspections, parades and of course the ROM Course. That was difficult but we learned enough about calculators, plugs etc. and what went on behind radar screens, to take over if the men were posted abroad, where we were not allowed to go.

One wet day, my great-coat was soaking wet so I put it over a chair near one of the ghastly fires we had in the middle of the Nissen hut. Someone pushed it too near the fire and there appeared a great burn down the front. I took it to Stores but they told me to patch it. What with?

Kay and I went out of Yatesbury a few miles and found a delightful pub. There we met up with lots of pilots from a nearby station. We even found a way back into camp missing the Guard Room. There were a few WAAF officers there that night as well as mere AC2s, LACWs and corporals. The next morning Kay and I were summoned to the CO's room. Imagine our horror to be suddenly faced with our own CO who was at the party the night before. But she was human after all. She told us in future to get a late pass and issued us with several, and as I had been grumbling about my great-coat – a disgrace to the RAF etc. – she issued a chit to the store for a new one.

From Yatesbury, we were posted to RAF Barkway, near Royston, Cambridge and there began another hard and concentrating job. Naturally we did not know the importance and secrecy of it. But of course it enabled our bombers to go on low flying raids. The only recognition we received was when the crews came into the ops room to say 'thanks'. We were just a small cog in a big wheel but we were a proud lot. I still think of this on days when I see pylons scattered around the countryside.

I spent my next posting north of John O'Groats, the nearest town being Thurso. It was very bleak and wintery and to go to the ablutions we had to put on galoshes and wind-cheaters. I can only say that it was healthy. My last posting was to Truleigh Hill in Sussex. I can see the pylons from here.

I had met and married an RAF officer whom I had met at Cambridge but that is another story. I became pregnant and left the Service to give birth to my daughter Penny in 1945. My husband went over to France after D-Day and I came to live in this flat which belonged to my mother. Again, I had contact with the Australian Air Force. It was coming up to

VE Day and they were billeted in the Metropole Hotel and I used to go swimming with them. My home was an open one for them. They baby-sat for me and cooked. When VE Day arrived, we all celebrated but again with a tinge of sadness because all those boys were on their way back to the Pacific War.

Many of them had been killed and some were still missing. For two years after the war, I had letters from wives, mothers and sweethearts. A parcel of goodies came from Myers and invitations to come and see them. Even jobs were offered to us. We didn't make it and went to live in the Channel Islands. In Jersey I joined the RAFA and became their secretary 1952–7. Our chief aim was to raise money for those who were worse off than us and Jersey was one of the best fund raisers. They support several RAF homes. I think I shall soon have to reserve a room.

Unfortunately, my marriage failed in 1961 and I came back to England. I then met Eddie, ex RAF, also stationed at Dyce, and we lived together for twenty-five years. He started to lose his sight with cataracts and died three years ago. Now I muster alone, still do a job of work, swim indoors and enjoy the company of friends.

Writing this has brought back a lot of vivid memories and I must admit a few tears and laughs but all those wonderful friends are laughing down at us. So with my best salute, I salute them for the unforgettable years I spent with them in the best Service in the world, the Royal Air Force and the Women's Auxiliary Air Force.

Vivien Turner
Brighton, Sussex

WHEN THE POPPIES BLOOM AGAIN

Marjorie Smith in her story tells of Lincolnshire's spacious skies and fields of poppies. I have always thought of our Australian mallee country as the country of the big sky. Recently, when I visited Binbrook, the station where Elizabeth and I met, I was struck by the great open space, the strong winds and there the open sky so blue and almost inviting. I had forgotten the snow and ice of Christmas 1944. Marjorie reminds us of this in her story:

Let me begin by saying that I have had some enjoyment in putting together some of my memories of those far-off days spent in the WAAF.

I lived in Manchester with my parents and in July of 1943, at the age of twenty-three, I was called up into the WAAF and recruited at Innsworth near Gloucester. After all the preliminaries – vaccinations, square bashing etc. – I was assessed for a trade which turned out to be Wireless Operator.

The first part of training was at the RAF Radio School at Blackpool, where we were billeted in houses. I always remember marching through streets on 'bath parade' to the Derby Baths, sometimes in pouring rain, wearing those rubber camouflage ground sheets. The water ran straight off into one's shoes.

One bright spot at Blackpool was the Station Choir which I joined, where we sang 'Messiah' and carols at Christmas time and 'Hiawatha's Wedding Feast'.

The training sessions in morse signalling procedures and radio equipment were held in rooms above various shops. The course was completed at Compton Basset in Wiltshire, a lovely rural spot. With fellow WAAFs I visited the little village churches decorated with primroses for Easter. One of my friends now lives in Devon and we still exchange cards at Easter and look back to those spring days.

Eventually, in May 1944, complete with 'Sparks' badge on my sleeve, I was posted to SHQ Signals, RAF Binbrook and became one of the dozen or so occupants of Hut 23 on the WAAF site. This was some distance uphill from the main camp, so we were issued with bicycles. We had our own Sick Bay and NAAFI of course.

As wireless ops we worked shifts sending and receiving messages between Binbrook and satellite stations at Kelstern, Ludford and Group HQ at Bawtry. Outdated code was used, apparently to cause interference on frequencies used by the enemy. Sometimes we had a turn on the traffic desk when reports were coming through on the teleprinters from crews as they came in from ops – anxious moments waiting to see if certain 'kites' had landed.

Sometimes, on a free day, following night duty, we would treat ourselves to a trip by bus to Grimsby or Lincoln, perhaps with a visit to a cinema. There were cycle rides to Tealby for tea and home-made cake or over the Wolds on summer evenings. I always remember spacious skies and poppies in the cornfields. One day, several of us cycled all the way to Louth to attend the wedding of one of our hut-mates, much to her surprise.

I well remember the steep hill into the village, where you met your wife-to-be in such dramatic circumstances. I do not remember the Beaufighter incident. Perhaps I was on leave at the time.

One winter, there was so much snow and ice the bread vans could not climb the hill and we were temporarily reduced to 'hard tack' biscuits. We used to be detailed in twos to get large flasks filled with tea at 'Smokey Joe's' for the signals staff.

On one occasion, having been on night watch, I tried to sleep during the day, and, the weather being very warm, I took my 'biscuits' into the field by Hut 23 and dozed off. On waking, I returned to the hut and to my horror on looking into a mirror, discovered that I had a black eye. The only explanation seemed to be that some insect had stung me. The worst of it was that I had a first date that evening with the WOP of the crew of K2, whom I had met at a station dance, and he introduced me to several other crew members at a get-together. I think it was at the 'Marquis'. I braved it out and nobody made any rude remarks, but it was somewhat embarrassing!

As the war drew to a close, WAAF W/Ops became redundant and we were transferred to other trades and sections. I was given a short course as a radar mechanic and the rest of my time at Binbrook was spent working in the Base Radar workshop under a Canadian corporal and later in Squadron Radar with a Canadian officer.

I do not remember where the Tailors' Shop was, but there was one occasion when I should have visited it, as I learned later. One wet day I got my great-coat soaked and hung it over a chair by the stove in the hut to dry – too near, as I soon found out, as a small area in one sleeve was singed, leaving a hole. I patched it up with a small piece of material from the inside of the coat and it was hardly noticeable but the eagle eye of the WAAF officer spotted it on a parade and put me on a charge. I had to appear before an officer and write an explanation. She let me off lightly and said that I had made a neat job of it, but cutting pieces from one's uniform was an offence and it should have been taken to the Tailors' Shop. If I had, then maybe I would have met Elizabeth.

I am still in touch with several old Binbrook friends and several years ago, we had a reunion at the home of one who lives at Sleaford near RAF Cranwell. She married a Wing Commander at Uxbridge and they still have RAF connections, especially at Cranwell. Eight of us, including husbands, visited Binbrook in various cars and were entertained to lunch in the Officers' mess as guests of the CO. How young he seemed. We were taken on a tour of the camp, the airfield and the hangars and we were given the chance to view the interior of a Lightning at close quarters.

I little dreamt, as a humble LACW, that one day I would dine in the sacred precincts of the Officers' mess.

The film *Memphis Belle* was made at Binbrook. Even the Lightnings are no more and I believe a housing estate has replaced the station. There is a memorial to 460 Squadron in the village.

To end my story, in November 1945, I was posted with two of my friends to RAF Sudbury and sadly left Binbrook. Sudbury, Suffolk, was a Recruiting Centre where we were mis-employed in various jobs – in my case in the kitchen of the Officers' mess and later in the Catering Office. I eventually went to Cranwell, just filling in time until my demob number came up. This was in June 1946. So it was back to civvy street and my old job in the Civil Service. This took a good deal of adjustment. I was married in 1949 to an ex soldier who had served in France and Germany and we have lived at this address ever since.

I hope that our two sons will never be called up to go to war, but I shall never forget those days in the WAAF and I am glad to have had that experience. There was something very special about the camaraderie and I think I returned a better, more mature person, with some of the corners knocked off.

I hope that *Spit, Polish & Tears* will be successful as it is a worthy tribute to Elizabeth.

Marjorie Smith (née Spencer)

488177

Cheshire

MEMORIES LIVE LONGER THAN DREAMS

Yes, memories live longer than dreams and so many of us wish that we could turn the clock back, as does ex LACW Leonard. She mentions in her story how she and other WAAFs in the hut at night listened as a Scottish WAAF sang in a haunting, lilting voice such songs as 'Memories'. Happy times and sad times, times of great company and times of great sadness come back to all of us, but we must go on for we are the custodians of those wonderful memories given to us by those who were so close to us both during the war and after. We owe it to them to treasure and even pass on those memories to those who still wish to know. Here is a story full of memories:

I had a slight shock at seeing your late wife's photos. She had a very strong resemblance, at first glance, to one of my fellow WAAFs. It isn't the same, but I had a little flutter when I saw it.

I always loved the shiny peak on our caps. I remember going with others to a cinema and the girl next to me put her cigarette on the floor and then she kept saying that it wouldn't go out. When she came out she realized that her cap had been on the floor and it had two great holes in it. Others thought it was very funny at the time.

When we first got our uniforms, I seemed to go around the hut teaching girls how to tie a tie. No one seemed to know how to do this and I thought it strange for tying a girdle around a gym slip was just the same.

I came from Derby but never did meet anyone else from there. After training, I was stationed at Wick. Have you heard of it? It's just a few miles from John O'Groats and I thought I was never going to get there. An airman took me in hand at Carstairs and we travelled nearly to Wick together. A Scottie had laughed when I said, 'Wick', and he said that after the train I would join a mule train over the mountains and the hours I was on the last train almost made me believe him. It was the end of the line!

It was a dry town owing to the fighting that used to take place, so nearly every pub was a tea room. The pumps were still there. There was one doubtful blessing about being there as the lines were blocked in winter. One girl I knew was in a train that got stuck in the middle of nowhere. She laughed about it afterwards but not at the time.

I had never seen so much snow as I saw up there and the wind. You had to bend nearly double against it but the little children had bare feet and hardly any clothes on, just little trousers.

I went from Wick, on loan at first, to Skithen, just down the road, and my first job was to make sandwiches for the RAF Regiment who had to go out to the wreckages of planes. On one of these the Duke of Kent was killed. Near by it was flat, then two mountains. The plane hit one of these. The men were searched in case they had gathered souvenirs.

I was in Coastal Command until the war finished and ended up in a transit camp where those from abroad stayed to clear before being demobbed. The tiny village of Bourne near Cambridge had a hall for dancing so that was where I went on Saturdays. I had danced with a boy and was sitting down when another asked me and I told him I was a 'big' one but he didn't mind as it was his first dance for four years.

While I was at Milksham, a Scottish girl used to sing when we were all

in bed. As you know, they were sentimental then and her favourite was
'Memories Live Longer than Dreams'. It must have been very sad for her
as her fiancé died at the beginning of the war but she still sang to please
us. I always seemed to have Scotties as pals, followed by Geordies and
Yorkies.

There have been 'characters'. One was called 'Frenchie' and she used
to smoke a clay pipe. When the stem broke she still had a go. When we
walked down the passage, we'd enter the mess like chorus girls and neither
of us was sylph-like. I got to be 11 stone of muscle; now, at seventy-one,
am 10½ stone of flab!

I know it is the wrong time to say that I wish the clock could be turned
back. I had many good friends and I knew that being demobbed would
lead to a life of loneliness. I had had one friend and she married while I
was still in the Forces. I saw her once by chance in 1954. I did have mates
at work but once I was home that was it until I married. I am now back
to the loneliness as I am a widow. To have conversations, I go to Bingo
twice a week. It is pricey if you don't win but that is the price needed to
be able to speak to someone. I am always glad when the festive season is
over as it seems twice as lonely. I was never on leave at Christmas as I
really didn't want to be!

W. Vickerstaff (née Leonard)
Derbyshire

A TRIBUTE TO ELIZABETH

We volunteered, we volunteered, we volunteered to join the Air
Force.
Ten bob a week, nothing much to eat, great big shoes, and blisters
on our feet.
We volunteered, we volunteered to serve our King and Country.
If it wasn't for the War we'd be where we were before.

I was working as a Civil Servant, and unable to get my release to join the
RAF until 9 December 1941. I became a Driver, DMT Group V. Then
we used to sing!

I will always remember the morning I enlisted on the spree,
To be a greasy Driver in the RAF MT

My heart is aching till it's breaking, to be in civvy street once
   more.
You ought to see the WAAFs on a Saturday night,
Polishing up their buttons in the pale moonlight, 'Cos there is
Going to be inspection in the morning. Flt/Sgt. Williams will be
   there.

and many more.

As an only child the impact of War was bewildering to say the least. I was
also sent to Bridgnorth, Shropshire and Innsworth. After kitting I was sent
on a ten-week driving instruction course at Blackpool, and North Wales.

In North Wales, we were told how to maintain heavy trucks, and
instructed how to change crash gears without too much noise. Also how
to drive in the dark with shielded headlights along winding narrow lanes.
I did my first solo drive in a truck in the dark, from Pwllheli to Nefyn,
N. Wales.

During the day we were not alone on the road. Nearby was a camp of
WRENs also learning to drive. On this same route were Indian soldiers
teaching our English soldiers how to manage horses with packs, ready for
overseas service. We certainly had to keep our eyes on the road.

From Wales I was sent to 4MT Coy, Lords Cricket Ground, St John's
Wood, London. This was great for me because I was born near Primrose
Hill, Regents Park and went to school in the Hampstead Garden Suburb.
I knew my way around. My first job there was in a 15 cwt Bedford. My
first time around London was dodging taxis and buses and I was so scared
I cannot remember too much about it.

After a while, I was posted to RAF Spitalgate, Grantham, Lincs.,
12 Pilots' Advanced Flying Unit, Training 21. Most of the pilots were
Australian or New Zealanders. They were training on Ansons, Airspeed
Oxfords and later on Blenheims. We also had other nationalities beside
our own British pilots.

Late spring they asked for a volunteer to stand by flying on our satellite
'drome called Harlaxton where the pilots used to practise circuits and
bumps. I volunteered and each day I had to take a different pilot with
me. We were placed next to the fire tender to make the emergency team
during the day. We were familiar with this farm clearing because prior
to this job I used to go out with the duty officer to lay Goose Neck Flares.

Looking back now, how primitive it all seems. Still, it was over half a century ago.

One day, somebody called 'Smoke', and the fire tender raced off with me following right behind. A Wellington bomber, without bombs, was out on a training session, and had crashed about half a mile away on to farmland.

When we arrived there were men strewn all over the place badly injured. Thank God, they were all alive. The main station had been signalled and before long an Albion ambulance arrived as back-up.

The man I went to was the pilot. He was very badly hurt, his face dreadfully disfigured. His nose was practically torn off. I tried my best to reassure him. He said, 'Is my face all right?' I tried not to show my horror and told him he had the cutest turned up nose I had ever seen. He smiled at me, a smile I shall never forget. They transported him to hospital. Later on, nearer the end of the War, I was sitting in the Fernleaf Club near Trafalgar Square when I noticed an Australian airman looking at me. He was with a pretty young woman, so I could not understand his interest in me. Suddenly, he got up and came across to me. He said, 'You do not remember me, do you?' I apologised, and said, 'Sorry, I cannot place you.'

It turned out to be the pilot I have just mentioned. He said, 'I shall never forget you.' He called the young lady with him. She had nursed him after his accident. 'I would like to introduce you to my wife,' he said. 'I have been repatriated to Australia.' I know his name was Crouch, and he was either a Squadron Leader or a Wing Commander. It would be nice to think they had a very happy life together.

The other injured man was a Canadian. He asked me if I was an angel. The poor man thought he had died. I cannot think of anybody who looked less like an angel than I did that day.

To round this incident off, the plane blew up and I caught a terrible blast from it. Thank God everybody else was clear. They sent me on leave. For a time I lost my memory, but it gradually came back.

After several postings around England, they sent me to the Air Crew Receiving Centre, Abbey Lodge, Regent's Park, London.

As I was trained for ambulance work, and attendant, I joined two more ambulance drivers, Jeannot and Yvonne, in the ambulance flat on the ground floor of Abbey Lodge. Our ambulance was always parked outside the front door.

The V2 bombs started just after I arrived, and we had a busy time. When the sirens sounded, we had to disperse our doctors to various medical centres. It was a very frightening time. My one fear was being bombed going across the River Thames, and being blasted into the water. One evening on my way back from duty, I was badly caught by the blast for the second time. On this occasion I found it nearly impossible to breathe in. It was late at night and there was nobody to help. It is a moment I hope never repeats itself.

One awful day the sirens went, and I had to go to a block of flats called Embassy Court opposite the London Zoo. The Zoo had been evacuated of all its animals, and the airmen used to have their meals in the Refectory. After lunch they had to parade at 2.00 p.m. approximately and a V2 dropped in the midst of them. There was chaos, with ambulances everywhere. The Americans blocked my way and said I could not go through. I told them it was my area – try and stop me. I took a very injured Free Frenchman to St Thomas's Hospital, London. He had obviously been injured by splintered glass and his face was no longer a face. Sadly, he died on arrival at the hospital. Maybe it was merciful!

Shortly afterwards, I was called to the Pay Office to be informed that I would receive 15/– every three months as 'danger money'. It had taken them all that time to realise we were out whilst the raids were on.

By the time 6 June 1944 had arrived, I was staff car driving. I had taken an Intelligence Officer to RAF Netheravon early that morning, and had been invited to watch a practice jump of 1,000 paras., dropping from planes and gliders. What a sight – never to be forgotten. By the time I returned to London, D-Day had commenced.

To conclude, I would like to say THANK YOU to all the RAF personnel whatever their job. We all needed each other. One could not work without the other.

I would also like to thank all the Servicemen who came from all corners of the world to fight, to protect the British Isles, and free Europe, remembering those gallant men and women who did not survive. God bless them. Rest In Peace.

Josephine Harriott
Brighton

AUSSIE ANTICS AT
BINBROOK 460 SQUADRON

Their wild parties became something of a legend – a legend which is still discussed today by people who were around in the Binbrook area in those last two years of war.

There was the time they 'liberated' a donkey from the Marquis of Granby in Binbrook and decided to paint it Air Force blue.

On another occasion, the Sergeants' mess was turned into an impromptu polo arena; cycles were horses, brushes mallets, and for a ball they used a tea cup. The following day there wasn't a surviving cup in the mess.

The piano in the Sergeant's mess needed replacing at least once a fortnight because of the amount of beer poured into it.

Gp. Capt. Edwards was always on hand at briefings to give out advice but despite all his experience, he never really mastered landing a Lancaster. Everyone would turn out to watch him land and there were a lot of comments about him flying on kangaroo juice.

One of 460's Lancasters carried a neat sign on the fuselage by the Elsan chemical toilet. It read, 'Do not pull the chain while the train is standing in the station.' Below which was added, 'Except over enemy territory.'

At the Yarborough Hotel in Grimsby one night they ordered a lobster for one of the crew who hailed from the Alice Springs area. He had never seen the sea before he left for England, let alone a lobster. It took him all night to eat it.

THE HORSE-DRAWN TRAIN

Years ago, even in Australia, we had horse-drawn trams but I had never heard of a horse-drawn train. If you think that's Irish, well, it was. Isobel of Northern Ireland tells of going on leave and completing the journey in a train that was once horse-drawn:

My name is Isobel Beattie and I was a WAAF MT Driver from 1942–6. I trained at Gloucester and Morecambe Driving School. I was then posted to RAF Limavardy from 1942–4 and then to RAF Killadeas until being demobbed in 1946.

I drove the Padre on his rounds to isolated DF Stations. He was a dedicated man who was always ready to help. Of course we had to drive other vehicles as necessary.

I always remember coming back to camp after a day off. The train was very slow as it came from Belfast in the blackout. To reach the camp, it was necessary to change at Fintona Junction to an even slower train. This particular train was, before the war, pulled by a horse. We arrived at Enniskillen at about 11 p.m., and I had to book in to the Guard Room at midnight. The only way to get there was to run those last couple of miles. In those days, we could be alone in the blackout. Nowadays it would be too dangerous to be out at all!

Isobel Beattie
Bangor, N. Ireland

THEY SHALL NOT BE FORGOTTEN

Dorothy McCandless, writing from Northern Ireland, says:

I am an ex WAAF, not Irish, but an English lassie from Cheshire. It was vital for us to do war work so I went into the WAAF. I was Dorothy Hassall, LACW 2059407.

At first, I was a balloon operator on Coastal Command at Southampton and then I was posted to London to help protect the Palace. While at Lewisham, we received a message which really came from the Jerries. It was made out like an order of our own Command and it was to bed all balloons. The result was that the school at Lewisham was bombed and around thirty children died.

The guns firing around us were frightening as planes flew up the roads like cars. The Germans did not care whom they killed.

After the sandbags for bedding balloons were changed for concrete blocks, the RAF had to train men to man the balloons for it became too heavy for girls.

I then took a driving course and was posted to Cranwell and later to Scampton and Scunthorpe in Lincolnshire with Bomber Command. This was where I met my late husband. He was a pilot and we had many happy times together with the crew, but his kite was reported missing and neither he nor the crew returned. The whole camp was saddened.

I am enclosing my photo with the Queen, when she presented new Colours to the RAF. It was a great honour for me and we had a wonderful day. I told the Queen that the WAAF was a forgotten force. The Queen's reply was that not by her had we been forgotten.

Dorothy McCandless

Co. Down, Northern Ireland

BRIDGNORTH

Back in December 1993, Geoff Hill of Halesowen, West Midlands, wrote telling me that a Shropshire newspaper, the *Express & Star*, had in September published an article telling of 'The Day Bridgnorth saw Freedom First'. I wrote to the *Express & Star* and then in March 1994, they sent me a copy of the article written in the *Bridgnorth Journal*, 17 September 1993. I am most grateful for their kindness and their interest, but when I read the article I was a little dismayed.

The article pointed out that over a million RAF had passed through the gates of the Bridgnorth camp, Stanmore, in war and peace. This city of Bridgnorth became the first to award the RAF the Freedom of the City. In 1950 history was made when a casket of oak containing a scroll giving the Freedom of Entry to the city was presented to G/Cpt. G.J.L. Read, Commanding Officer of Bridgnorth.

The article goes on to list the top personnel of the RAF who were present. Since a unique reunion was being held at Bridgnorth during the Battle of Britain week in 1993, then this account of that ceremony held in 1950 was written up again. Splendid photographs were shown and there at the side of the article was the old crest, once the pride of RAF Bridgnorth. It was pointed out that the Latin inscription reads in translation: 'These are the gates; the walls are men.'

Now among the million must have been thousands of WAAFs and I do suggest that when that crest was designed, there may not have been many WAAFs in the RAF, but the whole article telling of 'the unprecented impact during its tenure, mostly good . . . ' on the city of Bridgnorth by the RAF, does not once mention the WAAF. What a pity! In my opinion, the walls were men but they were often propped up by the women of the WAAF.

IF IT DOESN'T WORK — BRING IT BACK!

If it doesn't work — bring it back! I doubt if these are encouraging words to hear when you are issued with a parachute. When Molly, a flight mechanic, took her first test flight, those were the very words she heard from a bod in the parachute section.

Molly, who now lives in Australia, begins her story at the very beginning of the war when she was just thirteen. This is a story for those who were not there; those who knew little about the real dangers of war; those who really didn't have to go without things such as eggs, oranges and bananas; those perhaps who lived in Australia or Canada where rationing existed but which never hit as hard as in Britain.

Molly's story was written as an address to the Geelong Branch of the War Widows' Association. It must have brought back memories both sad and joyful to many who heard her as I feel it will to those who now read it:

The war started four months before my fourteenth birthday. All children and expectant mothers had to be taken out of London into the quiet countryside. All schools were closed and the teachers who hadn't joined up went with the evacuees.

We went to relatives at Billericay in Essex and could attend school only on every second day, owing to the shortage of teachers and the overflow of pupils. I returned to London on my fourteenth birthday and worked in tailoring.

Church bells were to be the warning of the invasion of England so during the war we didn't hear a church bell. When peace was declared in 1945, every church bell in England, Scotland and Wales was ringing from the smallest village church to the largest cathedrals.

Gas masks had to be carried everywhere and firms made handbags with zippered sections at the base to put the masks in.

Food rations were small – two ounces of each butter and margarine, four ounces of tea, two ounces of cheese per week and one egg per month. These were just for babies, children and older folk when convoys did get through. Children of two years or more didn't know what a banana was. Confectionery was rationed too. Meat was tightly rationed and all tinned food was on a points system. It was very difficult for mothers feeding families. There were no ingredients for cakes at Christmas or on birthdays.

Cinemas and theatres closed during the blitz but re-opened when the bombing eased. If a raid was on, it was announced, and if people wished to leave they went to shelters.

During the Battle of Britain blitz on London, I didn't go to bed for six weeks. We had air raid shelters in our back yards and spent nights there from 7 p.m.–6 a.m. usually. Bombers would come over in waves all night long. Anyone caught out had to rush to the nearest street shelters built all over London. Some people felt safe in the underground stations and one had to step over people who were sleeping on the platforms.

The horrible sound of high explosive bombs screaming down one after the other and the guns blazing at the bombers was like a horrific nightmare. The sound of any siren which is like an air raid warning still sends shivers down my back after all these years. Casualty lists were posted up at buildings such as theatres, dance halls and in any place where a large number of people were killed or injured or missing. The King, George VI, visited bombed sites as did Mr Churchill. Sometimes people were dug out days after a raid and they were on occasions still alive.

The only men to help were very young or old or those unfit for the Service. They did a wonderful job with the ARP etc. Sometimes when a building was hit, there could be one wall remaining and it could have such things as an unbroken mirror on it. In one case I saw a large picture of Jesus with the words, 'I am the Light of the Word', hanging on the wall amid all the rubble.

One day, I was at Charing Cross Station and there were rows and rows of ambulances to meet hospital trains from the coast bringing men from the beaches at Dunkirk. It was a dreadful sight for a fourteen-year-old and I decided there and then that I had to do something.

In the City of London one day I was passing a recruiting office for the RAF. I went in and applied to join. I was sixteen, but said that I was seventeen. Mum, as guardian, signed her permission and said that once I was in I had to stay there. Actually 17½ was the minimum age, so I had to wait until 27 July, when I was really 16½. On 4 August 1942, I was enrolled as a member of the WAAF. We were drafted to a place in Shropshire for three weeks for discipline training, lessons, lectures and marching.

During the first week we had vaccinations and I was very sick and miserable and of course homesick! Our mattresses were three biscuits, straw filled and we had a round, neck-breaking bolster. Our bedclothes had to be stacked blanket, sheet, blanket, sheet and then the last blanket folded lengthwise and folded round the lot. Your gas mask and tin hat were then placed on top.

There was no leniency because we were girls for we marched that parade ground day after day seemingly for hours on end. We quick marched, slow marched, right wheeled, left wheeled, about-turned and did every move until we had blisters on our blisters. All our drill instructors were RAF sergeants and warrant officers and could they bellow! We soon learned to obey orders no matter how we felt.

At the end of three weeks we went to Bedminster, where we were in a field with American camps on either side, divided by a railway. Two girls were on guard all night for two-hour shifts, armed with a truncheon and a whistle. Officers used to check us during the night. Later, it was one girl alone for one-hour shifts.

One of the things we had to learn was how to splice ropes and wire cables. Officials soon realized that lugging cement blocks and sandbags around plus other heavy work was too much for girls and we had to remuster to high tech trades.

On one occasion, after days of really bad weather and battling to save the balloon, we couldn't take any more. Our only dry clothes were our pyjamas. We all reported sick and the MO came out to us on the site as we all felt so wretched.

Leave was seven days plus forty-eight hours every three months and we were constantly reminded that it was a privilege and not a right. We always had to sign out of camp and in again. The normal time for a pass was until 22.00 or 22.30 hours and a Late Pass until 23.59 hours.

I remustered as Flt./Mechanic Engines and was sent to a large training school at St Athan in South Wales for a very intensive five-month course. We were given one week's leave half-way through that course.

Breakfast on Sunday was always a real egg so we used to race across to the mess with battledress over our pyjamas and then back to bed to listen to the Vera Lynn Forces Request Programme.

Fortunately, I passed my course and was posted to RAF Charterhall in southern Scotland. This was a Night Fighter Operational Training Unit and we were the first female Flt./Mechs. to arrive on the station. This caused quite a sensation and it was pretty rough having to prove that we could do the job and that we weren't there just for the airmen's benefit.

The site for our sleeping quarters was a long way from the actual 'drome area and we were issued with cycles for getting about. At first, our washing facilities were a piece of pipe sticking out of the ground at the side of the track with a cold water tap on it. From this came ice cold water and it was in the open air! To get to the bath huts, we had to walk across open fields in all weathers. The baths were closed to admin. staff for two nights a week, so we could be sure of getting a hot bath on those nights. One WAAF used to boil water for her hot water bottle and the next morning we would use that for our cat-licks.

Wartime 'dromes were usually built in the quiet countryside and we could cycle along glorious country lanes when off duty in summer. The owners of the estate allowed us to cycle through the grounds and pick the primroses and violets. It was a wonderful place.

At first, I worked on Beaufighters in hangars and then on Mosquitoes. After any repairs, one of us had to go on the air test and in our crew it was usually me. The first time I went to the parachute store for a 'chute, they strapped me into it and said, 'Right, if it doesn't work, bring it back!' I was terrified!

At night, we would listen to the planes taking off and wonder how many would come back.

It was about three miles to the local railway station and if we were going on leave we had to walk there and back. Local pubs were our meeting places for dates.

While we were preparing for D-Day all leave was cancelled, except compassionate leave for Londoners whose homes had been bombed. My turn came for that. Earlier my Mum and brother came up for a week to get away from buzz bombs and to have a sleep. The Scottish people were wonderful and could not do enough for us.

In early December 1944, I was posted to RAF Stoney Cross in Hampshire. Previously it had been an American glider 'drome and it was deserted when I arrived with a few other WAAFs. It was decided that half of us could go on leave straight away and the other half at Christmas. I went in the first lot to save my Mum worry. Christmas on a station was always fun as officers had to serve the ranks and wait on the tables for Christmas dinner in the ground crew mess. It was a great occasion. The first Christmas there it was thick fog and we couldn't find our way around.

The 'drome was in the New Forest and our huts were built in among the trees. Sometimes the ponies would come and put their heads in our windows. We walked through the forest to reach the local pub where there was a social club rather than a drinking club.

Eventually aircraft arrived and they were four-engined Stirling bombers now being used as transports. The aircrews were ex Bomber Command on rest after two or even more tours of operations. Some were highly decorated men from all parts of the Commonwealth. The ground crews were men who had returned from service in the Middle East. These men had never seen WAAFs before, let alone Flt./Mechs., instrument technicians or electricians who were WAAFs. So once again, we had to prove ourselves capable of doing the job. Once we were accepted, I made some very good friends. One mechanic was allotted to each engine and one girl to each crew where possible. The men really looked after me as even the age I was using was young for service life and the job I was doing.

On freezing winter mornings, we had to turn the engines over by hand with a long starter handle. The cockpit was about twenty-five feet from the ground. We had to get this long steel rod through a small hole in the engine cowling. It was a very difficult task.

Our winter clothing was undies, shirt, sleeveless pullover then long sleeved, round-necked jumper, battledress and overall over all that lot. Our socks were thick seamen's socks and turned down wellington boots over the trousers. On our heads we wore a beret with a scarf tied over it. We often used to laugh about it and say that we weren't asked for a date because of our glamorous looks while working. Usually there were streaks of oil or grease somewhere on my face and the men often wiped a smudge off my nose.

There was always a NAAFI canteen on the camp for ranks up to corporal but if going out with an officer it had to be the local pub. These were more like clubs and there always seemed to be someone who could play the piano or mouth organ and of course sing. We used to have some great sing-songs. Wartime companionship was something apart and very special as most just lived from day to day. Even with the married men, it was just a special friendship and nothing to interfere with their marriage.

We found that the really brave men did not talk about things much. It was the small ribbons and emblems on their chest that told the story. The ones who bragged a lot usually hadn't done much.

Even on the four-engined aircraft, I was still the one to go on air tests. The men weren't keen on going. One day, I climbed aboard and noticed a couple of Australian uniforms. I said, 'Good morning, Sir,' and sat down in my seat behind him. We flew around for a while and all was checking out OK, when suddenly it was obvious that something was wrong. I looked out the port side and my engine had stopped. I raced up to the pilot and found that he had feathered it and promptly started it again. I then realised from the grins on the faces of the crew that they knew which engine was mine and were playing a joke on me. I didn't think it was a bit funny and told them so, very politely of course, and said that I would never go on an air test with that pilot again. I didn't either but I married him instead. That of course is another story.

Molly Woolnough
Newcomb, Victoria, Australia

TO ELIZABETH

Elizabeth has a very special place
In this ancient land;
There is an ancient seabed
Where a billion, billion fish swam
In sand strewn caverns,
Now in a safe and sacred place,
She lies resting.

The Australian bush opens
To that vast unending sky
Where cumulus roll and
Mares' tails stream out;
Where rainbow birds
Flash their glorious colours.
They have come home
From a far land
Just as Elizabeth lies here;
But her beauty and her love
Have returned
To Scotland's ancient hills.

'Bunny rabbits!' she used to say,
And now they leap and play,
Around the stone
And nibble the roses.
Under the everlasting stars
Of the soft Australian night,
From a distance comes the mournful cry
Of the black Australian crow.
The screech of the galahs

As they flock in the scrub
And once again we hear
The magnificent music,
As magpies carol and warble.

Here, Elizabeth lies resting,
To her I say,
'Fear no more the heat
Nor sand storms and lashing rain;
You have fought and won
An honoured place.'

When that glorious, golden
Harvest moon
Paints the sky and trees,
And men of sinew
Bustle and rush,
To win that precious grain;
Then, dear Elizabeth
May all the beauty
And serenity of this place
Be your harvest once again.

The cold hard hand
Of winter,
Will come and sparkle and glisten;
But spring will stir
And come again,
When the wild boronia bursts,
And songs of young birds
Are heard again.
As the seasons
Come and go,
Your echoes shall roll.
From soul to soul,
And never pass away.
Though few may know
Of your courage,
Your wry and beautiful smile
And soft grey loving eyes,

I shall tell the world
For I loved you.

And when I am gone
And a thousand storms
Have passed
Over our resting place,
Then that love
Shall linger on
With the cry of the birds,
And the skittering paw of a rabbit,
And as I hear you cry,
'Bunny rabbits!'
I shall know,
You love me still.

Norman Small

ELIZABETH IN AUSTRALIA

When Elizabeth was made a Life Governor of the Elanora Hospital at Brighton, Mrs A.P. Nissen S.S. St J., Commandant Red Cross, wrote, 'The love, kindness and friendship that you have given to the folk at Elanora for so many years I know has had its own rewards, but it is grand for these old folk to show their appreciation in this way. You have given help and assistance so untiringly and so freely.'

The work which Elizabeth did at this hospital and the many hours she also spent at home sewing and doing other tasks such as writing letters was only part of the Red Cross work she did.

After years of study and practical work, she obtained the highest qualifications in First Aid and Home Nursing that the Red Cross could offer. This led to her work as an Examiner for Red Cross and St John in First Aid, as well as qualifying her as a lecturer in First Aid. Her work with Red Cross First Aid classes in Ouyen demonstrated a quality seldom surpassed.

Her further voluntary work at hospitals such as the geriatric hospital at Cheltenham, Heidelberg Hospital, Heatherton and Larundal, was done when there were shortages or strikes by nursing staff. She also assisted at the Sisters of the Holy Name Orphanage at Brighton, Melbourne Airport during the East Timor crisis, and migrant hostels during that same crisis. As a member of a Red Cross Disaster Team she attended bush fires on the Mornington Peninsula and Lancefield and floods at Flemington in the 1970s to assist with First Aid.

Primary Schools at Hampton and Ouyen were visited for tests and lectures in First Aid for Year 6 students.

Her church work with the Anglican Church was wide, both in the type of work and in the number of churches. Anglican churches at Red Hill, Dingee, Kyneton, Hampton, Manangatang and Ouyen all benefited from her Guild experience as an ordinary member and as a member of the executive.

From 1956–9, at Kyneton, she was President of the RSL Ladies' Auxiliary, where she showed a very firm, but kindly leadership. During those same years she became the Secretary of the Mothers' Club at the Kyneton Primary School.

In two private schools, All Saints College, Bathurst and Haileybury College, Brighton, she acted voluntarily as a house mother to boys who were boarders. The ages of these boys ranged from five years to eighteen years.

Before coming to Australia as a war bride in 1946, Elizabeth served in the Royal Air Force, from August 1941 to September 1945. Her initial training was done at Bridgnorth, Derbyshire, and her first posting was to a Fighter Command Station at Dyce, near Aberdeen, in Scotland. In 1943, she was posted to Binbrook, Lincolnshire, England, where she became a member of 460 Squadron Royal Australian Air Force. This squadron was in Bomber Command, flying Lancasters, and it was there that she met her future husband, Norman.

Only those who were on an operational squadron in Britain would know of the dangers faced by WAAF personnel. Much has been written about fighter pilots and other Air Force heroes, but not nearly enough tribute has been paid to the thousands of women who gave so much support to Australian ground staff and air crews while they served in Britain. Their lives were always in danger and they often and unwillingly had to witness the loss of life of aircrews. This Australian squadron lost one thousand men – many died on takeoff and many more on landings.

Elizabeth was born at Carluke, Lanarkshire, Scotland, on 4 February 1919. She attended the Carluke Primary and Secondary Schools and distinguished herself as a fine literature and language student.

With her husband she came to live in Ouyen in 1977. For a short time

Elizabeth and Norman retired to Castlemaine. It was here that she had a stroke in early 1981. Many thoughtful people in Castlemaine and Ouyen gave her tremendous support and encouragement. With their help and her own determination she overcame great difficulties.

It was however a great disappointment that one who for years had given love, consolation and effort to helping the sick and those who care for them, should suffer the frustrations, humiliations and downgrading that are so often, and so unthinkingly, passed on to those who because of their condition, are unable to protect themselves.

Elizabeth was a proud woman, fiercely independent and even craggy, but she had the qualities of the Scottish Highlands – granitic and rock solid. As those Highlands have a grandeur, a softness and a quiet loveliness, so had this Scottish lass who served both Scotland, her native land, and Australia, well.

Elizabeth passed away at Ouyen on 18 August. May she have honour, rest and peace for she has gone beyond our ken; no longer is she just westering hamewards; she has gang awa' hame.

The 460 Squadron Memorial at Binbrook.